Pro Service-Oriented Smart Clients with .NET 2.0

Sayed Y. Hashimi and
Scott J. Steffan

Apress®

Pro Service-Oriented Smart Clients with .NET 2.0

Copyright © 2005 by Sayed Y. Hashimi and Scott J. Steffan

ISBN (pbk): 1-59059-551-3

Printed and bound in the United States of America 9 8 7 6 5 4 3 2 1

Lead Editor: Jonathan Hassell
Technical Reviewer: Jason Mitchell
Editorial Board: Steve Anglin, Dan Appleman, Ewan Buckingham, Gary Cornell, Tony Davis,
    Jason Gilmore, Jonathan Hassell, Chris Mills, Dominic Shakeshaft, Jim Sumser
Associate Publisher and Project Manager: Grace Wong
Copy Edit Manager: Nicole LeClerc
Copy Editor: Marilyn Smith
Assistant Production Director: Kari Brooks-Copony
Production Editor: Linda Marousek
Compositor: Linda Weidemann
Proofreader: Liz Welch
Indexer: Valerie Perry
Artist: Kinetic Publishing Services, LLC
Interior Designer: Van Winkle Design Group
Cover Designer: Kurt Krames
Manufacturing Director: Tom Debolski

Distributed to the book trade worldwide by Springer-Verlag New York, Inc., 233 Spring Street, 6th Floor, New York, NY 10013. Phone 1-800-SPRINGER, fax 201-348-4505, e-mail orders-ny@springer-sbm.com, or visit http://www.springeronline.com.

For information on translations, please contact Apress directly at 2560 Ninth Street, Suite 219, Berkeley, CA 94710. Phone 510-549-5930, fax 510-549-5939, e-mail info@apress.com, or visit http://www.apress.com.

To my parents Sayed A. and Sohayla Hashimi

—Sayed Y. Hashimi

To my wife, Trina, my children, Christin and Lane,
my parents, Herman and Lavinia, and my brother Steven Steffan

—Scott J. Steffan

Contents at a Glance

Contents

About the Authors

SAYED Y. HASHIMI was born in Afghanistan and now resides in Jacksonville, Florida. His has expertise in the areas of health care, logistics, scientific computing, and civil/structural engineering. In his professional career, Sayed has developed large-scale distributed applications with a variety of programming languages and platforms, including Fortran, C++, J2EE, and .NET. He has published articles in major software journals on topics that range from low-level programming techniques to high-level architecture concepts. Sayed holds a Master of Engineering degree from the University of Florida. You can reach Sayed by visiting http://www.sayedhashimi.com.

SCOTT J. STEFFAN has worked in IT for more than 20 years. He has been employed by multiple Fortune 100 companies as an enterprise IT architect and member of senior technical management. Scott earned his Bachelor of Science in Engineering and has a Master of Business Administration degree. He has worked on state-of-the-art computer systems and process improvements in a variety of industries. He is currently pursuing a postgraduate degree in the fields of control theory and machine intelligence. Scott is a member of the North Florida Rational User Group and the Central Florida Architecture Council.

About the Technical Reviewer

■**JASON MITCHELL** is a software consultant in Jacksonville, Florida. He is the creator of Autobahn (`http://www.newroadsoftware.com/newroad/products/autobahn2.asp`), a business-process workflow designer and engine. Jason has published papers in the areas of system architectures and virtual data sources. His current research areas include JavaSpaces, J2EE, C#, relational data storage, business-process workflow, and middleware architecture. He has a Master of Science degree in Computer Science from the University of North Florida.

Acknowledgments

Writing a book requires the efforts of many people besides the authors. Therefore, we would like to acknowledge the fruitful and timely efforts of the following Apress staff: Jonathan Hassell, Grace Wong, Marilyn Smith, Linda Marousek, Linda Weidemann, Nicole LeClerc, Kari Brooks-Copony, Tina Nielsen, and Liz Welch. We would also like to thank the technical reviewers, Jason Mitchell and Scott Smith, for their watchful eye. Lastly and most importantly, we wish to thank our families for their support throughout the entire project.

Introduction

This book shows you how to build smart client applications and how to exploit them using a service-oriented architecture. So, the best way to introduce the book is to define just what a smart client is.

What's a Smart Client?

A smart client is not a technology. Rather, a smart client is a concept for a client application with specific features. Many of these features already exist in the thin and thick client architectures.

From our experience in building thin clients, we know that if we build a web application and deploy it to a web server, it instantly becomes available to users all over the world. Moreover, we are aware that if the application needs to be updated, all we need to do is drop the new files on the web server.

Similarly, we recognize that if we build a thick client, the client will have a rich and dynamic user interface, and that it will be deployed directly to the user's desktop. On the desktop, the thick client application will have access to all of the local resources. For example, the application will be able to access and use the file system, printer, processes, threads, and so on. More important, the application can also easily integrate with other applications installed on the machine.

We can conclude that thin client applications have a global reach and are easily deployed and updated, and thick client applications have a rich user interface and can use and integrate easily with local resources.

A smart client inherits the following features from both thin and thick clients:

- Global reach

- Easy deployment and updates

- Rich and dynamic user interface

- Ability to use local resources

- Easy integration with installed applications

On top of these features, the smart client adds a few capabilities of its own:

- Ability to perform its functions without a network connection (offline)

- Ability to use XML Web Services for integration and interoperability to support a service-oriented architecture

So, if the smart client is not a technology, then what technology or technologies do we use to build smart client applications? Since a smart client has a rich user interface and can access local resources, we need a technology that provides the capability to build such an application. This turns out to be Windows Forms. That's not to say that you use only standard technologies to construct a smart client. In fact, the smart client's critical advantage of being easy to deploy and update is implemented through a new technology called ClickOnce, which will be released with Visual Studio .NET 2005.

Who Should Read This Book?

This book is written for designers, developers, and IT managers who want to understand how to build the next generation of client technology. In covering smart clients and their related technologies, we assume that you have some experience in developing applications for Microsoft Windows. We expect that you have built a few Windows Forms applications. If you haven't, we suggest that you build a few simple examples before reading past Chapter 1.

The examples in Chapters 3 through 5 use web services without discussing what they are or how to build them. We do, however, give a speedy introduction to a subset of the web services platform in Chapter 8 (as an introduction to our discussion of service-oriented architecture in Chapter 9 and service-oriented smart clients in Chapter 10). If you have not developed any web services using .NET, we suggest you start with Chapter 8 and spend a half a day working with the technology before diving into Chapter 3.

We also assume that you have a general knowledge of design patterns and UML, but you do not need to be an expert on these subjects.

What's in This Book?

This book covers the different types of smart clients and the technologies around them. We explore the practical features of smart clients, and as we go along, we give you some theory here and there.

The first part of the book (Chapters 1 through 7) shows you how to build and deploy smart client applications. Most of this portion of the book is hands-on, with a lot of screen shots to guide you through the examples. The second part (Chapters 8 through 11) extends the concept of a smart client to the service-oriented smart client (SOSC). This smart client adds a few features to the smart client to make it more agile. You can think of the SOSC as a "really, really smart" smart client.

Here's a summary of what each chapter contains:

Chapter 1, An Introduction to Smart Clients: We open our discussion of smart clients by looking at the clients of the past. Specifically, we talk about the characteristics of thick and thin clients and their benefits and shortfalls. We then look at the characteristics of smart clients and SOSCs.

Chapter 2, Types of Smart Clients: In this chapter, we provide an overview of each of the three main types of smart clients: Windows Forms (WinForms) smart clients, Office smart clients, and mobile smart clients. This chapter prepares you for Chapters 3, 4, and 5, where we discuss building each type of smart client.

Chapter 3, Windows Forms Smart Clients: This chapter is all about building WinForms smart clients. We dissect two reference implementations of a smart client (TaskVision and IssueVision), guiding you through downloading, installing, configuring, and running the applications. Along the way, you'll learn all of the implementation details specific to smart clients.

Chapter 4, Microsoft Office Smart Clients: Microsoft has made radical improvements to Office and Visual Studio .NET to allow developers to build applications that use the power of the Office products. Additionally, two other Microsoft products—Visual Studio Tools for Office (VSTO) and Information Bridge Framework (IBF)—help you build applications that leverage the power of Office. In this chapter, we discuss these technologies and demonstrate how to build both VSTO-based and IBF-based smart clients.

Chapter 5, Mobile Smart Clients: The demand for applications that target smart devices is increasing every day. This chapter starts with an introduction to the Windows mobile platform, and then dissects a reference implementation of a mobile smart client (FotoVision). We also address the difficulties associated with writing smart device applications, packaging and deploying mobile smart clients, and the upcoming changes to the mobile development tools in Visual Studio .NET 2005.

Chapter 6, Offline Support: In this chapter, we discuss a feature that is common to all types of smart clients: offline support. We explain why smart clients need offline support, the best strategy for implementing this support, and how to easily achieve it using prebuilt libraries supported by Microsoft.

Chapter 7, WinForms Smart Client Deployment: One of the primary and fundamental properties of a smart client is easy deployment coupled with automatic updates. This chapter is one of the more important chapters of the book because it discusses solutions to deploying WinForms smart clients. We describe each of the deployment options, focusing on ClickOnce, a technology that allows you to deploy rich-client-type applications using a thin client deployment model.

Chapter 8, XML Web Services and Smart Clients: This chapter is a prelude to our discussion of service orientation and how smart clients can gain interoperability by using a loosely coupled model. Here, we introduce XML Web Services and give the business case for them. We also provide an overview of the technologies associated with XML Web Services: the Extensible Markup Language (XML), XML Schema Definition (XSD) language, Simple Object Access Protocol (SOAP), Web Services Definition Language (WSDL), and Universal Description, Discovery and Integration (UDDI).

Chapter 9, Service-Oriented Architecture: In this chapter, we describe the service-oriented architecture (SOA) and talk about its benefits. We then dissect the elements of an SOA, including message-oriented middleware (MOM), the horizontal service bus, and message-oriented architecture (MOA). Finally, we introduce how a smart client can use this technology.

Chapter 10, Service-Oriented Smart Clients: XML Web Services and the SOA are integral to building service-oriented smart clients (SOSCs). The SOSC is a new type of smart client that extends the capabilities of the smart client by adding agility. This agility allows smart clients to choose and bind to the correct web services.

Chapter 11, SOSC Testing: In this chapter, we discuss the difficulties associated with testing agility in smart clients. We start with the fundamentals of testing and conclude with testing communication, state, and concurrency in the SOSC.

Accompanying all the examples discussed in this book are instructions for downloading, installing, and running the sample applications.

Again, our goal in writing this book was to help you to build smarter applications. We hope that you find this book useful and educational.

CHAPTER 1

■ ■ ■

An Introduction to Smart Clients

The expectations placed on software today are enormous. Years ago, it was acceptable for software to attempt an operation and just quit if it failed. For example, legacy software could merely issue an error message if a credit card wouldn't validate. Failure is not an option in software anymore. Today's software must be agile, robust, and intelligent. It must be able to perform the operations and processes that humans used to do, adapting to unknown situations and opportunities. For example, it must try several systems to verify a credit card, and if the card cannot be verified, accept alternative forms of payment, such as an electronic check.

The *smart client* is the natural evolution of client architecture and is the direction for the future. Smart clients give the user and the business a new and distinct technological advantage. Microsoft defines a smart client as follows:

> *Easily deployed and managed client application that provides an adaptive, responsive and rich interactive experience by leveraging local resources and intelligently connecting to distributive data sources.*

A smart client exploits local resources already available on desktops and connects to remote services to perform complex business operations. The smart client will not increase hardware costs, but will use the available idle cycles that are wastefully ticking away while users are connected to a remote resource. Users isolated from the network or Internet will be able to continue to perform their duties by using the offline capabilities of a smart client. Information collaboration can also take on new heights with smart client technology, which will significantly reduce development costs and increase user efficiency.

Information must be exchanged and processed in a timely manner if it is to have any meaning in the current business world. The smart client can use multiple threads to ensure the application has the horsepower to perform an operation to give users the experience they want. As the power of mobile handheld devices (such as phones and PDAs) increases, so will the need to develop smart clients that are device-adaptable to maximize the businesses deployment options. Using a smart client and .NET technology, developers can take advantage of numerous external remote services to make deployment of feature-rich applications cheaper and easier.

Smart clients that are service-based are called service-oriented smart clients (SOSCs). An SOSC is an intelligent application that possesses the agility to use multiple web services

1

and local resources effectively. The SOSC is more dynamic than the smart client, allowing organizations to keep up with constantly changing business markets.

As you'll learn in this chapter, smart clients solve many of the problems that client architectures faced in the past. The smart client gives the user sophisticated controls and features normally only available in a thick client, while offering the easy deployment and global reach of the thin client. We'll begin this introduction to the smart client by tracing its evolution from previous client architectures. We'll then take a closer look at the architecture, anatomy, user experience, communication, development, and deployment aspects of thick clients, thin clients, smart clients, and SOSCs. With this foundation, you'll be ready to enter the world of smart client development.

Evolution of the Smart Client

Computers have been evolving to meet business needs ever since their inception. This maturation has led us to the smart client and inevitably the service-oriented smart client. As shown in Figure 1-1, smart clients have been developed from lessons learned from stand-alone applications and two very popular methods of building solutions: thin and thick clients.

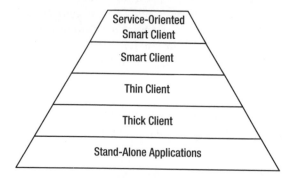

Figure 1-1. *Client evolution*

Thick client applications, which run on a user's desktop, are called thick because they generally have a heavy footprint due to their full functionality. They suffer from a lack of portability and flexibility in moving from one platform to another, as well as the significant processing and memory space required to physically execute the application. As the use of the Internet expanded, thin clients offered better connectivity and a lighter footprint. Thin clients typically trade rich features and responsiveness for versatility and connectivity. Both types of clients have benefits and drawbacks, leaving users with a less than adequate experience. Smart clients enjoy the advantages of stand-alone, thick, and thin clients, while avoiding their disadvantages.

Client evolution follows the path of computer architecture development, as shown in Figure 1-2. In this section, we'll explore this evolution.

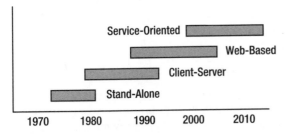

Figure 1-2. *Computer architecture evolution*

Stand-Alone Applications: From DOS to Windows

As businesses needed to the reduce cost of executing repetitive processes that were typically done by groups of people, they turned to computers to automate these processes. Stand-alone systems were built completely from scratch to meet this need. The original user of the system was grateful because the system automated a manual, cumbersome process, so the user experience was considered to be good. The business benefited from the application since fewer mistakes were made and fewer people were needed. However, the stand-alone application rarely had external communication, and the user experience was isolated. A single department had no effective way to get information to other departments or individuals within the corporation, so the productivity gain was restricted to a single user or a group of users in proximity.

The entire application resided in the operating system, which was layered on top of a single microprocessor. In most cases, this was the Disk Operating System (DOS) developed by IBM and eventually owned by Microsoft. The application was responsive to the user, since applications ran one at a time, but were also platform-specific, which removed the flexibility of moving the applications between devices.

Developers had to contend with limited development tools. Stand-alone applications were not developed as components. Most were written as a custom entity in a single language using minimal support software. The costs for creating and modifying applications were significant. Most applications went through only a single life cycle. Once that life cycle expired, the application was typically rewritten from scratch. In the process of developing the new application, it was difficult to capture all the learned business requirements that were achieved through maintenance cycles following the initial release, since a new team did not share the learned experience. Therefore, much of the investment in the original application was lost.

As computers became more commonplace, users required more functionality. This led to the development of an integrated window-based operating system called Microsoft Windows. Microsoft Windows resided on top of DOS and allowed multiple applications to be viewed simultaneously by a single user. Microsoft Windows developed a common look and feel, and established the initial standards for the user interface. This reduced training costs as new employees entered the workforce and used the application.

Deployment of stand-alone applications was slow, difficult, and unreliable. Deployment was accomplished using diskettes and a manual process informally known as "sneaker net." This forced businesses to increase the time to market due to deployment costs, since only a few software releases could be afforded each year.

Separation of the Client: Tiered Architecture

Even though a new microprocessor was being introduced to the market every 12 to 18 months, as described by Moore's Law,[1] application functionality and complexity continued to outpace the single microprocessor's capacity to deliver adequate performance to the user. To compensate, complex applications were divided into two or three parts and placed on different computers or platforms. This *tiered*, or divided, architecture labeled the local computer the *client* and the remote computer as the *server*. This architecture took advantage of the growing availability of network resources. The evolution of network bandwidth and availability has a lot to do with client evolution.

This client is known today as a *thick client*, given that label retroactively due to the amount of memory and disk space it consumed in comparison to the thin client, which followed it. Without formal standards, the actual content or functionality that a particular thick client needed to support varied on an application-by-application basis. Typical functionality included providing support for the user interface, cross-checking the user input syntax, verifying the business logic, managing session state, and assisting in communication with the server component.

The server contained the centralized information that was previously duplicated in each application by different business solutions. The server supported persistent data, managed the global state, validated the business logic using this persistent data, and assisted in communication with the client. Because network bandwidth was limited at that time, if a large quantity of information were placed on the centrally located server, this could result in a slow or nonfunctioning system.

The centralization of the server functionality offered only minor relief in the management and delivery of software. The thick client footprint had increased in size, and the available media and network bandwidth to distribute it were limited. A large number of people were required to walk around and manually load the clients using numerous 1.44MB floppy disks. This increased the length of the release cycle, and thus did not decrease the time to market, since the cost of a release was exorbitant.

The separation of the client from centralized information on the server using a network established the foundation of a community that could interact via computers. Individuals, departments, and the corporation as a whole could now collaborate, resulting in productivity gains and cost reductions. Computers were connected through local area networks (LANs) and wide area networks (WANs). The communication between the client and server was typically point-to-point using a variety of network protocols. Each industry used a different protocol, so business-to-business interoperability was limited, unless information was translated or both were using the same type of protocol. The next evolution of the client was to expand business collaboration globally using the largest network in the world, the Internet.

---

1. Gordon E. Moore is credited with stating that the number of transistors in the integrated circuit would continue to double every 12 to 18 months. This has become known as Moore's Law.

Enter the Internet: Web-Based Clients

In the middle of the 1990s, the National Center for Supercomputing Applications (NCSA), located in Champaign, Illinois, developed a revolutionary new client application that was to have a broad-reaching impact on the global business community and inevitably how people in general would look at the computer. This client application extended the user experience by bringing users in contact with a worldwide community of networked individuals and information. Used for perusing or browsing networked information, it was called a *graphics browser* and named Mosaic. Focusing on text and simple graphics, this client gave the user an interface experience similar to that provided by HyperCard, which was developed in the late 1980s by Bill Atkinson of Apple. HyperCard was a stand-alone application that allowed a virtual stack of cards to be manipulated via links. The graphics browser used pages versus cards and presented networked information seamlessly to the user using the link metaphor.

Lacking support for any of the advanced features available in a thick client, the overall footprint of the browser was small, so the computer industry labeled it the *thin client*. Another significant characteristic of the browser was that applications running within it had to play in a "sandbox," which meant the applications could not get to local resources, such as files on the disk. This stemmed from a fear that data on the Internet could corrupt local data if resources were integrated. At the time, the information technology industry had only a limited understanding of how to set up appropriate security policies and procedures.

Realizing Mosaic's business potential, the newly formed Mosaic Communication Corporation undertook a commercial venture. This company was later renamed Netscape. Coupling the technology of the Internet with Netscape's first public browser, called Navigator, had a significant effect on the public and business landscape. Within a year, Microsoft introduced its own browser, Internet Explorer.

Once loaded on the desktop, this simple client application allowed small businesses and large corporations to advertise and reach out to an extended population. Advertising on the Internet reached new customer bases—local, national, and even international. As more and more individuals and countries connected to the Internet each day, a business was automatically exposed to new customers. This significantly lowered advertising costs for small companies and allowed them to compete in niche markets that large corporations did not want to engage in or had overlooked. Small advertising-based applications also gained the benefit of deploying once to a centralized server and being quickly downloaded by the user. Advertising is still one of the primary uses of the Internet today.

Although the backbone and large data conduits of the Internet are maintained by the Metropolitan Area Exchanges (MAEs), located in the east, central, and west for the United States, individual access to this backbone can sometimes be limited. Individuals have seen an increase in bandwidth from 14,400 bits per second in the 1990s to 1,540,000 bits per second today.[2] This increase in bandwidth allows additional functionality to be transferred, and businesses are using this capability to move applications toward financial transaction processing.

Financial transaction applications that involve the exchange of money for services or products require more sophisticated client logic than simple advertising. This has been the challenge

---

2. The net result of faster user access to the Internet has not changed much in some ways, since application size has also increased. A 1990s typical application was approximately 750KB in size and, using a 14.4 Kbps (1,800 bytes per second) modem connection, took approximately 6.9 minutes to download. A 2005 typical application is approximately 80MB in size and, using a 1.54 Mbps (192,500 bytes per second) cable or DSL modem connection, takes 6.9 minutes to download.

of using thin clients to perform the functions that were previously performed by thick clients. Users expected the feature-rich client they had before, and many were disappointed by the lack of controls available with the Hypertext Markup Language (HTML) used by the thin client. Even though additional controls are now available with Dynamic HTML (DHTML) and ActiveX, these fall short or cannot be used due to security policies in place by various corporations. In a nutshell, the user experience is less than satisfactory using a thin client.

An even larger challenge in developing transaction processing for business applications on the Internet is the fact that the Internet is stateless. Thin client pages retain no history of the overall transaction. Once the page is sent to the server, the state and session information must be established and retained on the server. If the transmission is interrupted, the client must reestablish session information and possibly also state information. This issue, and the fact that all information must be exchanged back and forth through the user's *access point* to the Internet, can make the responsiveness of the client very slow, which is typically why the request/response interaction between the thin client and the server is minimized. Mission-critical business applications using a customer's narrow access points can hinder or lose clientele and cost the company business opportunities and revenue.

Service-Oriented Clients

Corporations wishing to stay in business and achieve a competitive advantage will need to have a global market reach and use strategic technological advantages to get into that position, as illustrated in Figure 1-3. Mapping these strategies, each client technology presents a specific business opportunity. Figure 1-4 compares the client's market reach with its functionality.

Figure 1-3. *Market reach versus technology advantage matrix*

The typical business desktop today is configured with thick client applications such as Microsoft Excel and a few specific line-of-business (LOB) applications. This suite of applications delivers a rich, responsive experience that offers advanced interaction mechanisms for the user using local resources. Isolated from local functions, Microsoft Internet Explorer typically supports only access to remote resources. Local resources are bound to local activities, and remote resources are bound to remote activities. Employees, customers, and users employ thick client applications in an offline mode, and they work with thin client applications while in an online mode. Most exchanges between these two worlds require a user to stop and start individual applications and use simple cut-and-paste operations. Text-based e-mail is one of the few smart clients that employs both online and offline functionality and allows this interaction to satisfy a single business objective.

The *smart client* addresses this lack of interactivity between these two worlds and offers all of the advantages of past clients. This list includes the ability to automate repetitive processes, centralize common information assets to avoid costly replication, decrease time to market by offering better deployment techniques, make the reach to global markets easier, and provide rich and responsive user interfaces. By using both local and remote resources, such a client will make customer and employee experiences more pleasant. As illustrated in Figure 1-4, aligning the smart client directly with the needs of the business delivers the shortest route for a corporation to achieve that strategic business competitive advantage.

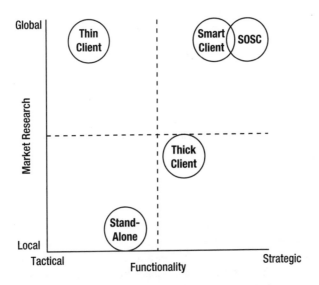

Figure 1-4. *Market reach versus client functionality matrix*

A *service-oriented smart client* (SOSC) uniquely extends the capability of the smart client by incorporating intelligence and agility into its *service-oriented architecture* (SOA). Using the principles and practices associated with constructing a smart client, the SOSC can deliver high-end business solutions, as illustrated in Figure 1-5. These solutions can adapt in real time to information changes using *smart agents*. Smart agents are intelligence entities, or components, that are delegated specific tasks of intelligence that can be leveraged by the application. Smart agents are a key to the loosely coupled smart-client architecture. Smart agents give the SOSC a dynamic property to keep up with constantly changing business markets. Using an SOSC with an SOA will lower software development costs, increase the return on investment, and reduce the time to market.

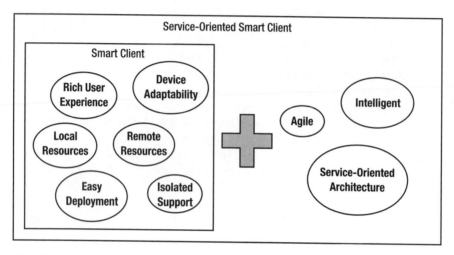

Figure 1-5. *The service-oriented smart client*

Smart clients are the future of business applications, and SOSCs deliver the future directly aligned to business opportunities. To fully understand the advantages of smart clients and the business opportunities of SOSCs, you need to know exactly how thick and thin clients work.

Thick Clients

As the network became a viable technology solution, businesses used thick client technology to remove the duplication of functionality existing in multiple stand-alone systems. Centralizing common business resources and functionality on a single computer offered the opportunity to lower costs and increase efficiency. Functionality that was not centralized became the responsibility of the client. The thick client was created in the advent of the new client/server architecture and is still used today for many applications.

Thick Client Architecture

Three basic models of client/server architecture were developed, and each one differed in the degree of functional centralization. Each of these models equipped the client with the complete functionality of a user interface and varied the other logic that was to be distributed.

The first model, shown in Figure 1-6, offers the most profitable arrangement for business, but due to bandwidth limitations, is employed only for small applications that minimize its overall business impact. The difficulty in developing a large application based on this model stems from the need to validate and verify a large quantity of user information across the network. When dealing with a quantity of data needed by a standard business application, the additional network traffic and centralized processing typically cripple the central server and the system. This lack of response generates a dismal user experience. The model should not be confused with the architecture of the thin client, since a significant amount of presentation logic is embedded in the user interface. Nor should it be confused with the connection of a terminal or monitor to a central mainframe, where only keystrokes and screens are transmitted back and forth.

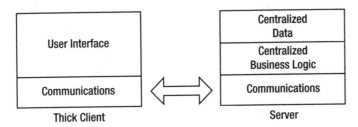

Figure 1-6. *Thick client centralized business logic model*

The next model, shown in Figure 1-7, decentralizes, or distributes, the business logic. This model is the most commonly used configuration of a thick client and the least profitable for the business when trying to centralize business functionality or remote resources. Limited network bandwidth in most corporations forces the developers to place only the data that is necessary on the central server. Centralized servers typically contain a database and, in some cases, only files. The bulk of logic is left on the client to perform the business objective of the application.

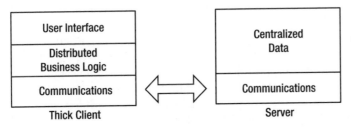

Figure 1-7. *Thick client distributed business logic model*

The third model was developed as a hybrid of the other two. It distributed business logic between the two systems, placing client-centric information with the client and centralized business logic on the server, as shown in Figure 1-8. For the rest of this section, we'll focus on the distributed and hybrid models, because they are the most prevalent and share the same thick client configuration.

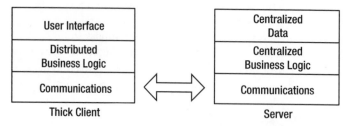

Figure 1-8. *Thick client distributed and centralized business logic model*

Thick Client Anatomy

All the logic for the presentation of the application is contained in the thick client. This logic is placed on top of the Windows operating system and business logic. The business logic supports syntax verification for the user input, as well as for managing the user's session state. High-level communication logic, such as data connection pooling or asynchronous communication, is also integrated into the business logic. Windows includes many resources—such as rich toolkits and support for presentation, networking, storage, graphics, and animation—that make the thick client a rich environment for both the user and the developer.

As shown in Figure 1-9, with Windows present, two or more applications residing on the same thick client have numerous ways to interact at the presentation and business logic layers. Simple and complex mechanisms, such as Object Linking and Embedding (OLE) and cut-and-paste, allow the user to seamlessly maneuver text, graphics, and complex objects between applications. This gives the user a distinct advantage when working with information that may need to pass through a number of applications.

A limitation affecting the reliability and availability of the thick client to perform its business objective was the lack of management or control for local common resources. These common resources are called dynamic link libraries (DLLs). They are basically runtime libraries that can be used to segment custom and common functionality used by the thick client applications. Since Microsoft Windows allows multiple applications to run simultaneously, one application could corrupt the common resources on the client that another application needed. This is known as "DLL Hell." A poorly constructed application had the potential to bring down the client as a whole, resulting in lost revenue, productivity, and opportunities.

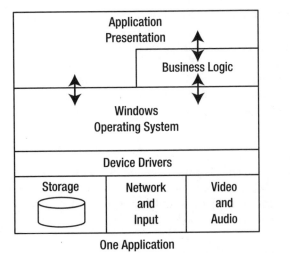 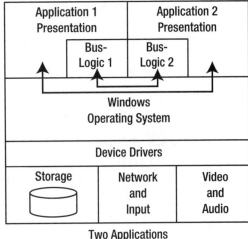

Figure 1-9. *Thick client anatomy, single and multiple applications*

Thick Client User Experience

The thick client user experience is excellent as it relates to the user interface and processing of local resources. The desktop workstation, which contains a single microprocessor, is dedicated to a single user and offers more computing power than most user applications require. This excess capacity results in the development of sophisticated user interfaces and advanced integration capabilities that can deliver critical technological advantages.

Early user interface controls for these clients contained only the most rudimentary controls (buttons, text boxes, labels, panels, lists, simple grids, and so on), but as Microsoft introduced new operating systems and enhanced integrated development environments (such as Visual Basic, Visual C++, and .NET), the suite of controls continued to grow. These tools give the developer the leading edge of technology to supply the user with a rich experience.

Depending on the application's need, the thick client can contain a lot of business logic. Logic is typically hard-coded into the user interface controls or contained in separate hidden components. The number of components required depends on the complexity of the application.

Another aspect of the client's functionality is the way it uses state information. Persistent state information is usually held on the server, but if a client is continuously requesting information over a slow network, the client might cache state information internally to increase performance.

Unfortunately for the user, when connecting to or using remote resources, the thick client can be less than eloquent. The thick client can make a point-to-point data exchange with its server, but the client has limited online reach.

Thick Client Communication

For the most part, communication used by thick clients is point-to-point. Protocols for point-to-point communications initially varied significantly across each industry. Many applications used IBM's LU6.2 protocol to get to the mainframe. The gaming industry using the IPX/SPX protocol to develop multiplayer scenarios. Microsoft Windows applications used NetBEUI and TCP/IP.

The industry standardized on TCP/IP and Remote Procedure Calls (RPC) using WinSock as the primary exchange between the server and the thick client. RPC sends a message to the server requesting a set of business logic to be executed, and then the server returns the result of the request to the client.

Two types of network topologies were developed: point-to-point and later multidrop client connections. The point-to-point topology restricted the exchange between the thick client and multiple systems. This limited its reach in the business community, and inevitably, the business impact of the solution or objective. The multidrop communication topology changed the value the thick client had on the overall business. This topology extended the thick client, allowing it to support corporate initiatives and increasing its business impact.

Messages followed three communication styles: synchronous, asynchronous, and broadcast. Most thick clients used synchronous communication style, as shown in Figure 1-10, which gave the most responsive exchange with the server.

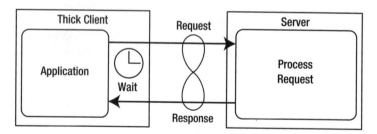

Figure 1-10. *Synchronous communication*

Synchronous communication had one primary drawback: the client could not perform any other business function once this communication had been initiated. Although this was not a problem when exchanging a small quantity of data, executing RPC to request a large amount of data could effectively tie up the thick client, preventing it from using local resources and interacting with other applications, which is the thick client's biggest advantage.

Asynchronous communication, shown in Figure 1-11, was introduced using a point-to-point topology, but it is best used in the multidrop topology. Introduced as a standard with Digital Equipment Corporation's DEC Message Queue and followed with IBM MQSeries and Microsoft MSMQ, the message-oriented middleware (MOM) gives the thick client the ability to make a request to a single or multiple servers, and allows the user to perform other business objectives while the request is being processed. Harder to configure and develop, asynchronous communication increases the user's productivity by removing the idle period between requests to the central server.

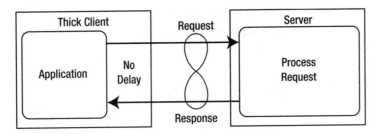

Figure 1-11. *Asynchronous communication*

Broadcast communication is monodirectional, as shown in Figure 1-12. The client or server does not expect a response to be delivered. For example, a broadcast message might alert the user or server of a business opportunity or critical situation.

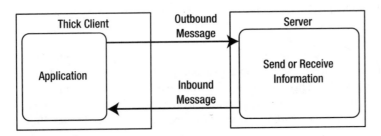

Figure 1-12. *Broadcast communication*

Thick Client Development

In the early days of thick clients, the developer was expected to develop all custom or advanced controls needed by the thick client. Custom controls gave the user a welcomed experience, since they were fitted directly to the needs of the business for the particular application under construction. However, in many ways, the limited number of controls increased the cost of developing applications and removed the adaptability, longevity, and flexibility of the client. This started to change as Microsoft and other software development vendors identified and reintroduced controls, which were considered to be a staple of their software development toolkits.

Supplementing these controls, the developer added custom syntax checkers to verify user input. For example, a U.S. Social Security number represented by nine integers had to be verified using a string type since it was actually a label. This custom code was eventually replaced by verification masks (such as ###-##-#### for a Social Security number) and other components that were associated with a particular visual control.

Aggravated by the common resource issue (DLL Hell) and the increasing size of thick clients, the ability to establish highly reliable applications decreased. To combat reliability and flexibility problems, the developer was introduced to new object-oriented concepts promoting reusability. A large undertaking was made in all areas of development to adopt design and construction standards, and segment each functional area of the business into reusable entities or objects. This promoted a degree of longevity for those segments of the client that were designed and implemented according to formal object-oriented concepts and standards.

To decrease the time to market, interface standards were also introduced for a few of the critical connectivity channels to allow integration of components and to make overall system development quicker and easier. Unfortunately, this effort required highly skilled developers, which increased the cost of development.

Thick Client Deployment

Deployment was another costly undertaking with a thick client, limiting the number of releases that a business application could receive. The footprint of the thick client was large, so it could not be downloaded via a server on the network. This forced deployment using removable media, such as diskettes and CD-ROMs, at each client.

Performing a thick client release was (and still is) an orchestration. Deployment had to occur in a quiescent period when the business could afford to have the system outage and when the support resources were available. This was usually the middle of the night, weekends, and holidays. Servers and clients had to be synchronized manually to ensure the upgrade worked. Failure in the client installation or server loading resulted in scores of hours of troubleshooting to find the cause. This made deployment inefficient and delayed the delivery of critical business upgrades until an appropriate time was available.

Thin Clients

Thin clients offer what thick clients cannot deliver: easy deployment and upgrades. Thin clients are web-based solutions that are deployed to a server and accessed via a web or graphics browser.

Sparked by the Internet, business executives started to order anything and everything to be built as (or migrated to) thin clients. Businesses realized significant cost reductions by being able to deploy an application in a single step and reach a global community. When discovered, defects could be fixed and redeployed onto the server quickly.

On the downside, thin clients require a constant connection and cannot use local resources. If the network is down, the thin client is useless and cannot support users with their business objectives.

Thin Client Architecture

The basic intranet (internal network) or Internet thin client architecture involves a client and a server platform. On the hardware level, this architecture pattern is similar to a standard client/ server model using an *n*-tier structure, but that is where the similarity ends. The thin client consists of an operating system and a web browser, such as Microsoft Internet Explorer. The web browser's principle duty is to render web pages developed in HTML. The web pages are transferred to the thin client via the Hypertext Transfer Protocol (HTTP) over a network or the Internet. These basic components allow businesses to develop web sites that reach the global community.

Basic Web Server

To present HTML pages on the Internet or intranet, you need a connection to a server that runs a process called a *web server*. Microsoft Internet Information Server (IIS) is this web server process, and it serves up static HTML web pages to a browser once the user requests them. The server has an operating system, which must support the particular web server process.

Web pages are files that are stored on a hard drive and located in a specific directory configured with IIS. These files use a common file extension or a Multipart Internet Mail Extension (MIME) type. Web pages are typically transmitted and received across the Internet via HTTP (unsecured) or HTTPS (secured). The web server can be configured, if necessary, to request a user to enter authentication information before being allowed to receive the content. Authentication information such as user names and passwords can be stored in a database contained in the web server. Figure 1-13 illustrates the basic web server architecture.

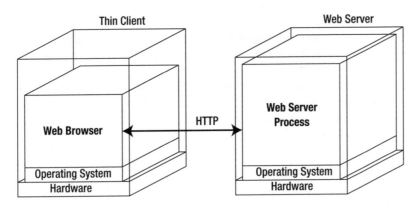

Figure 1-13. *Basic web server architecture*

Web servers worked well in advertising, but they could not capture or exchange rudimentary user information because of HTML's limitations. To extend the web server functionality to support persistent storage and state variables for user information, the architecture must be enhanced by using web server interfaces.

Web Server Interfaces

Information that requires data to be stored cannot be processed by the web server process. Instead, it must be passed off to an external process. Each web server has a set of application programming interfaces (APIs) that allows an external process to be called. Web servers can exchange user information through rudimentary interfaces such as the Common Gateway Interface (CGI), Netscape Server API (NSAPI), and Internet Server API (ISAPI) or through more advanced mechanisms available with Microsoft's Active Server Pages (ASP) or Sun's Java Servlets. Figure 1-14 illustrates the use of a web server interface.

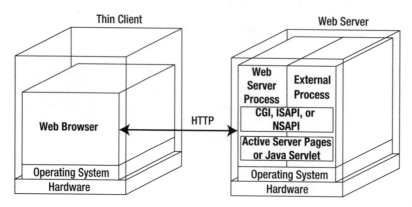

Figure 1-14. *Web server interface*

Separating the software into different processes offers the advantage of modularity and reliability, and it extends the basic function of the web server. The disadvantage of using some of the early mechanisms was that a new process was typically started for each user request, adding a significant amount of overhead and decreasing the server's responsiveness. Microsoft's ASP and Sun's Java Servlets removed this problem by allowing a persistent process to be maintained on the server, as shown in Figure 1-15.

These external processes perform business logic. When connected to some form of persistent data store, they also give the user the ability to enter user information and exchange data between the web server and the thin client. This configuration, with the appropriate security in place, supports thin client transactional business applications.

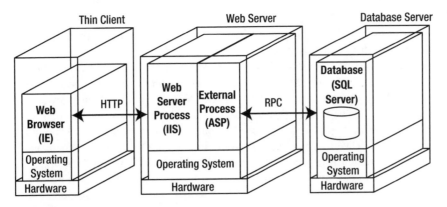

Figure 1-15. *Microsoft Active Server Pages*

Application Server

As applications added users and required more business functionality, the business logic located in the external processes continued to expand. This caused the web server performance to suffer. To remove this performance problem, the revised architecture shuffles off the logic to a new server called the *application server*, while keeping the data in a central database server, as shown in Figure 1-16. The application server concentrates on working with business logic and the user's session state. This architecture adds complexity and continues to evolve.

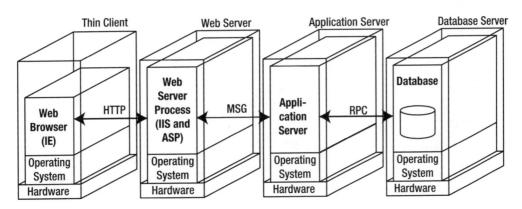

Figure 1-16. *Application server*

Thin Client Anatomy

As illustrated in Figure 1-17, the thin client anatomy centers on an application called a *browser*. With its small size, the primary purpose of the browser is to present HTML web pages. HTML displays text and static pictures, and has no binary executable. Designers can manipulate fonts and text placement easily by using specific HTML tags. This way, the user and thin client got an attractive presentation, much like looking at paper magazine or periodical (which is why it works well with marketing and advertising).

Also integral to the browser is a scripting interpreter. Netscape developed the JavaScript language and embedded the interpreter into its browser, and Microsoft did the same with JScript and Internet Explorer. Scripting gives the browser a programming capability, which develops logic that can run on the thin client. This gave the browser the ability to execute rudimentary syntax checking, along with some robustness. Both Netscape and Microsoft also developed a Document Object Model (DOM) to assist in the creation, management, and control of forms. Forms give the thin client the basic functionality to exchange data with the server. Scripting languages could affect the applications running within the browser or launch different browser windows, but these languages were not given the ability to write to files or control resources outside the browser for security reasons. Scripting and the DOMs have improved significantly since their inception and have a much broader functionality today.

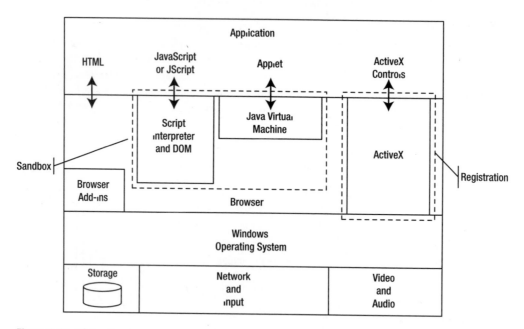

Figure 1-17. *Thin client anatomy*

It was difficult to create a viable business application using the initial versions of JavaScript or JScript. Sun Microsystems introduced the *applet*, which allowed an application to be created using the Java programming language. The applet used a Java Virtual Machine (JVM), which was loaded into the browser at startup. The JVM is a bytecode-level interpreter, which runs a fully functional business application developed in Java to execute in the memory space of the browser. Similar to the scripting languages, an applet could not use local resources. The applet could use only its own resources, browser resources, or resources from the server where it was loaded. The control and restriction over the applet is called a *sandbox*. A sandbox is a space where the application can function without affecting local resources. The sandbox is actually a special filter that allows only selected applications from the remote source to execute in the browser. Even with this protection, many businesses were, and still are, hesitant to use applets across the Internet.

Microsoft developed ActiveX to allow a Visual Basic, Visual C++, or .NET application to run within the memory space of the browser. Microsoft developers also realized that a number of desktops were running a Windows operating system and Internet Explorer. Instead of implementing a sandbox, they used a registration system, which allowed the user to accept or reject the application or control. The registration system in ActiveX released the untapped potential of its operating system to the application created in the browser.

Thin Client User Experience

Initially, the thin client could perform only simple advertising tasks. It was easy for the business to generate static advertising content and broadcast this to the user. In this static environment, the thin client performs well. The browser controls are relatively straightforward, and the user needs to learn only a few navigation techniques.

However, some difficulties started to hinder the user experience. First, user interface controls available to build mission-critical applications were limited to the forms available in the DOM. These forms supported only simple text boxes, combo boxes, labels, and buttons. Replacing the thick client environment with the thin client environment left users feeling they were in the kitchen, but there was no refrigerator, stove, or sink.

To make matters worse for business transactional applications, the Internet is stateless, which means each web page has no history of the other pages that preceded it or will follow it. As each page is presented to the user, this history or state must be tracked on the web server. This requires additional information to be sent back and forth over the network, decreasing the application's overall responsiveness. The stateless environment of the Internet is also reflected by the necessity of a refresh button on the browser. Information must be continuously refreshed at the user's request, since only the server, not the thin client, has this knowledge. This is in contrast to the thick client, which has the ability to write state and history information into memory, to a local file or a database. This gives the thick client application the ability to forecast where the user will go by determining where the user has been in the application.[3]

Keeping some form of state in the client increases the application's responsiveness and productivity of the user. The controls and capabilities currently available are moving toward providing responsive transactional applications as thin clients evolve, but they still have a long way to go to catch up with the rich functionality of thick clients.

Thin Client Communication

Thin client communication is based on TCP/IP, which is used by the Internet. Users type a Uniform Resource Locator (URL) in the address bar of the browser to request information from a server on the Internet or intranet. The URL is broken into specific sections that direct the user's request by defining a particular protocol, the target server or domain

---

3. An example of such forecasting is how Microsoft Excel uses this technique. When the user starts typing into a new cell, Excel completes the entry with the contents of a cell where the user previously typed, to see if this meets the user's criteria.

name, port, path, and if necessary, input parameters. The composition of a URL is as follows for a CGI request:

```
protocol://<server name or domain name >[:port]/
<CGI path and program name>/[extra path info]?[query string]
```

To access any server on the Internet, a unique TCP/IP address is required. The domain name portion of the URL is resolved automatically to the server's TCP/IP quadded decimal address, such as 123.12.133.15. Each address can have a number of ports assigned to it, but the two primary ports of the web server are port 80, which is used for unsecured information transfer, and port 443, which is used for secured (private) information transfer. Figure 1-18 illustrates web server-to-browser communication.

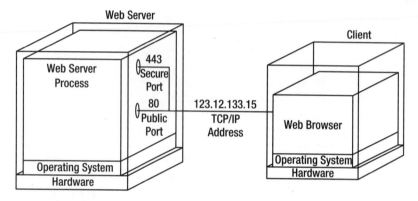

Figure 1-18. *Web server-to-browser communication*

Security is a major concern for any thin client implementation, since information is being sent via a public network. Information being transferred to or from port 443 can be encrypted. *Encryption* means that all information is scrambled using an advanced algorithm (mathematical polynomial) before being transmitted by the web server. This encryption algorithm is sold by organizations (such as VeriSign) fronted by the U.S. National Security Agency (NSA). Specific encryption algorithms (128-bit) are available for use only within the United States, and other algorithms (40-bit) can be used in foreign countries.

Thin Client Deployment

The deployment model for the thin client is excellent. Coupled with its community reach, deployment ease is the major selling point for developing business applications that use thin clients. Since all resources are deployed to the servers, upgrading and performing maintenance involves only a single move to these localized resources. Corporations or hosting services typically own all the hardware and software, and locate these resources in a central area to make deployment operations easy. Businesses can schedule releases more readily, and align them directly with business initiatives and strategic movement.

Smart Clients

The smart client employs the best features of stand-alone applications and the thick and thin clients. Stand-alone applications work best in isolation. The smart client will give the user the ability to function when disconnected from the network or remote resources. The thick client gives a rich user experience and access to local resources on the device, whereas the thin client gives the user access to global remote resources. The smart client uses both local and remote resources, while supplying a highly interactive environment to give the user a rich experience. The thin client supports easy single-point deployment and using advanced techniques. The smart client will also supply this cost-effective feature.

Unlike its predecessors, the smart client is easy to deploy on multiple devices. This gives it a distinct advantage, since only one application needs to be developed to support a variety of devices and business roles.

Smart Client Architecture

The architecture of the smart client varies based on the business needs that it is expected to solve. The smart client architecture works well in a Model-View-Controller (MVC) approach. These three components aggregate the logic of the application into three entities: The model is the state or perisistent data, the view is the presentation or graphical user interface (GUI), and the controller is the business logic. The basic smart client architecture extends this model by separating local and remote resources into additional components. Local resources are code, runtime libraries (DLLs), or software applications, which could be deployed or are already available on the mobile device. These resources offer speed and execution advantages. Remote resources are code, runtime libraries, or software applications, which could be deployed or are available to connect with over a network. Remote resources offer a broad reach, but typically have a performance impact associated with them.

If connectivity to remote resources is available, the smart client will require the sophistication to determine when it is appropriate to use a remote resource rather than a local resource, as shown in Figure 1-19. However, if remote resources are disconnected, the smart client will rely on business logic and local resources contained within the smart device, as shown in Figure 1-20. Likewise, if local resources are not available, but remote resources are, the smart client could rely on the remote resources to keep the user working, as shown in Figure 1-21. In rare cases, if both local and remote resources are not available, the smart client may still be able to perform the function the user is requesting. These scenarios demonstrate the high reliability smart clients can achieve to keep the user productive.

The architecture of the smart client will need to address the appropriate balance between the resources and their availability, as illustrated in Figure 1-22. The smart client in isolation a large percentage of the time will need to focus on the usage of local resources. As the percentage of the time that both local and remote resources are available increases, so does the degree of sophistication required to deal with both sets of resources.

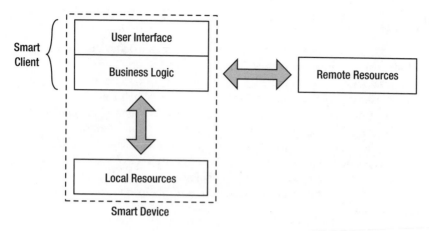

Figure 1-19. *A smart client using both local and remote resources*

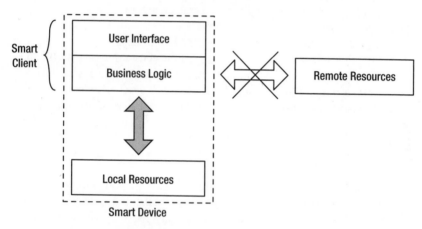

Figure 1-20. *A smart client using local resources if remote resources are disconnected*

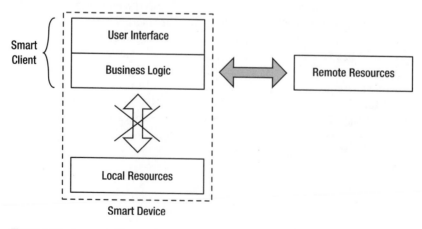

Figure 1-21. *A smart client using remote resources if local resources are unavailable*

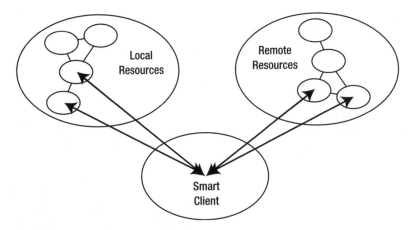

Figure 1-22. *Smart clients balance local and remote resources.*

Smart Client Anatomy

The smart client has a variable size depending on the business solution. The smart client sits on top of the Windows operating system and offers developers tools originally available only to thick clients. These tools exploit all the benefits of Windows to allow developers to produce fully functional client-side applications, with rich user interfaces.

Concurrency plays a significant role in all aspects of the smart client, from its execution to its communication. The smart client supports multiple threads, which can be used to make the user interface responsive in more complex applications. Developers can set up communication using an asynchronous message approach to allow the user to concurrently perform operations while information is being exchanged with remote resources.

The smart client also uses the advanced technology mechanisms available with the .NET Framework to connect to remote resources. Smart clients have numerous mechanisms, both tightly and loosely coupled, including .NET Enterprise Services, .NET Remoting, and message queuing using MSMQ. They can also use a web services implementation.

Smart Client User Experience

The client technology of the thick and thin worlds segregated the local and remote resources, significantly diminishing the user experience. Simple interaction was limited to cut-and-paste or downloading. Using smart client technology gives the user a new set of experiences in a highly interactive environment, as illustrated in Figure 1-23. Local and remote services can be integrated seamlessly on a single screen, providing both the global reach of thin clients and the complex functionality of thick clients. This integration, coupled with sophisticated interactivity, can give the user advanced techniques to simplify activities, increase productivity, and obtain new solutions previously not available. Local and remote resource requests can be powered by the local hardware to give the user a highly responsive application, without experiencing any unwanted latency.

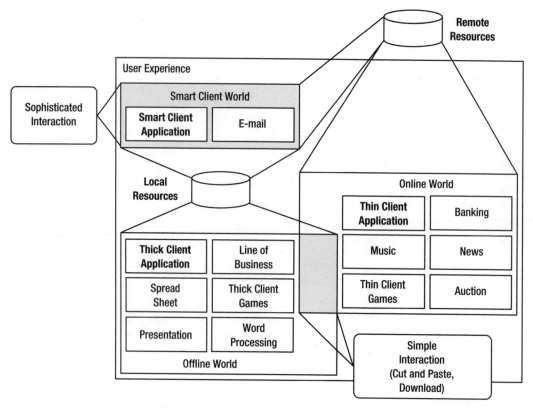

Figure 1-23. *Offline, online, and smart client world*

Smart Client Communication

Connected or isolated—the smart client can perform in both environments equally well with
the appropriate architectural considerations. Smart clients developed to support an isolated
application can be equipped with asynchronous communication via MSMQ. MSMQ messages
can be sent using a store-and-forward or asynchronous communication configuration. Using
this communication mode, if the smart client is disconnected, the messages are sent to an outbox located on the local platform's persistent storage device. The smart client will then return
operation to the user and wait for the device to connect to the network or Internet. Once the
device connects to the remote service, messages will be automatically sent and processed, and
the response will be placed in the centralized server's outbox. Again, when the device is connected to the network, the response will be sent back to the smart client.

Smart clients that have connectivity to remote resources can use a variety of communication styles—broadcast, synchronous, and asynchronous—depending on the responsiveness
needed by the user and the timeliness of the messages. Synchronous message transmission is
faster for short operations when a minimal wait is acceptable. Asychronous message transmission can be used if the request contains a large amount of data.

Smart Client Deployment

One of the biggest advantages of thin clients over thick clients is the ease in which they deployed. Smart clients expand on thin client deployment by offering intelligent deployment and upgrading capabilities.

Deployment involves getting a set of files or an executable onto a local machine. This can be accomplished by downloading the files from a staging computer to the user's computer. More advanced mechanisms also exist using Microsoft IIS and the .NET Framework. The Information Technology (IT) department could stage the files to the web server and let it perform the release or upgrade. Microsoft labels this operation "No-Touch." Other No-Touch options include downloading a small application called a *stub*, which, in turn, downloads the larger quantity of files or executables, potentially in the background while the user works with another application. Another option, if enough network bandwidth is available, is to centrally locate the smart client on a file share. Using this method removes the requirement of having the smart client installed on the local hardware and executes it from a remote network resource. However, the application still executes on the local hardware. Another deployment option is to use a Windows installer, which will download and install all the necessary files and the .NET Framework to make the smart client function on the user's local machine. These options provide a diverse set of alternatives to install the smart client and provide incremental updates that will not impact the user's overall productivity.

Smart Client Development

The .NET Framework offers a robust development environment using Visual Studio that allows the developer to create and debug controls. You can leverage Visual Studio's full power and functionality to develop the smart client. You also no longer need to worry about common resources being corrupted by more than one application. The problem that was associated with DLL Hell has been removed. Application isolation ensures that one application will not affect another. This improves the developer's experience when building a smart client.

Service-Oriented Smart Clients (SOSCs)

The SOSC extends the smart client to perform better business analysis and deliver a variety of solutions, and potentially an optimal solution. The SOSC requires greater intelligence and agility in its design than the smart client to optimize its performance. The SOSC uses a service-oriented architecture (SOA) and its principles and practices to accomplish its business objective. An SOA promotes reusability by creating and using reusable services. A web service separates the business functionality of the service from the user presentation, enabling the service to be accessed directly using the Extensible Markup Language (XML).

A large benefit of deploying an SOSC is the alignment with the real-world business services. These real-world services are executed and implemented by real people.

For example, a book distribution company that has sales, shipping, and customer support departments might develop a web service mirroring the functionality of each real-world service. Customers at a warehouse wishing to determine the status of their order could call the shipping department on the phone to speak with an individual, or they could use an SOSC that would connect to the registry of the corporation, activate a conversation with the shipping web service, and retrieve the order status directly. A detailed look at the shipping department would reveal that, when a customer is calling on the phone, the shipping clerk is also retrieving the order status using an SOSC connected to the corporate intranet. Figure 1-24 illustrates this example.

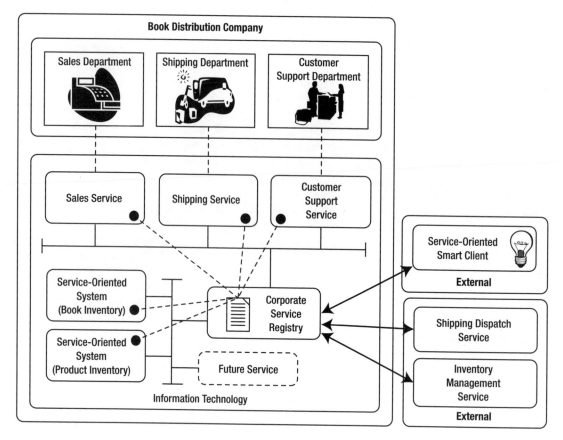

Figure 1-24. *A service-oriented smart client business case*

SOSC Architecture

An SOSC employs web services that are directly aligned with real-world business services. The SOA leverages the technologies of XML and its ancillary languages. It then couples XML technology with the technology of web services. XML is a mature markup language, which extends interoperability to different systems using a message-based format. Messages are transmitted via the Simple Object Access Protocol (SOAP). XML technology in this context also refers to XML Schema Definition (XSD) language and Extensible Stylesheet Language Transformations (XSLT), which are used to develop XML documents.

Each web service in the architecture is expected to implement business logic through a well-defined interface. The web service publishes information about itself to a registry using the Web Services Definition Language (WSDL). The WSDL identifies the interface, the interface binding, and the location of the service. The Universal Description, Discovery and Integration (UDDI) specification defines all aspects of the registry. Figure 1-25 shows the SOSC architecture.

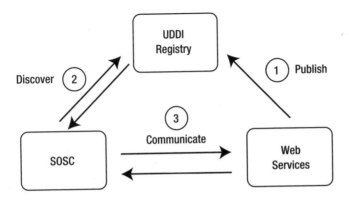

Figure 1-25. *Web service interaction*

The registry is a centralized lookup facility, which contains information about all the available web services. A client would discover what web services are available at a web site through the use of the Web Services Inspection Language (WSIL) by communicating with the registry. Once the web service is located, a direct communication between client and the web service would commence using SOAP. Figure 1-26 illustrates the web service model.

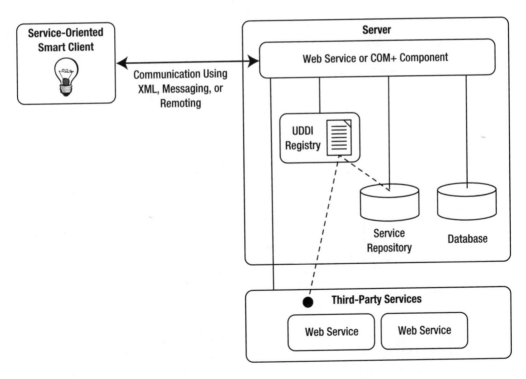

Figure 1-26. *Web service model*

The SOSC principle asset is intelligence, which gives it agility, and when coupled with basic smart client technology, gives new meaning to the word *smart*.

SOSC Anatomy

The critical components of the SOSC are the smart agent, a local service registry, local service repository, and local data store, as shown in Figure 1-27. The local service registry stores web services and provides facilities to lookup services. The local service repository contains running instances of services and provides facilities to use them. The local data store provides a location to persistently store data for the SOSC. These three components give the SOSC the ability to function in isolation and extend the ability of the user to perform business objectives when not in an online mode.

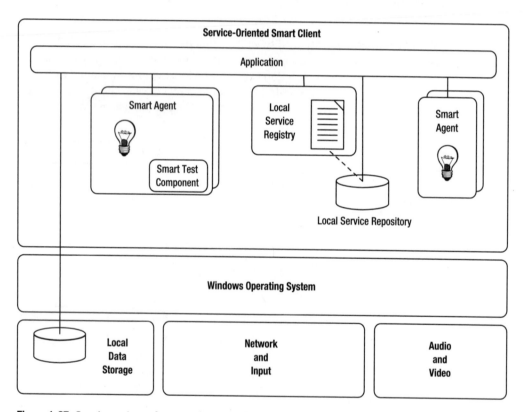

Figure 1-27. *Service-oriented smart client model*

The SOSC can use remote resources when online. Similar to their local counterparts, the typical server components consist of a service registry, service repository, and data store. As a business application, an SOSC has the responsibility to be agile and intelligent in determining which and how many remote services it should connect to. These components can vary depending on the needs of the business solution.

The smart agent is one of the most critical components of the SOSC. As a pluggable intelligent agent, this component has at its disposal both local and remote resources. The smart agent will know if remote resources are available, and balance local and remote information as it is processed by the SOSC. If remote resources are unavailable, the SOSC will optimize itself for isolation. When connected, the SOSC uses the smart agents to increase its community reach and explore a greater number of available remote resources. If the local resources are unavailable for a reason other than a critical system failure, the smart agent could make sure that remote resources keep the user productivity intact.

The smart test component will reside as an integral part of the smart agent. Applying an embedded smart test component will ensure ample testing is being done once the smart agent is plugged in and integrated with SOSC. The smart test component would check for changes at initialization or during a change of state in the SOSC, similar to the way Microsoft Windows uses Plug-and-Play to check for new hardware.

The smart test component has two principle missions. Its first is to ensure the integrity of the SOSC is maintained and make the user aware of potential issues in this environment. This is accomplished by the smart test component establishing and maintaining communications with local and remote resources by referencing state information held in the local data store. The second is to ensure that the smart agent is performing its functions correctly. Periodically or on demand, the smart test component will test itself using a facsimile of a request from the application.

The local services registry makes the SOSC aware of what services are available when in isolation and what services can be established once connected. This local registry establishes what services have been historically called and can be called upon by the SOSC. The local services repository stores services for local utilization—most important, those critical services needed by the SOSC in isolation.

SOSC Testing

An SOSC presents a number of challenges and opportunities from a testing perspective. One aspect of an SOSC that will improve testing is the alignment of departmental business processes with IT services, to make it easier to ensure requirements are being satisfied. However, there are many more challenges to testing an SOSC.

The architecture of an SOSC distributes business logic and persistence in both local components and remote components. This adds complexity that is not readily apparent. One of these complexities is in the system's state engine. The system may need to use local persistent data prior to trying to access remote persistent data or vice versa. A chronology or timestamp may need to be introduced within both persistent data structures to accommodate the relationships between local and remote resources. This will require the creation of sequenced event-based tests to check out the local-to-remote configurations.

The intelligence of the smart agent within the SOSC presents another testing challenge. A smart agent can elect to override local resources and connect to multiple remote services to obtain optimum data for the SOSC. This intelligence comes with a cost by extending the amount of testing. This testing can be accomplished by embedding a smart test component to maintain the health and integrity of the SOSC.

SOSC User Experience

The SOSC reaps the benefits of a smart client and adds an intelligence that will work seamlessly with the user experience. The SOSC will automatically inform the user of local and remote resource availability. When connected, its intelligence gives the user a broader reach, allowing the user to make more informed decisions. When isolated, the SOSC will ensure critical data and functionality are available to the user. This gives the user the best experience and support for making the right business decisions, whether offline or online.

SOSC Communication

The SOSC communicates with the corporate or third-party web services as described earlier using XML through a messaging interface. Alternatively, it can use .NET Remoting, which allows access and use of remote objects and gives the SOSC more flexibility. .NET Remoting works well with HTTP listeners with XML when traversing the Internet. Additionally, if the SOSC is deployed on an intranet, you may be able to speed up communication by using the various forms of customizations possible with .NET Remoting.

Asynchronous and synchronous communication will both be used based on input from the smart agent. If isolated from remote resources, the SOSC will use asynchronous store-and-forward mechanisms to preserve communications with remote resources. This communication style guarantees delivery once the SOSC is reconnected. When the SOSC is connected, the smart agent can balance communications between a synchronous and asynchronous communication style, depending on the size and urgency of the request. This optimizes the user experience based on the available communication bandwidth.

SOSC Deployment

The SOSC uses the deployment techniques and mechanisms of the smart client. In addition, the intelligence in the SOSC's smart agent can assist in determining when the SOSC needs an upgrade. The smart agent is also a pluggable self-contained entity, which gives the SOSC a smaller footprint and makes it more flexible in deployment.

Summary

In this chapter, we introduced the smart client and SOSC. First, we described the evolution of the smart client, in the context of the evolution of client architecture: from stand-alone applications, to thick clients in client/server applications, to thin clients in web-based applications, and to the new smart client architecture. Then we explored thick and thin clients in more detail, because smart clients are designed to have the advantages of both of these types of clients, while avoiding their disadvantages. Finally, we looked at the makeup of smart clients and SOSCs, which are the subject of this book.

In the next chapter, you'll learn about the various types of smart clients.

CHAPTER 2

∎∎∎

Types of Smart Clients

Smart clients come in three distinct types: Windows Forms smart clients, Office smart clients, and mobile smart clients. Windows Forms smart clients are built with the WinForms technology and resemble traditional rich user interface applications that run on the desktop. Office smart clients are applications built with the Office 2003 suite of technologies. Mobile smart clients are applications written with the .NET Compact Framework for smart devices (such as a Pocket PC). These types of smart clients are built to support the mobile worker.

In this chapter, we'll describe the different types of smart clients and discuss when to use each type. This chapter sets the stage for the next three chapters, where we discuss how to build each type of smart client.

Overview of Smart Client Types

Here are brief descriptions of the three main smart client types:

Windows Forms (WinForms) smart client: The most popular type of smart client, the WinForms smart client represents the next generation of thin and thick clients. Generally, a WinForms smart client functions while offline, makes heavy use of the client's resources (disk space, threads, and so on), and can interact with local applications. WinForms smart clients offer a tremendous cost savings because organizations can avoid needing to buy the hardware required to host and run alternative solutions (for example, web applications).

Office smart client: This type of smart client come in two flavors: those based on Visual Studio Tools for Office (VSTO) and those based on the Information Bridge Framework (IBF). VSTO-based smart clients are smart clients whose core functionality extends Word or Excel. IBF-based smart clients are clients that connect Office products to line-of-business (LOB) systems. This type of smart client greatly reduces costs associated with getting data from LOB systems to users of Office of products. Office smart clients leverage Microsoft Office 2003, the .NET Framework, and the rapid application development (RAD) integration within Visual Studio. This variation of an Office smart client is applicable only when an organization has users who spend most of their workday using an Office product and who often need to stray to one or more LOB systems to complete their work.

Mobile smart client: Mobile smart clients are smart clients that run on Windows CE devices, such as Pocket PCs and Smartphones, on top of the .NET Compact Framework. Mobile smart clients have features similar to WinForms smart clients, such as support for offline use. This type of smart client is meant for companies who have mobile workers or who can gain a competitive edge by offering a mobile solution.

As you can see, the smart client space spans all of Office, the .NET desktop, and the .NET Compact Framework. Each type of smart client targets a specific problem space at the enterprise level. For example, we can now build *n*-tier Office smart clients.

Note that the types of smart clients don't include web-based technologies. With the investment that Microsoft is making in smart clients, the direction of application development is moving away from web-based applications and back toward desktop applications. As you'll see, WinForms smart clients offer the same advantages web-based solutions provide, without the disadvantages, so there will definitely be a reduction in the number of web-based applications we'll build in the future.[1]

We'll cover each smart client type in more detail in the remainder of this chapter.

Windows Forms Smart Clients

Windows Forms (WinForms) smart clients are the next generation of rich user interface applications. This is the most popular type of smart client because it extends the advantages of the traditional thick clients and also offers the best of thin clients. A WinForms smart client has a client-side footprint. In other words, the WinForms smart client runs on the client's machine, and thus has full access to local resources. The application can cache data locally, use threads, access the network, access printers, and so on. This allows the enterprise to shift load off servers while putting to use rather extensive resources on the desktops.

WinForms smart clients have the following main features:

- Thick client style user interface, with dynamic controls, responsive behavior, and so on

- Thin client style deployment, so you can deploy an application to a web server, and clients anywhere can download it from there

- Smart client updates, so applications can be versioned instead of having the user download and run only the latest version

- Smart client offline support, so applications can function without a network connection and resynchronize when network connections resume

Offline Capabilities

Offline capability is a feature often found in WinForms and mobile smart clients. In fact, some applications already have this capability. For example, if you launch Microsoft Outlook 2003 with a network connection, Outlook connects to your configured accounts. You can then send and receive e-mail, add journal entries, and so on. If you then disconnect from the network and choose to work offline, you can still use Outlook as if you were online; that is, you can continue to send e-mail, add journal entries, and perform other work in the program. When you decide to go back online (when you have a network connection), Outlook connects to your accounts and sends any messages you may have in your outbox.

Figure 2-1 shows an example of working offline in Outlook. You can see that Outlook has a Work Offline menu item under the File menu. When you go offline, Outlook displays the

---

1. This doesn't mean that web-based applications will completely disappear. We will still build web-based applications, just fewer of them.

offline indicator at the lower-right corner of the user interface. When you go online, Outlook resynchronizes with the server to update your messages, journal, and other items.

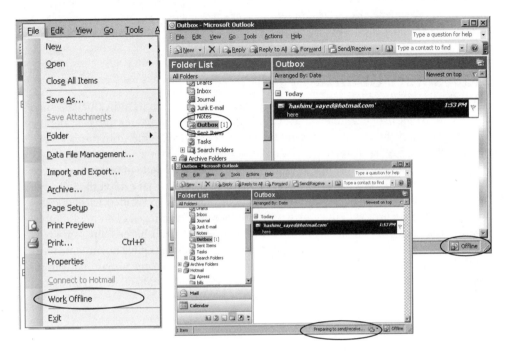

Figure 2-1. *Outlook's offline capabilities*

Providing offline capabilities is one of the features that make this next generation of client-side applications smart. This is one way that applications stay a step ahead of the user.

Deployment Solutions

Over the past decade, technology decision makers (chief technical officers, architects, senior designers, and the like) have chosen to deliver less functionality with thin clients, even though thick clients have more functionality and allow users to get a lot more done in the same amount of time. The primary reason for this decision is that web solutions are easy and cheap to deploy, while thick clients are difficult and expensive to deploy. A web-based application can be deployed in a matter of minutes, because all you need to do is copy the files onto the web server. The same is not true for thick clients. To deploy a thick client, you must first build an installer for the application, and then possibly burn CDs/DVDs of the installer. You then need to get those copies to your installation base. In other words, deploying thick clients is time consuming and costly.

Perhaps the most attractive feature of a WinForms smart client is that it is easy to deploy. WinForms smart clients offer a better deployment solution than thin clients, while providing the same benefits of a thick client. Deploying smart clients is supported with technologies that not only allow smart clients to be deployed similar to how web applications are deployed, but also to be updated and versioned easily. We'll talk all about deploying WinForms smart clients in detail in Chapter 7.

WinForms smart clients are applicable in most places where thin clients have been deployed to circumvent deployment costs and efforts. WinForms smart clients also are applicable wherever thick clients have been deployed in the past.

Office Smart Clients

The WinForms smart client is not entirely new, because we have seen its individual offerings in other solution types; for example, offline capabilities in e-mail programs and easy deployment of thin clients. Office smart clients, on the other hand, are different from the types of clients with which we're familiar.

Office smart clients are applications built with the Office 2003 suite of technologies. You can use Visual Studio Tools for Office (VSTO)[2] to build applications that exploit the full power of Word or Excel. These types of applications often consume complex Word or Excel documents and provide the user with the Office user interface and a managed code-behind file.

Additionally, you can build Information Bridge Framework (IBF)-based Office smart clients. This type of Office smart client adds functionality to existing Office documents (created in Word, Excel, Outlook, and so on). For instance, you can add some functionality to the task pane of Word to call a web service to retrieve context-sensitive data related to an open Word document.

Here, we'll look at both types of Office smart clients.

VSTO-Based Office Smart Clients

VSTO-based Office smart clients are clients that leverage the power of the .NET Framework, Visual Studio, and Word or Excel, all in one solution. For example, envision opening a Word document that shows a customer's name that is hyperlinked. When you click the link, the customer's orders and contact information appear in the task pane.

In a nutshell, a VSTO-based smart client is a client that is built with Visual Studio, whose user interface is either Word or Excel, and whose code-behind is in managed code (such as C#). You can build these types of smart clients because VSTO enables an intimate relationship between Visual Studio and Office (2003 and later versions).

Figure 2-2 shows the Visual Studio 2005 New Project dialog box and an example of a VSTO-based Office smart client user interface. Notice that Visual Studio 2005 supports two types of VSTO-based smart clients: Word and Excel. Also notice that VSTO-based Office smart clients run within their corresponding Office product, which is Excel in the example in Figure 2-2. If the smart client is based on Excel, then Excel is launched; if it's based on Word, Word is launched.

---

2. Visual Studio Tools for Office is actually a shorter name for the product. The full name is Microsoft Visual Studio 2005 Tools for the Microsoft Office System.

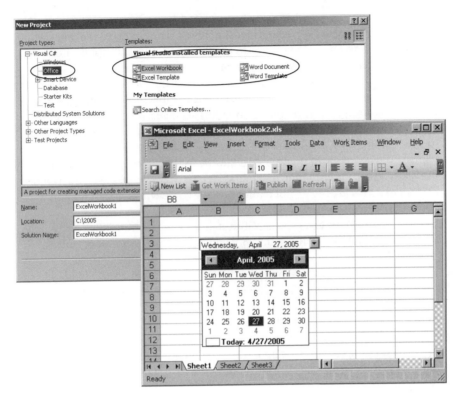

Figure 2-2. *A VSTO-based Office smart client*

The figure also shows that the smart client has a DateTimePicker WinForms control within the Excel worksheet. This demonstrates one of the features that makes VSTO-based smart clients powerful: you have full access to the .NET Framework and Word or Excel. In addition, you can use Visual Studio with the RAD style development to rapidly build applications whose core functionality is based on either Word or Excel. The technology is powerful enough to support an enterprise application capable of deploying across an *n*-tier architecture. We'll cover this type of deployment in Chapter 4, where we discuss Office smart clients in detail.

VSTO-based Office smart clients are a good choice when you need to write an application whose core functionality is either in Word or Excel. For example, if you have complex Excel spreadsheets and need to build an enterprise application on top of Excel, then developing this type of smart client makes sense.

IBF-Based Office Smart Clients

The other type of Office smart client is based on IBF, a technology that brings the data from line-of-business (LOB) systems directly to Office documents (Word, Excel, Outlook, and InfoPath). This enables employees to complete their job directly from the Office product and not need to learn several LOB systems.

IBF-based Office smart clients are best described with a real-world scenario. Consider an actuary, named John, who works for a medical insurance provider. John's job is to build and support the risk (cost) associated with the company's list of products. He builds new cost models and maintains existing cost models using Excel spreadsheets. Because his job is solely to support the company's products, John spends most of his workday in Excel, playing around with the product spreadsheets. Often, John needs to use the company's LOB applications for doing cost analyses. For example, John uses the company's customer relationship management (CRM) system to get details about a customer, and he uses the billing system to find out last year's monthly premiums for the customer. It takes considerable time for John to log in to these systems and navigate around to find the information he needs. (Imagine the additional wasted time, effort, and cost if the company had a half dozen actuaries doing this.)

It would be nice if John could access these LOB systems directly from within the Excel spreadsheet. Perhaps the task pane of Excel could show the list of customers and allow him to drill down into their contact information and billing details. That would save John a lot of time and enable him to do his job better, not to mention the cost savings to the company. An IBF-based Office smart client is the solution.

IBF-based Office smart clients can expose LOB systems directly within Office documents. Not only can you interface with the LOB systems, but you do so with the power of Office and .NET at your disposal.

Let's look at another example. With the power of IBF, Office, .NET, and Visual Studio, you can build an IBF-based Office smart client that hyperlinks critical data within an Outlook e-mail message. Clicking links within the e-mail message provides readers with context-sensitive data related to the message (displayed directly within the e-mail). Suppose that a customer representative of a telecommunications company receives an e-mail message from a dissatisfied customer. Rather than opening several LOB applications to find out who the customer is and what product she purchased, the rep can click the name of the customer in the e-mail message to find out all of this information.

IBF-based Office smart clients are applicable only in situations where an organization has a sufficient number of employees who spend most of their workday using the Office product to justify the cost of building the solution. It does not make sense to build a solution if you have only a few users that use, say Excel, for an hour a day.

Mobile Smart Clients

Mobile smart clients are built with the .NET Compact Framework. The fundamental features of smart clients apply across the board to all the types of smart clients. Conceptually, building mobile smart clients is similar to building WinForms smart clients. The difference is that the mobile versions have some added constraints due to the size of the mobile device and the limitations in the .NET Compact Framework. You'll learn about these constraints in Chapter 5, where we cover developing mobile smart clients.

With the release of Visual Studio 2005, developers will have major additions to the .NET Compact Framework, Visual Studio's integration with smart devices, and RAD development with respect to mobile development. For example, Visual Studio 2005 has a new project type targeting Smartphones and better debugging support for mobile applications.

Organizations need to find intelligent methods of getting information to their employees in order to stay competitive. A mobile solution makes sense when your applications are used by mobile workers. For example, the United Parcel Service (UPS) and Federal Express use mobile solutions extensively to support the core of their business.

Summary

In this chapter, you learned about the three main types of smart clients: WinForms, Office, and mobile smart clients. Each of these is designed to solve a different problem.

WinForms smart clients are intelligent applications that run on the desktop. This type of smart client is geared to replace web-based applications and the traditional thick client. Although web-based applications still have their place, we will build fewer thin clients in the future.

Office smart clients come in two types: VSTO-based and IBF-based. VSTO-based Office smart clients run within the Office product (Word or Excel), and thus are geared to extend the functionality of the product with the .NET Framework. IBF-based Office smart clients are meant to connect Office documents to LOB systems and to circumvent the cost and effort required to gather information from these systems. This type of solution is meant for organizations that have a considerable number of employees who use one or more of the Office products and must frequently access LOB applications to do their work.

The mobile smart client is built on the .NET Compact Framework and can add a competitive advantage for organizations that have mobile workers.

In the next chapter, we'll get to the nuts and bolts of building WinForms smart clients.

CHAPTER 3

■ ■ ■

Windows Forms Smart Clients

As you learned in Chapter 2, Windows Forms (WinForms) smart clients are the most popular type of smart client, offering a rich user interface similar to traditional desktop applications.

In this chapter, we will get into the nuts and bolts of building WinForms smart client applications. Rather than build an application from scratch, we'll look at two reference implementations of smart clients: TaskVision and IssueVision. These two applications are complete solutions. Both can be downloaded in C# and VB .NET. In addition, TaskVision can be downloaded for the Pocket PC.

TaskVision is a problem-tracking application that demonstrates the fundamental concepts behind building WinForms smart clients. IssueVision is a help desk application. IssueVision and TaskVision are not related. However, IssueVision corrects some of the problems in Task-Vision by using design patterns and best practices. TaskVision, nevertheless, is the starting place for building smart clients for Windows. Once you understand TaskVision, understanding IssueVision will be easier. Therefore, we are going to thoroughly dissect TaskVision to ensure that you understand the core of what smart clients are all about. We will augment this by discussing the important aspects of IssueVision. Understanding these two applications will thoroughly prepare you for building your own WinForms smart clients.

Getting Started with TaskVision

The TaskVision application demonstrates some of the fundamental concepts related to building WinForms smart clients. To get started with TaskVision, go to its home page on MSDN at `http://msdn.microsoft.com/library/default.asp?url=/library/en-us/dnwinforms/html/wnf_taskvision.asp`. You'll see that three different downloads are available for TaskVision:

- The client download is a Microsoft Installer package (MSI), which contains only the client binaries. This client, by default, is configured to run against a public web service for its server.

- The server download is also an MSI, and this MSI creates the TaskVision database on a locally running SQL Server and installs a few web services.

- The source code MSI installs a VB .NET version of the solution, because TaskVision was initially developed in VB .NET. The C# version was developed later and can be downloaded from the following location as a zip file: http://www.windowsforms.net/ Applications/application.aspx?PageID=20&tabindex=8.

Go ahead and download the client, server, and solution. We'll begin by getting the Task-Vision client up and running.

Installing the TaskVision Client

As noted, the TaskVision client, by default, is configured to execute against a few public web services. This means that you don't need to install the server locally to get the client up and running.

To install the client, double-click taskvisionclient_1.0.0.0.msi and follow the directions. After a few simple screens, the application should install under the TaskVision program group, unless you specified another location.

Next, run the application from the Start menu. When you start the application, you'll be presented with the TaskVision Login dialog box, as shown in Figure 3-1. To log in to the application, use **jdoe** as the user name and **welcome** as the password.

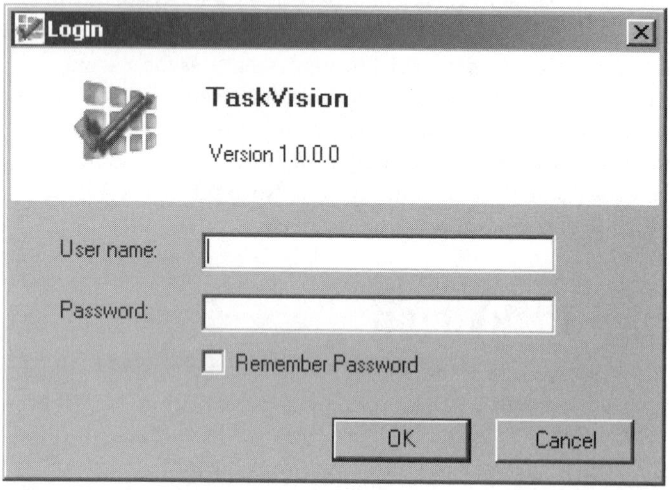

Figure 3-1. *The TaskVision Login dialog box*

After you log in, the TaskVision user interface should load tasks, as shown in Figure 3-2. The web service that provides data to TaskVision is publicly available on the Internet and may be updated by someone using the web service, so TaskVision probably won't show the same tasks as you see in this figure. Clicking a task shows its summary just below the data grid pane. Double-clicking a task brings up a dialog box with the tasks details, including history. You can add new tasks, as well as add new users and projects, and edit existing users.

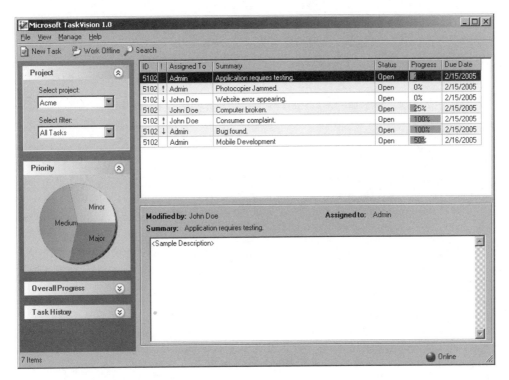

Figure 3-2. *The TaskVision user interface*

As you would expect from a WinForms smart client, the application provides offline and online capability. You can click the Work Offline button on the toolbar to work without updating the server, and then click Work Online to reconnect to the back-end server. If you work offline and then go back online, the application automatically synchronizes your changes with the back-end server.

TaskVision supports exporting tasks to Excel. You can do this by choosing File ➤ Export to Excel (or use the shortcut Ctrl+E).

Play around with the application a bit to get familiar with it. (Note that the web service is reset nightly, so don't expect to make changes and have these changes persist overnight.) When you feel comfortable with the program, continue to the next section to install the server.

Installing the TaskVision Server

Before you run the MSI to install the server, review the following checklist and ensure that you have satisfied the installation requirements.

- The logged-in user is an admin on the machine (must belong to local administrator group).

- You have SQL Server running locally. Note that it is also helpful if you have either SQL Server Enterprise Manager or another SQL Server management tool installed locally.

- The logged-in user has SQL Server administrator privileges using integrated security.

- Internet Information Server (IIS) is installed and running.

If you have satisfied the installation requirements, run `taskvisionserver_1.1.0.0.msi` to install the server. After the installation completes, you should have the following installed:

- *TaskVision database on the local instance of SQL Server.* Verify this by running SQL Server Enterprise Manager and check under the local instance ➤ Databases ➤ TaskVision.

- *TaskVisionWS:* This is the TaskVision web service. If you chose the default install path, the virtual directory probably points to the physical path: `C:\Program Files\ TaskVision Server\TaskVisionWS`. You should verify that the virtual directory was created by checking under the Default Web Site in IIS.

- *TaskVisionUpdate.* This is the TaskVision update web site. If you chose the default install path, the virtual directory probably points to the physical path: `C:\Program Files\ TaskVision Server\TaskVisionUpdates`. You should verify that the virtual directory was created by checking under the Default Web Site in IIS.

If you have any installation problems, you can get support through the TaskVision forum at `http://www.windowsforms.net/Forums/ShowForum.aspx?tabIndex=1&tabId=41&ForumID=15`.

The next step is to point the client application to the locally installed server. The Task-Vision client application, by default, points to the public web service we talked about earlier. The client application finds its server by looking at a configuration setting in the application's configuration file. To modify this setting, find the TaskVision client configuration file, `TaskVision.exe.config`, located in the same directory where the application was installed. If you chose to install the application in the default path during installation, this is `C:\Program Files\TaskVision\1.0.0.0\`. Open this configuration file in a text editor. The original file looks like this:

```
<?xml version="1.0" encoding="utf-8"?>
<configuration>
  <appSettings>
    <!--   User application and configured property settings go here.-->
    <!--   Example: <add key="settingName" value="settingValue"/> -->
    <add key="AppUpdater1.UpdateUrl"
value="http://www.notouchdeploy.com/taskvisionupdates/updateversion.xml"/>
    <add key="TaskVision.AuthWS.AuthService"
value="http://www.notouchdeploy.com/taskvisionws/authservice.asmx"/>
    <add key="TaskVision.DataWS.DataService"
value="http://www.notouchdeploy.com/taskvisionws/dataservice.asmx"/>
  </appSettings>
</configuration>
```

Modify the file as follows to point to the local instances:

```
<?xml version="1.0" encoding="utf-8"?>
<configuration>
  <appSettings>
    <!--   User application and configured property settings go here.-->
    <!--   Example: <add key="settingName" value="settingValue"/> -->
    <add key="AppUpdater1.UpdateUrl"
value="http://localhost/taskvisionupdates/updateversion.xml"/>
    <add key="TaskVision.AuthWS.AuthService"
```

```
value="http://localhost/taskvisionws/authservice.asmx"/>
    <add key="TaskVision.DataWS.DataService"
value="http://localhost/taskvisionws/dataservice.asmx"/>
  </appSettings>
</configuration>
```

After you change the configuration file so that the client now points to the local running database and web applications, bring up the TaskVision client and log in with the same user name (jdoe) and password (welcome). After logging in, you should see the TaskVision user interface, showing two projects and six tasks. Experiment with the application to see how it works with the client and server installed on the local machine.

Installing the TaskVision Solution

So far, you have installed the TaskVision client and server. Now, you will install the source, so that you can look at the architecture and implementation of the solution. However, because the server installation installed the virtual directories and the TaskVision database, you need to first either remove these items or uninstall the application altogether. The easiest approach is to run the uninstaller from Add Remove Programs to clean up properly. If you don't uninstall the application or fail to delete the web applications installed by the server, you will see the error message shown in Figure 3-3 when you attempt to install the source MSI.

Figure 3-3. *The error message you'll receive if you don't uninstall the server before trying to install the source MSI*

The TaskVision solution is available in VB .NET and C#. If you want to install the VB .NET version, all you need to do is run `taskvisionsource_1.1.0.0.msi`. However, getting the C# version up and running requires a bit of work.

Installing the C# Version of the Source

To install the C# version, you first need to download the C# version of the Data Access Application Block (a reusable component designed to simplify data access), which is not included in the zip file but is required by the solution. Then, because the C# version is a zip file rather than an MSI, you will need to do some manual setup in IIS.

To get the C# version of the solution working, follow these steps:

1. Unzip the TaskVision C# solution (TaskVision_FullSource_CS.zip).

2. Download the Data Access Application Block for .NET version 1.0 from http://www.microsoft.com/downloads/details.aspx?displaylang=en&FamilyID=76FE2B16-3271-42C2-B138-2891102590AD.

3. Run the installer.

4. Open the Default Web Site in IIS and add a virtual directory named TaskVisionWsCsVs, pointing to {ZIPFILE_INSTALL}\ TaskVisionWsCsVs, where ZIPFILE_INSTALL is the directory where you unzipped the C# solution zip file.

5. Open the solution in Visual Studio .NET.

When you load the solution into Visual Studio .NET, you will likely get an error concerning the path to the Data Access Application Block you installed in step 2. If you don't get this error and the solution works just fine, you're finished. Otherwise, you need to resolve the path to the Data Access Application Block, because the solution is pointing to the wrong path. The easiest way to handle this is to remove the project in the solution, and then add it again from the correct place. In the Solution Explorer, right-click Microsoft.ApplicationBlocks.Data and remove the project from the solution. After you remove the project, right-click the solution in the Solution Explorer, choose Add ➤ Existing Project, and browse to where the data application block was installed (be sure to choose the C# version of the project). If you chose the default installation options when you installed the block, the C# version of the project will be in C:\Program Files\Microsoft Application Blocks for .NET\Data Access\Code\CS\. After you add the project, open the TaskVisionWsCsVs project and add the Data Access Application Block project as a reference.

Migrating to Visual Studio 2005

The TaskVision solution was built with Visual Studio 2003, but you can easily migrate it to Visual Studio 2005. To migrate the solution, start Visual Studio 2005 and open the solution (File ➤ Open Project/Solution). In the Open Project dialog box, browse to the TaskVision solution. When you choose the solution file and click Open, Visual Studio 2005 displays the Conversion Wizard. The Conversion Wizard guides you through a few questions, and then converts the solution file to the Visual Studio 2005 file format. The conversion process is depicted in Figure 3-4.

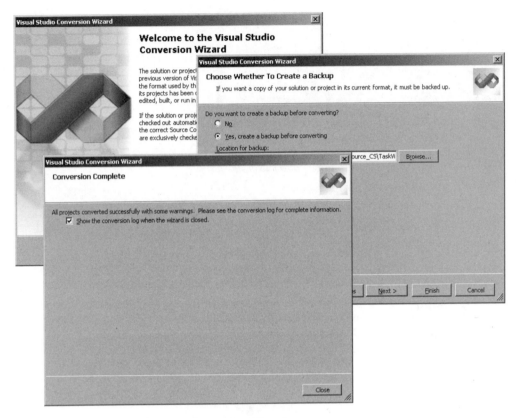

Figure 3-4. *The Visual Studio 2005 Conversion Wizard*

Running the Project

At this point, you should have the solution loaded into Visual Studio and be able to build the solution. If you get a build error concerning Excel, it is likely that you do not have Excel 2002 (or above) installed on your machine. You can either install Excel 2002 or just comment the references to Excel.

· Next, make sure that TaskVision is the selected project in the Solution Explorer and run the application. When the Login dialog box appears, use the same login you've used before (the user name jdoe and the password welcome).

The TaskVision client is configured to run against the remote web service at http://www.notouchdeploy.com. If you didn't change that, you probably passed authentication and now see the user interface with some tasks listed. If your Internet connection was down, you'll see the error shown in Figure 3-5.

Figure 3-5. *The error message you'll receive if you run the TaskVision project without an Internet connection*

Since you want to have the entire solution running locally, you need to modify the Task-Vision app.config file so that the client points to the locally installed web service. Open the configuration file in a text editor and change the settings to the following:

```
<configuration>
    <appSettings>
      <add key="AppUpdater1.UpdateUrl"
value="http://localhost/taskvisionupdates/updateversion.xml" />
      <add key="TaskVision.AuthWS.AuthService"
value="http://localhost/taskvisionwscsvs/authservice.asmx" />
      <add key="TaskVision.DataWS.DataService"
value="http://localhost/taskvisionwscsvs/dataservice.asmx" />
    </appSettings>
</configuration>
```

After your make the configuration changes, run the TaskVision project again. At this point, you may get the error message shown in Figure 3-6.

Figure 3-6. *Yet another error message*

Troubleshooting the Project

Unfortunately, as we've noted, the C# version of the application is difficult to get up and running. The error message shown in Figure 3-6 doesn't tell you what the problem is, but it's informative enough to indicate that something is wrong and needs debugging. Debugging leads to a SQL exception, and on inspection, you'll find that the locally installed TaskVision database was removed, which happened when you uninstalled the TaskVision server. Now that the source code is installed, you can safely run the server MSI again to re-create the database. After you reinstall the server, verify that the TaskVision database was installed properly using SQL Server Enterprise Manager, and then try running the application again.

If the application still won't run, check the ASP.NET user account privileges. The locally installed web service `TaskVisionWsCsVs` communicates with SQL Server to execute authentication and retrieve data. The login method with the database is Windows Authentication, and because the ASP.NET worker process runs under the ASP.NET user account, you need to make sure the ASP.NET user has sufficient SQL Server privileges. Alternatively, you can use impersonation.

If you're still having problems, visit the TaskVision forum at `http://www.windowsforms.net/Forums/ShowForum.aspx?tabIndex=2&tabId=41&ForumID=15`. See if someone else is having the same problem and whether any solutions are recommended.

By now, you should have the source code installed and the client configured to run against the locally installed web service. Depending on which version of the source code you installed, this was either an easy exercise or a more difficult undertaking. Either way, you should be up and running, and we can now start to look at the architecture.

TaskVision Architecture

In this section, we are going to look at the TaskVision architecture and discuss some of the design decisions. Understanding this application's components and design will help you in developing your own WinForms smart clients.

The TaskVision application is based on an *n*-tier architecture. In this architecture, the presentation, business logic, and data are separated into individual tiers. The diagram shown in Figure 3-7 identifies the major components of the solution and shows the communication methods used between the client and server.

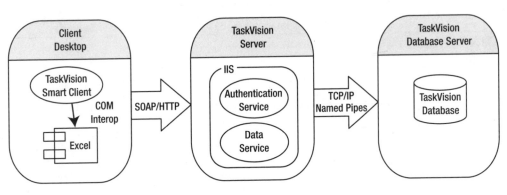

Figure 3-7. *TaskVision architecture*

Client and Server Communication

The TaskVision client uses two web services: an authentication web service to authenticate users and a data retrieval service to provide data. From an architectural perspective, it's important to understand why the client was designed to use web services for this information and not, for example, .NET Remoting.

When you think of the possible methods of communication, the solution comes down to answering this question: how should you do distributed component development? In other words, if you are building components that will be distributed over a network, how can they talk to each other? This question has been around for years, and some big vendors have answered with various technologies: Microsoft introduced Distributed Component Object Model (DCOM), Sun Microsystems introduced Remote Method Invocation (RMI), and the Object Management Group came up with a specification called the Common Object Request Broker Architecture (CORBA).

The problem with all of the named technologies is that they work very well in an intranet setting, where the execution environment is known, but not in an Internet environment. Attempting to use these technologies in an Internet environment poses several interoperability issues, along with coupling problems. This is because these approaches deal with objects and methods (they are RPC approaches), and they make assumptions about the programming language and platform.

This leaves two technologies: .NET Remoting and XML Web Services. .NET Remoting works over the Internet, because the only restriction to using .NET Remoting is that the endpoints must support .NET Remoting, which .NET does (and so do other platforms, such as Intrinsyc's Ja.NET). So why choose XML Web Services rather than .NET Remoting? To answer this, let's take a look at a side-by-side comparison of these two technologies. Table 3-1 compares XML Web Services with .NET Remoting, considering performance, interoperability, scalability, and security. These are all architectural considerations that can make or break a system.

Table 3-1. *XML Web Services and .NET Remoting Architectural Considerations*

	Performance	Interoperability	Scalability	Security
XML Web Services	Okay	Excellent	Okay	Okay
.NET Remoting	Excellent	Okay	Excellent	Okay

As you can see in Table 3-1, the choice depends on your system's main consideration, as follows:

Interoperability: If the most important consideration in a system is interoperability, use XML Web Services. XML Web Services is built on well-known and widely accepted standards, and you don't need to worry about programming languages or platforms.

Performance and scalability: If performance or scalability is the primary consideration, then .NET Remoting is the best choice. .NET Remoting is much better suited for mission-critical and highly available systems because of the many options available to customize transport protocols, the serialization format, and the hosting environment. .NET also gives you the ability to customize the endpoint object's life cycle to singleton, single call, or client-activated.

Security: If security is your main concern, either one will do. Neither of the two has a security model, but both can be extended to support one. Both XML Web Services and .NET Remoting will ultimately be hosted by some container, such as IIS, and so you can use the hosting environment's support for security.

Simplicity: XML Web Services is simpler to implement than .NET Remoting, because .NET hides most of the plumbing. This is one factor that can lead developers to go with XML Web Services rather than .NET Remoting.

So, what was the critical factor that led the TaskVision team to use XML Web Services? Was it performance, interoperability, scalability, or security? We can discard interoperability, because the back-end web services are used by only the front-end smart clients, which is in .NET. Performance, scalability, and security are usually not concerns when writing demos. Simplicity is most likely the reason why the TaskVision team decided to go with XML Web Services.

When writing your own WinForms smart clients, you should consider your requirements carefully when deciding between these two communication technologies.

Finally, note that the client-to-server communication link shown in Figure 3-7 is not a hard dependency, because the application can function while offline.

Server and Database Communication

The TaskVision web services talk to the back-end database server using ADO.NET. From an architectural perspective, it is important to understand how this communication is designed. The architecture diagram in Figure 3-7 shows TCP/IP and Named Pipes as examples. By default, the web services are configured to use TCP/IP. This is controlled with the database connection string in the web service's `web.config` file:

```
<appSettings>
    <add key="dbConn.ConnectionString" value="data source=localhost;initial
catalog=TaskVision;integrated security=SSPI;persist security info=False" />
  </appSettings>
```

This connection string does not specify the protocol, so the default library (DBMSSOCN) is used. You supply the method of communication using the Network Library key. For example, supplying `Network Library=DBMSSOCN` specifies TCP/IP as the protocol.

System Security

Security is an ever-growing concern in IT. TaskVision communicates with a server, and the server pulls data from a database. From an architectural perspective, one might ask the following security-related questions:

- How is the server authenticating the client?

- Is the authentication encrypted or over a secure line?

- Is the server using Windows Authentication or SQL Server Authentication when communicating with the database?

The TaskVision client authenticates users by presenting a login form to capture the user name and password. The user name and password are sent to the server in clear text, and then an encrypted ticket is sent back by the server. The encrypted ticket is then used to communicate with the server on subsequent queries. The TaskVision server communicates with SQL Server using Windows Integrated security, rather than putting SQL Server credentials directly in the configuration file.

Although using Integrated security here is acceptable, TaskVision does not do a good job of securing system assets (such as user credentials and connection strings). For most real-world applications, TaskVision's behavior would not be acceptable from a security perspective. You will learn much more about protecting system assets when we talk about IssueVision, because that application properly secures system assets.

TaskVision Implementation

The TaskVision solution is composed of three projects: the TaskVision client, a web application (the server), and a utility data block project. In this section, we will examine the implementation of the solution. Decomposing the solution piece by piece will assist you in understanding the details of smart clients.

TaskVision Server: TaskVisionWsCsVs

Figure 3-8 shows the server project in Visual Studio.

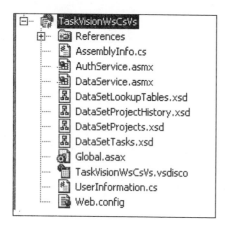

Figure 3-8. *TaskVision Server in Visual Studio 2003*

The server project is made up of only two web services, a few XML schemas, a custom class named UserInformation, and the application configuration file. AuthService.asmx is the authentication web service, and DataService.asmx is the data-retrieval web service. The four XML schema files were created to support typed datasets, and UserInformation is a class that is passed between the client and server by the authentication service. We'll start by looking at the authentication service.

Authentication Service

The purpose of the authentication service is to support authenticating users and to provide services to add new users and modify existing users. The service does this by providing specific web methods. For example, the service defines GetAuthorizationTicket() to allow clients to authenticate users, as shown in Listing 3-1. When the smart client is launched, the user is presented with a login form to supply a user name and password. Ultimately, the client makes a web service call to this method to get an authorization ticket for the user.

Listing 3-1. *The GetAuthorization Ticket() Method*

```
public string GetAuthorizationTicket(string userName, string password)
{
    string userID;

    try
    {
        userID = SqlHelper.ExecuteScalar(dbConn, "AuthenticateUser", userName,
password).ToString();
    }
    finally
    {
        dbConn.Close();
    }

    if (userID == null)
    {
        return null;
    }
FormsAuthenticationTicket ticket = new FormsAuthenticationTicket(userID,false,1);

    string encryptedTicket = FormsAuthentication.Encrypt(ticket);
    AppSettingsReader configurationAppSettings = new AppSettingsReader();

    int timeout = (int) configurationAppSettings.
GetValue("AuthenticationTicket.Timeout", typeof(int));

    Context.Cache.Insert(encryptedTicket, userID, null,
DateTime.Now.AddMinutes(timeout), TimeSpan.Zero);

    return encryptedTicket;
}
```

The web method shown in Listing 3-1 authenticates users against the system and returns an encrypted ticket. If the service fails to authenticate a user, the service returns null to indicate that the user doesn't exist in the system or the user name/password combination is not valid. Note that the service talks directly to the SQL Server using the data application block (Microsoft.ApplicationBlocks.Data).

SqlHelper.ExecuteScalar() is a static method that has several overloads. The version used to get an authorization ticket for the user calls a stored procedure named AuthenticateUser(), with the user name and password as parameters. ExecuteScalar() ultimately returns the first column in the first row as the result. In other words, ExecuteScalar() is used to return a single value. In this case, the stored procedure returns the user ID given the user name and password. It is also interesting to note that the user name and password are passed to the service in clear text. Moreover, after a successful authentication, an encrypted ticket is created and cached prior to returning the encrypted ticket.

The authentication service also defines a web method to add new users given an existing ticket and information about the new user, as shown in Listing 3-2.

Listing 3-2. *The InsertUser() Method*

```
public int InsertUser(string ticket, UserInformation userInfo)
{
    if (!IsTicketValid(ticket, true))
       return -1;

    try
    {
    object userID = SqlHelper.ExecuteScalar
(dbConn, "InsertUser", userInfo.UserName,
userInfo.UserPassword, userInfo.UserFullName,
userInfo.UserEmail, userInfo.IsAdministrator,
userInfo.IsAccountLocked);

        if (userID == null)
        {
           return -1;
        }
        else
        {
           return Convert.ToInt32(userID.ToString());
        }
    }
    catch (SqlException ex)
    {
        if (ex.Number == 2627)
        {
                      return 0;
        }
        else
        {
           throw ex;
        }
    }
}
```

```
    finally
    {
        dbConn.Close();
    }
}
```

Adding new users seems simple enough. The InsertUser() method takes an encrypted ticket and the new users details and adds the user. Before adding the new user, however, the method first checks to see if the ticket is a valid logged-in user. The method IsTicketValid(), shown in Listing 3-3, decrypts the encrypted ticket and checks the cache to make sure that the user has logged in and the session has not timed out.

Listing 3-3. *The IsTicketValid Method*

```
private bool IsTicketValid(string ticket, bool IsAdminCall)
{
    if (ticket == null || Context.Cache[ticket] == null)
    {
        return false;
    }
    else
    {
        int userID = int.Parse(FormsAuthentication.Decrypt(ticket).Name);

        DataSet ds;

        try
        {
        ds = SqlHelper.ExecuteDataset(dbConn, "GetUserInfo", userID);
        }
        finally
        {
            dbConn.Close();
        }

        UserInformation userInfo = new UserInformation();

        DataRow dr = ds.Tables[0].Rows[0];

        userInfo.IsAdministrator = (bool) dr["IsAdministrator"];
        userInfo.IsAccountLocked = (bool)dr["IsAccountLocked"];
        if (userInfo.IsAccountLocked)
            return false;
        else
```

```
        {
            if (IsAdminCall && !userInfo.IsAdministrator)
                return false;
            return true;
        }
    }
}
```

If the user's credentials are valid, the method proceeds to adding the new user using the `InsertUser()` stored procedure, passing in the user's details. After the user is added, the user ID of the new user is returned. Why does the `InsertUser()` method require an encrypted ticket? It needs this ticket simply because someone must be logged in to the system in order to add new users. This also goes for updating users.

The authentication service is quite simple. The service provides a few web methods to add, update, and insert users, and a few other utility methods used by the service itself.

Keep in mind that the entry into the authentication service is `GetAuthenticationTicket()`. Once a client has logged in to the service, the service passes back to the client an encrypted ticket that the client keeps. From then on, every time the client needs to perform an action, the client passes to the service its credentials (the encrypted ticket).

Now, that we've examined the authentication service, let's take a look at the data service.

Data Service

The TaskVision server uses a web service to serve data to clients. If you've experimented with the client, you know that there isn't all that much to it. The application, in a nutshell, tracks problems. To track anything, you need to know what it is you are tracking. In this case, the application tracks tasks that belong to projects. That's pretty much it.

The Database

You know that TaskVision uses SQL Server, but you don't know anything about the database yet. Let's take a peek into the database. Figure 3-9 shows the TaskVision database schema.

As expected, at the heart of the schema is a table called Tasks. A task captures information specific to a particular problem. You can see that a task belongs to a project and has a status. In addition, tasks have histories and can be assigned to and modified by users. Finally, tasks have a priority.

That's the data storage end of it. Now what about data access? You have already gained some insight into that from the authentication service; you saw that the authentication service uses stored procedure calls to get data. If you bring up SQL Server Enterprise Manager (or some other SQL Server management tool), you'll see that the TaskVision database has about a dozen stored procedures. The stored procedures, as you would expect, simply allow for manipulating users, tasks, and projects. Also note that there are no custom views or functions defined in the database, just stored procedures. So that's the background. Now, let's take a look at the web service, `DataService.asmx`.

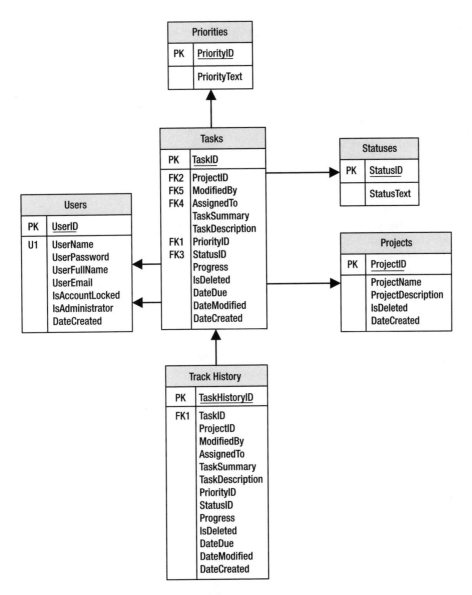

Figure 3-9. *The TaskVision database schema*

Typed Datasets

One of the first things you see when looking at the data service, DataService.asmx, is that the TaskVision team has used typed datasets. One of the reasons for this is the level of support for typed datasets from Visual Studio itself.

WHY ARE TYPED DATASETS SO POPULAR?

If you have used .NET for any reasonable amount of time, you know that the concept of a DataSet is littered in the .NET literature and is at the core of ADO.NET. The .NET documentation defines a DataSet as "an in-memory cache of data retrieved from a data source. . . ." DataSet just may be the most popular class in the .NET class libraries.

Developers like the DataSet not only because it's complete in its support of tables, relationships, and constraints, but also because of the level of support from Visual Studio IDE. The IDE, for example, directly supports generating typed datasets. Typed datasets became popular when developers realized that they were losing type-safety when working with datasets.

A DataSet knows only about tables, the relationship between them, and constraints; it knows nothing about the data that is stored in the tables. For example, if you retrieve your Customers table from your database and shove it into a DataSet, then you've lost the fact that that each row in your table really represents a customer. When developers realized this, they either stopped using the DataSet and went to an object-relational mapping layer or decided to extend the DataSet class. For example, you might create a typed dataset named CustomerDataSet. So now, if you retrieve your Customers table, you get a CustomerDataSet, and when you look at the rows in your Customer table, the rows give you a Customer object. Then you can use IntelliSense to look at the properties defined for your Customer object.

How does Visual Studio support typed datasets? To demonstrate the support, let's create a typed DataSet for the Tasks table. Follow these steps:

1. Open Visual Studio and create a new web application named MyFirstTypedData➡ SetProject.

2. Open WebForm1.aspx in design mode.

3. From the Toolbox, select the Data group and drag-and-drop a SqlDataAdapter onto the form. As soon as you drop the component onto the form, you should see the Data Adapter Configuration Wizard. Click Next.

4. Now, you need to create a data source connection. Choose New Connection and create a connection to the TaskVision database. Then click Next.

5. Next, you need to tell the wizard what data to pull from the database. You can choose to supply a SELECT statement, create a new stored procedure, or use an existing stored procedure. The simplest method here is to just type the following SELECT statement: SELECT * FROM tasks.

6. Choose Next on the following page, and then click Finish.

7. At this point, you have a SqlDataAdapter created and configured with a SqlConnection. Choose the SqlDataAdapter in design mode and choose the Properties tab.

8. In the Properties tab, select the link titled Generate DataSet . . .. Be sure to change the name of the DataSet from DataSet1 to TasksDataSet, and then click OK to finish.

At this point, Visual Studio should have created an XML schema called TasksDataSet and a class named TasksDataSet. You can verify the class by choosing View ➤ Class View. Notice that the IDE generated the following classes: TasksDataSet, TasksDataTable, and TasksRow. If you peek into TasksRow, you'll find that it has all the columns in the Tasks table mapped as public properties.

Figure 3-10 shows the eight classes defined in the TaskVision server project: two web services, four typed datasets, Global.asax, and a help class named UserInformation. You can figure out that DataSetTasks and DataSetProjects datasets are probably wrapping the Tasks and Projects table, respectively. But what about DataSetLookupTables and DataSetProjectHistory? These two dataset names are not very clear. It turns out that DataSetLookupTables wraps three tables: Statuses, Users, and Priorities. DataSetProjectHistory wraps TasksHistory.

Figure 3-10. *TaskVision server classes*

At this point, we know all about the TaskVision database and what typed datasets have been generated. Now, we're ready to look at the data service implementation.

Data Service Implementation

Looking at the implementation, the first thing to notice is that all of the public methods expect a ticket; that is, someone must be authenticated prior to obtaining data. The data service provides a few accessor methods to obtain tasks, projects, and so on, and a few methods to insert projects and tasks. Notice the simplicity with which data is retrieved with the use of typed datasets now.

```
[WebMethod]
public DataSetProjects GetProjects(string ticket)
{
    if (!IsTicketValid(ticket, false))
        return null;

    DataSetProjects ds = new DataSetProjects();
    daProjects.Fill(ds, "Projects");

    return ds;
}
```

In summary, the server provides a service for clients to retrieve data. Data is accessible only to authenticated clients. Clients call web methods to get, insert, and update tasks, projects, and so on. The accessor methods return typed datasets to clients. The typed datasets are serialized into XML and sent over the wire within a SOAP envelope (we'll discuss SOAP in Chapter 8).

At this point, you know why the TaskVision team decided to use typed datasets for the data service implementation. But what are the consequences of using typed datasets? This turns out to be an important question that has been debated since the introduction of .NET.

Datasets have some advantages and disadvantages. As we noted earlier, an obvious advantage is that .NET provides incredible support for datasets in .NET. Within minutes, you can retrieve data using a data adapter and fill a dataset. You can auto-generate typed datasets, and even send them across the wire without even thinking about serialization.

The problem with datasets is that they have a serialization overhead, but that becomes an issue only if you include tables that have several thousand rows. For large distributed applications, it's important to accurately identify the size of the datasets that will cross the wire. However, even if the datasets are large, the performance may be acceptable.

If it turns out that datasets won't work, the other option is to use an object-relational mapping tool. These tools reverse-engineer a database and generate a data tier that maps to the database schema. Most of these tools capture table relationships and constraints, and build this information into the generated classes.

Before you throw out the idea of using datasets, however, be sure to carefully benchmark your system's performance requirements. In addition to looking at performance, take into account the fact that since smart client applications work while offline, they may need to merge data from the client after a network connection is restored. A dataset/data adapter combination has a built-in merge operation that can support this easily.

The bottom line is that you need to have clear reasons for not using datasets, because the alternative can add incredible development overheard to your project. Using datasets will work for most applications, but they are not suitable for all purposes. You need to understand your application well enough to decide whether datasets are for you.

TaskVision Client

The real meat in the TaskVision solution is in the client. In this section, we are going examine the guts of the client. We'll start by dissecting the project as a whole, and then slowly work our way inwards. We'll talk about several issues at the heart of building smart clients—specifically, offline support and automatic updates.

TaskVision Project Components

Let's start by looking at the project components, as shown in Figure 3-11.

The project has a collection of forms and a few folders, one of which contains the web references. The UserControls folder has one user control, TaskHistoryPanel, which is used to show a task's history. The Components folder contains a few helper classes. For example, there is the LogError class that logs errors to the event log. One of the more interesting classes in the Components folder is the DataLayer class.

The DataLayer class is a facade class that hides the calls to the web services and maintains the current state (data) of the application. If you are familiar with the Model-View-Controller (MVC) model, you can think of this class as the model for the primary user interface of the application. If you look at this class, the first thing you see is the datasets we talked about in our discussion of the server, as shown in Listing 3-4.

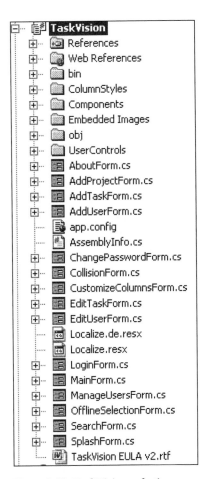

Figure 3-11. *TaskVision solution*

Listing 3-4. *The DataLayer Class*

```
public class DataLayer
{
    public DataSetTasks DsTasks = new DataSetTasks();
    public DataSetProjects DsProjects = new DataSetProjects();
    public DataSetLookupTables DsLookupTables = new DataSetLookupTables();
    public DataSetProjectHistory DsProjectHistory = new DataSetProjectHistory();
    public UserInformation CurrentUserInformation = new UserInformation();

    private string m_Ticket = null;
    private DataService m_WsData = new DataService();
    private AuthService m_WsAuth = new AuthService();
```

```csharp
private const int c_wsTimeout = 30000; // 30 seconds
public DataLayer()
{
    CurrentUserInformation.UserID = -1;
    CurrentUserInformation.UserEmail = String.Empty;
    CurrentUserInformation.UserFullName = String.Empty;
    CurrentUserInformation.UserName = String.Empty;
    CurrentUserInformation.UserPassword = String.Empty;

    m_WsData.Timeout = c_wsTimeout;
    m_WsAuth.Timeout = c_wsTimeout;
}
public DataLayerResult Login(string userName, string userPassword)
{
    CurrentUserInformation.UserName = userName;
    CurrentUserInformation.UserPassword = userPassword;
    DataLayerResult ticketResult = GetAuthorizationTicket();
    if (ticketResult == DataLayerResult.Success)
    {
        UserInformation newUserInfo;
        try
        {
            newUserInfo = m_WsAuth.GetUserInfo(m_Ticket);
        }
        catch (Exception ex)
        {
            return HandleException(ex);
        }
        if (newUserInfo == null)
            return DataLayerResult.AuthenticationFailure;

        // keep the returned information
        CurrentUserInformation.UserID = newUserInfo.UserID;
        CurrentUserInformation.UserName = newUserInfo.UserName;
        CurrentUserInformation.UserFullName = newUserInfo.UserFullName;
        CurrentUserInformation.UserEmail = newUserInfo.UserEmail;
        CurrentUserInformation.IsAdministrator = newUserInfo.IsAdministrator;
        CurrentUserInformation.IsAccountLocked = newUserInfo.IsAccountLocked;

        return DataLayerResult.Success;
    }
    else
    {
        return ticketResult;
    }
}
private DataLayerResult GetAuthorizationTicket()
```

```
    {
        try
        {
            m_Ticket = m_WsAuth.GetAuthorizationTicket(
CurrentUserInformation.UserName, CurrentUserInformation.UserPassword);
        }
        catch (Exception ex)
        {
            m_Ticket = null;
            return HandleException(ex);
        }
        if (m_Ticket == null)
        {
            return DataLayerResult.AuthenticationFailure;
        }

        return DataLayerResult.Success;
    }
    public DataLayerResult InsertUser(ref int userID,
UserInformation newUserInfo)
    {
        try
        {
            userID = m_WsAuth.InsertUser(m_Ticket, newUserInfo);
            if (userID == -1)
            {
                DataLayerResult ticketResult = GetAuthorizationTicket();
                if (ticketResult != DataLayerResult.Success)
                    return ticketResult;

                userID = m_WsAuth.InsertUser(m_Ticket, newUserInfo);
                if (userID == -1)
                    return DataLayerResult.AuthenticationFailure;
            }
        }
        catch (Exception ex)
        {
            return HandleException(ex);
        }

        return DataLayerResult.Success;
    }
    public DataLayerResult UpdateUser(UserInformation updatedUserInfo)
    {
        UserInformation uInfo;
        try
```

```
        {
            uInfo = m_WsAuth.UpdateUser(m_Ticket, updatedUserInfo);
            if (uInfo == null)
            {
                DataLayerResult ticketResult = GetAuthorizationTicket();
                if (ticketResult != DataLayerResult.Success)
                    return ticketResult;

                uInfo = m_WsAuth.UpdateUser(m_Ticket, updatedUserInfo);
                if (uInfo == null)
                    return DataLayerResult.AuthenticationFailure;
            }
        }
        catch (Exception ex)
        {
            return HandleException(ex);
        }

        return DataLayerResult.Success;
    }
    ...
}
```

Also note that since clients must authenticate and pass their encrypted credentials to the server when they need something, the DataLayer class defines two members to track this: m_ticket and CurrentUserInformation. The m_ticket member is the encrypted ticket, and CurrentUserInformation is the details of the logged-in user.

The DataLayer class turns out to be one of the core classes in the project. Because this class maintains the application state, virtually all of the forms in the application take this class in their constructor. At this point, you might wonder where the DataLayer class is constructed and how many instances of it exist? In other words, if this class maintains the state of the application and all of the forms use this class to get the current state, you should have only one instance of this class in order to maintain accurate state.

Looking at the code a bit leads us to the MainForm class. The MainForm class provides the main entry point for the application. As the name suggests, this form class is the user interface form that you see when you run the application. MainForm instantiates the DataLayer class, in the form-load event, and holds the reference to the instantiated instance as a member of the class. MainForm acts like a controller because it is responsible for handling events. So, for example, when you pull down a menu and choose a menu item, the handler called is in the MainForm class. This class instantiates a form (if necessary) and passes the DataLayer class to the constructor to use in populating itself.

So, you know that the client has a form class called MainForm, and this class is a controller for the application. The client has a class called DataLayer, which facades the web services and holds the application state. Classes that need to access the application state are constructed with the DataLayer class and can manipulate the state as they see fit. That's great, but since this is a smart client, what we're really interested in is how offline support is implemented.

Offline Implementation in TaskVision

TaskVision is a smart client application, and one of the things that makes a client smart is the ability for the application to function without a connection. Thick clients of the past that required a connection generally assumed that the connection was always available. If it turned out that the connection wasn't there, the application would issue an error message and give up on performing the operation. Smart clients are smarter than that.

In this section, we'll talk about how TaskVision supports some of the application's functionality while offline. In Chapter 6, we'll talk about offline support in much more detail.

The TaskVision smart client user interface has an offline/online indicator that tells you whether the application is running in offline mode or online mode. In addition, the user interface allows you to toggle the offline/online mode by clicking a button in its toolbar. These elements are highlighted in Figure 3-12.

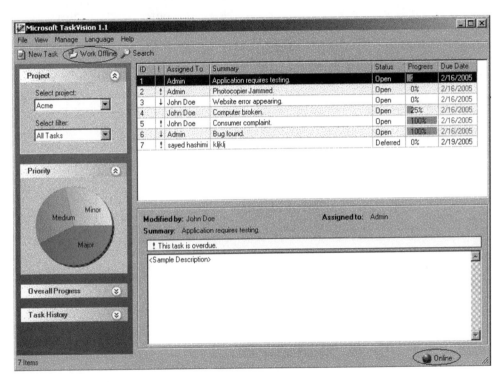

Figure 3-12. *Offline mode in TaskVision*

When you click the offline/online button, the click event is handled by the MainForm class. Ultimately, however, the SwitchOnlineMode() method is called in response to the click event. The MainForm class defines a Boolean member, m_IsOnline, to track whether the application is in offline or online mode. If the application is running in online mode (m_IsOnline==true), the user is presented with a dialog box to choose which projects should run offline.

> **■Note** In TaskVision, you cannot run one project in offline mode and another in online mode. You can select one or more projects for offline use, and then only those projects are available while the application runs offline.

An interesting thing about running in offline mode is that the application doesn't require authentication if you shut down and restart the application. Instead, the application waits until you go online, and then authenticates you before any changes are persisted to the server.

So how does TaskVision maintain the application state while you work offline? In our discussion of the server, we talked about the use of datasets in detail. It turns out that there is yet another benefit to using datasets: they know how to write their state as XML and rehydrate themselves from XML. Interestingly, when you choose to go offline, the application persists the state of the application (project, tasks, lookup tables, and so on) to the client's machine as XML documents and tracks changes in another XML document. Listing 3-5 shows how this is accomplished.

Listing 3-5. *Persisting Application State While Offline*

```
if (m_IsOnline)
{
    OfflineSelectionForm oForm =
new OfflineSelectionForm(m_DataLayer, m_ProjectID);
    DialogResult oFormResult = oForm.ShowDialog();

    if (oFormResult != DialogResult.Cancel)
    {
        try
        {
            m_DataLayer.DsProjects.WriteXml(m_MyDocumentsPath +
c_OfflineProjectsFile, XmlWriteMode.WriteSchema);
m_DataLayer.DsTasks.WriteXml(m_MyDocumentsPath +
c_OfflineTasksFile, XmlWriteMode.WriteSchema);
            m_DataLayer.DsLookupTables.WriteXml(m_MyDocumentsPath
+ c_OfflineLookUpTablesFile, XmlWriteMode.WriteSchema);

            try
            {
                File.Delete(m_MyDocumentsPath + c_OfflineTaskChangesFile);
            }
            catch
            {}

            ChangeOnlineStatus(false);
```

```
        }
        catch (Exception ex)
        {
            LogError.Write(ex.Message + "\n" + ex.StackTrace);
            MessageBox.Show(m_ResourceManager.
GetString("MessageBox.Show_Unable_to_write_files"));
            GetProjects();
        }
    }}
    else
    {
        if (DisplayLoginForm() != DialogResult.Cancel)
        {
            ChangeOnlineStatus(true);

            LockControls(true);
            GetProjects();
            LockControls(false);

            if (m_DataLayer.DsProjects.Projects.Rows.Count > 0)
            {
                if (m_DataLayer.DsProjects.Projects.Rows.Find(m_ProjectID) == null)
                    m_ProjectID =
                        (int) m_DataLayer.DsProjects.Projects.Rows[0]["ProjectID"];
            }
            else
            {
                m_ProjectID = -1;
            }

            cbProjects.SelectedValue = m_ProjectID;

            if (m_DataLayer.DsTasks.HasChanges())
            {
                foreach (DataRow dr in m_DataLayer.DsTasks.Tasks.Rows)
                {
                    if ((int) dr["ModifiedBy"] == -1)
                        dr["ModifiedBy"] = m_DataLayer.CurrentUserInformation.UserID;
                }
                    UpdateTasks();
            }
            else
            {
                GetTasks(m_ProjectID, true);
            }
```

```
        // get the latest lookup tables
        GetLookUpTables();

        DeleteOfflineFiles();
    }
}
```

As shown in Listing 3-5, the three datasets we talked about earlier are persisted first, and then the application deletes any old changes due to offline activity by deleting the file pointed to by c_OfflineTaskChangesFile (TaskChanges.xml). After deleting old changes, the application changes the offline/online flag and sets the connection indicator at the lower-right corner of the user interface to offline.

The application detects offline/online mode at application startup by looking for the offline files. If the files are found locally, the application assumes offline mode and reads the files into the datasets. If not, online status is assumed, and the user is presented with a login form. Listing 3-6 shows how the application tracks offline and online mode.

Listing 3-6. *Detecting Online/Offline Mode*

```
try
{
    if (File.Exists(m_MyDocumentsPath + c_OfflineTasksFile) &&
    File.Exists(m_MyDocumentsPath + c_OfflineProjectsFile) &&
    File.Exists(m_MyDocumentsPath + c_OfflineLookUpTablesFile))
    {
        try
        {
            ChangeOnlineStatus(false);
        m_DataLayer.DsProjects.ReadXml(m_MyDocumentsPath +
c_OfflineProjectsFile, XmlReadMode.ReadSchema);
            m_DataLayer.DsTasks.ReadXml(m_MyDocumentsPath +
c_OfflineTasksFile, XmlReadMode.ReadSchema);
            m_DataLayer.DsLookupTables.ReadXml(m_MyDocumentsPath
+ c_OfflineLookUpTablesFile, XmlReadMode.ReadSchema);

            m_DataLayer.DsTasks.Tasks.Columns["TaskID"].AutoIncrement = true;

            m_DataLayer.DsTasks.AcceptChanges();

            if (File.Exists(m_MyDocumentsPath + c_OfflineTaskChangesFile))
                m_DataLayer.DsTasks.ReadXml(m_MyDocumentsPath +
                  c_OfflineTaskChangesFile, XmlReadMode.DiffGram);


            if (m_DataLayer.DsProjects.Projects.Rows.Find(m_ProjectID) == null)
                m_ProjectID = (int) m_DataLayer.DsProjects.Projects.Rows[0]["ProjectID"];
        }
        catch (Exception ex)
```

```
    {
        LogError.Write(ex.Message + "\n" + ex.StackTrace);
        DialogResult mbResult = MessageBox.Show(m_ResourceManager.
GetString("MessageBox.Show(There_was_an_error_reading_theoffline_files)")
+ "\n\n" + m_ResourceManager.GetString("Do_you_want_to_go_online"), "",
MessageBoxButtons.YesNo, MessageBoxIcon.Error,
MessageBoxDefaultButton.Button1,
MessageBoxOptions.DefaultDesktopOnly);
        this.Refresh();
        if (mbResult == DialogResult.Yes)
        {
            ChangeOnlineStatus(true);

            DeleteOfflineFiles();
            m_DataLayer.DsProjects.Clear();
            m_DataLayer.DsTasks.Clear();
            m_DataLayer.DsLookupTables.Clear();
        }
        else
        {
            throw new ExitException();
        }
    }
}
    if (m_IsOnline)
    {
        if (DisplayLoginForm() == DialogResult.Cancel)
            throw new ExitException();

        ChangeOnlineStatus(true);
        if (!GetProjects())
            throw new ExitException(m_ResourceManager.
            GetString("ExitException(Unable_to_load_projects)"));

        if (m_DataLayer.DsProjects.Projects.Rows.Count > 0)
        {
            if (m_DataLayer.DsProjects.Projects.Rows.Find(m_ProjectID) == null)
            {
                m_ProjectID =
(int) m_DataLayer.DsProjects.Projects.Rows[0]["ProjectID"];
            }
            if (!GetTasks(m_ProjectID, true))
                throw new ExitException(m_ResourceManager.
GetString("ExitException(Unable_to_load_tasks)"));
            if (!GetLookUpTables())
                throw new ExitException(m_ResourceManager.
```

```
GetString("ExitException(Unable_to_load_lookup_tables)"));
            }
            else
            {
                m_ProjectID = -1;
            }
        }
        catch (ExitException ex)
        {
            ex.Show();
            this.Close();
            return;
        }
```

Now, you understand how the application tracks offline and online mode, and you know that the application's state is persisted locally by persisting the datasets as XML. Moreover, you know that any changes you make while the application runs offline are maintained in a separate XML file, and that only changes to tasks are allowed in offline mode (for example, you can't add new projects). If the application is shut down while in offline mode and then restarted, the application detects this by looking for the offline files.

Next, we need to discuss how changes are merged when you go from an offline status to an online status.

Merging Changes

As you've learned, the TaskVision smart client supports only task changes while offline. Changes made to existing tasks and added tasks are tracked by persisting changes to the client's machine as an XML document. Tracking changes to tasks turns out to be a lot simpler than you might think, due to the use of datasets. For example, when a new task is added in offline mode, the application simply adds a new task to the existing task's dataset. Internally, the DataSet handles the fact that the task was added by flagging the row appropriately. When the application shuts down, the MainForm's form-closing event gets the changes from the task's DataSet and writes the TaskChanges.xml file, as shown in Listing 3-7.

Listing 3-7. *The MainForm Closing Event*

```
private void MainForm_Closing(object sender,
System.ComponentModel.CancelEventArgs e)
{

    {
        if (!m_IsOnline && m_DataLayer.DsTasks.HasChanges())
        {
            m_DataLayer.DsTasks.GetChanges().WriteXml(m_MyDocumentsPath
+ c_OfflineTaskChangesFile, XmlWriteMode.DiffGram);
        }
        else
```

```
    {
        try
        {
            File.Delete(m_MyDocumentsPath + c_OfflineTaskChangesFile);
        }
        catch
        {}
    }

    SaveRegistrySettings();
    if (trayIcon != null)
        trayIcon.Dispose();
}
catch (Exception ex)
{
    LogError.Write(ex.Message + "\n" + ex.StackTrace);
}
}
```

When the application starts up again, it first processes old tasks by reading the
TaskChanges.xml file into the task's DataSet, and then appending the changes into the same
DataSet (see the MainForm's form-load event). When the user chooses to go online, changes are
persisted to the database by calling DataLayer's UpdateTasks() method. UpdateTasks() for-
wards the call to the data service, which ultimately calls the SqlDataAdapter to do the update.
SqlDataAdapter handles doing update, delete, and insert operations automatically. In a nutshell, managing updates and insertions is handled by the DataSet and SqlDataAdapter.

Data Corruption Detection

TaskVision even offers data corruption detection features. When we discussed the data web service, we didn't mention that the SqlDataAdapters were also used to help detect data corruption.

The data service implemented in TaskVision uses several SQLDataAdapters, and each of
these adapters is configured with update, insert, and delete stored procedures. The update
stored procedures have been written such that they verify that the row they are updating was
not updated since the data was retrieved. The data adapter internally keeps the original state
of each row. During an update operation, the data adapter passes the original values to the
stored procedure, along with the new values. The stored procedures do the update only if the
state of the row, prior to the update, matches the original values in the row. If it turns out that
the data was corrupted (someone else modified the row), the stored procedure will not modify
any rows, and the data service detects this and throws an exception.

The interesting thing about TaskVision's data corruption detection implementation is that
it allows the user to make a decision, as shown in Figure 3-13. When TaskVision detects data corruption, the user is presented with his changes along with the changes in the database. The user
can then either choose to save the changes he made or to keep the previous changes instead.

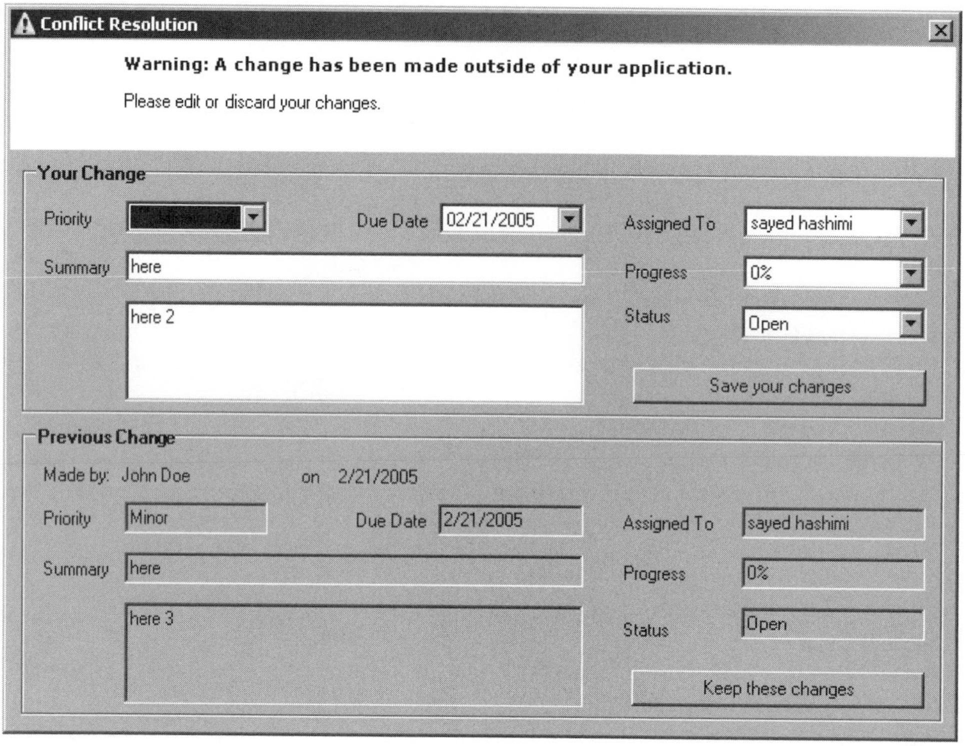

Figure 3-13. *Data corruption detection in TaskVision*

Automatic Updates

At the beginning of this chapter, we mentioned that TaskVision is a fairly complete example of a WinForms smart client. Automatic updates are one of the benefits of smart client applications, and TaskVision supports this via the .NET Application Updater component.

The Application Updater component allows applications to update themselves automatically. This component works by taking over launching of the application. Instead of launching, say TaskVision, users launch the Application Updater component, and this component then starts the desired application and ensures that updates are automatically downloaded.

Figure 3-14 shows how the Application Updater component works. In order to do updates, the Application Updater component sits as a sibling to the application being updated. The component looks at a local configuration file, AppStart.config, to determine the current version of the application and polls the server at predefined intervals (such as hourly). When a polling timer fires, the Application Updater component checks the server configuration file, UpdateVersion.xml, to see if the version on the server is greater than the version installed on the client. If a new version is available, the new version is downloaded, and the next time the application is launched, the new version is executed.

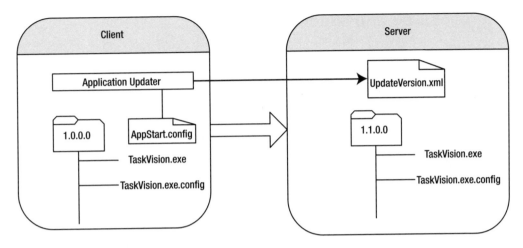

Figure 3-14. *The Application Updater component*

Here are a few things to keep in mind about the Application Updater component:

- The Application Updater component is a component because clients literally need to reference a component in their client application and configure it using the Properties window. Items that require configuring include how often to check for updates and where to check (where to find the UpdateVersion.xml file).

- The server configuration file contains a version number and a URL to the folder that has the new version.

- The Application Updater component uses HTTP-DAV to pull updates from the server.

- Updates are downloaded using a background thread.

■Note The Application Updater component has been around for some time and has been used in fairly large projects. You can find more information about this component (and download it) at http:// windowsforms.net/articles/appupdater.aspx.

IssueVision

IssueVision is another reference implementation of a smart client application. IssueVision is not related to TaskVision; however, some of the problems in TaskVision have been corrected in Issue-Vision. In addition, IssueVision uses some design patterns and defined best practices for smart client development. It's helpful to understand IssueVision if you plan on building enterprise-level smart clients.

Since we have already discussed TaskVision in great detail, we won't go into the same level of detail here with IssueVision. Instead, we will focus on the improvements of IssueVision and the best practices and design patterns.

Getting Started with IssueVision

To get started, download the IssueVision sample from the windowsforms.net site at http://
www.windowsforms.net/Applications/application.aspx?PageID=40&tabindex=9. After the
download completes, execute the downloaded MSI and walk through the installation steps.
The installer installs the source code, the SQL Server database, the back-end web service, and
the client application. The installer also creates an IssueVision program group, which has
shortcuts to all of the installed items, as shown in Figure 3-15.

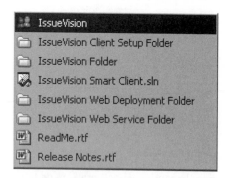

Figure 3-15. *The IssueVision program group menu*

From the Windows Start menu, find the IssueVision program group and run the client
application, which is named IssueVision (shown selected in Figure 3-15). When the client application starts, you're presented with a login form similar to the one displayed by TaskVision. Type
in **demo** for the user name and password, and then click OK. You should see the IssueVision user
interface, as shown in Figure 3-16.

The user interface shows a Views pane to the left and an Issues list view in the center.
As you choose various staffers from the Views pane, the Issues list for that staffer is shown in
the Issues list. As you select a particular issue, the issue's details and history is shown to the right.
As you select a staffer, the Issues Resolved list displays a Gant chart showing the resolved,
escalated, and open issues for that staffer.

You can create new issues by clicking the New button on the toolbar. You can edit an Issue
by double-clicking it or by choosing the Edit link from the Issue Details view. Notice that similar to TaskVision, IssueVision has an offline/online indicator at the bottom-right corner of the
window and a Work Offline/Online button on the toolbar. IssueVision also provides a Send/
Receive button that is used to synchronize with the back-end after an offline session.

Let's see IssueVision in action. For a quick demo, bring up two versions of the client. For
the first client, log in with **demo** for both the user name and password. For the second client,
use **dtibbott** for the username and **password** for password. (If you bring up a second user
interface and the application doesn't present the login form, select File ➤ Logout and Exit, and
then start another client to get the login form; the application saves your credentials after you
log in.) From the client where you logged in as the demo user, create a new issue by clicking
the New button in the toolbar. Assign the new issue to Diane Tibbott, as shown in Figure 3-17.

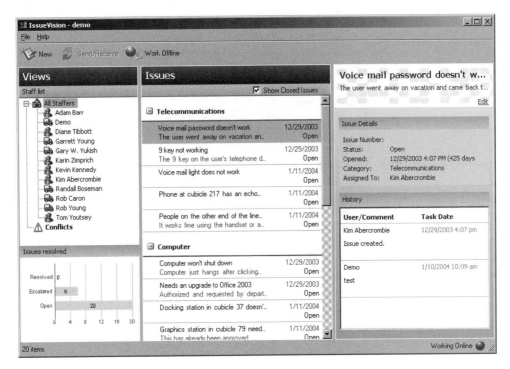

Figure 3-16. *The IssueVision smart client*

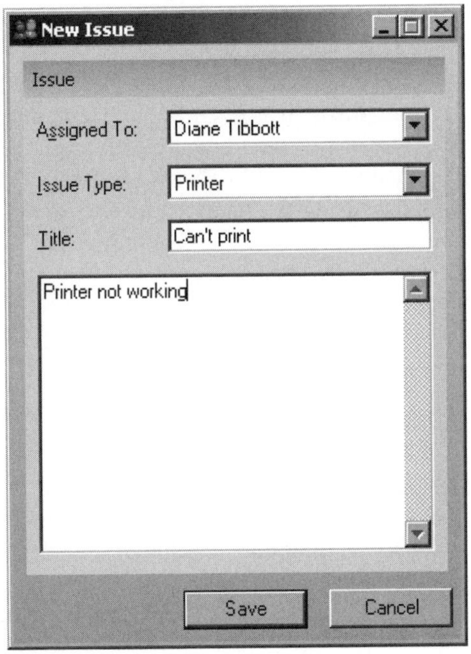

Figure 3-17. *A new issue created by demo and assigned to Diane Tibbott*

Pay close attention to what happens after you choose Save in the New Issue dialog box. If you have Diane Tibbott selected in the Staff List tree view, you'll see the issue show up in the Issues list, with a little icon next to it. The icon indicates that the issue has not been sent over to the server but has been queued for processing. A few seconds later, the status bar shows that issues are being processed, and then the icon goes away. This works very similar to how Microsoft Outlook sends and receives mail messages.

Now look at the client that has Diane Tibbott logged in. You should see the issue is already in her Issues list. Play around with this for a little while. Orient the two user interfaces so that you can see the dtibbott user's Issues list, and then add a few issues for her from the demo client. Notice that shortly after you assign an issue to her, that client's Issues list shows the new issue.

Exploring the Improvements in IssueVision

IssueVision doesn't have a lot of visible functionality; however, what is there is very robust. For example, you may have noticed that the application's user interface is much more attractive than the TaskVision user interface, and so is the offline/online experience. With just those improvements, you may wonder what makes IssueVision so nice.

IssueVision made improvements in three areas:

- The user interface, including design patterns, custom controls, Windows XP Themes, and overall user experience

- Encryption and code-access security

- Data management and data corruption detection

We are going to touch on each of these next. We'll start with the user interface.

User Interface Improvements

The TaskVision user interface was nice, but the code behind the interface was not implemented well. For example, there is a lot "spaghetti" code behind the forms. Extending the user interface, or using some of the code in your own application, is difficult. On the other hand, IssueVision implements several well-known design patterns, which allow for easier maintenance and extension. The Command pattern, for instance, is used for the menu items and toolbar buttons, and the Observer pattern is used to synchronize multiple views of the same data.

The client application is also built with reusable user controls, which allow for easier maintenance. The interface, as a whole, was built with Windows XP Themes, which isn't very difficult to do, but from a professional look-and-feel perspective and with regard to the user experience, it is an important addition.

Security Improvements

We noted that with TaskVision, the user name and password are passed to the server in clear text. In addition, most of the application doesn't pay too much attention to security. For example, the unencrypted database connection string is in the web service's configuration file.

For most real-world applications, these issues are important concerns and must be addressed adequately. IssueVision does a good job of managing security concerns by protecting the critical system information. Specifically, IssueVision uses the following security mechanisms:

- Protects user credentials by using a hash and salt

- Secures web service access using web service security

- Encrypts the database connection string

- Protects offline data through Data Protection API (DPAPI)

Data Improvements

Several data-related issues in TaskVision have been corrected in IssueVision. For the most part, all of the data-related improvements are in the area of handling concurrency issues, data corruption, and working offline. Again, even though the application has limited functionality, having proper solutions for these issues is important in real-world enterprise applications. IssueVision solves these nicely and in ways that you can use in your own applications.

Summary

In this chapter, we discussed two reference implementations of WinForms smart clients. We thoroughly dissected the TaskVision solution, and then highlighted the important aspects of IssueVision. Using these two implementations as guides, you can begin to build your own smart clients.

In the next two chapters, we'll cover Office smart clients and mobile smart clients. After that, we will talk in depth about deployment techniques and technologies specific to WinForms smart clients.

CHAPTER 4

■ ■ ■

Microsoft Office Smart Clients

Microsoft is marketing smart clients to be applications that span all of Microsoft Office development and Windows Forms applications, including mobile applications. Thankfully, this marketing is not filled with empty promises. Microsoft has built several products to support smart client development with Office and made radical improvements to Visual Studio and Office itself. Microsoft has also released the *Information Bridge Framework* (IBF), which is a tool set that allows developers to build Office-based smart clients.

Years ago, Microsoft found that users of the Office suite spend a considerable amount of their workday in one or more of the Office products, but often need to leave the suite to finish their work or perform additional tasks. In other words, users of Office products use these applications as containers of data and nothing more. This creates a disconnected user experience and costs companies money, because it takes longer to complete tasks and users need to have knowledge of several systems to do their work. With the release of .NET and the managed environment, Microsoft set out to extend the power of Office. With IBF, application developers can add context to the content contained in Office documents.

IBF is part of the story. The other part is Visual Studio Tools for Office (VSTO). In a nutshell, VSTO provides Visual Studio developers with a platform to build enterprise-level business applications based on the Office suite. VSTO is a technology that tightly integrates with Visual Studio and allows developers to build applications that are Office-centric, with the benefits of having full access to the .NET runtime, security model, deployment model, and so on.

This chapter is all about building smart client applications with VSTO and IBF. We'll start with VSTO.

Visual Studio Tools for Office (VSTO) Applications

VSTO allows developers to build Office-based enterprise applications using Visual Studio. It provides the full Excel and Word application environments within the Visual Studio designer, as well as support for data binding and data caching. In this section, we'll explore those features and build a VSTO-based Office application that showcases some of the power of VSTO.

■**Note** Currently, VSTO 2005, part of Visual Studio 2005, supports only Excel and Word, using only C# or VB .NET. However, Microsoft plans to support the entire product suite.

VSTO Facilities for Smart Client Construction

Visual Studio provides an Office project type that allows you to create Excel- or Word-based applications. As you can see in Figure 4-1, the four Office project types are Excel, Excel Template, Word, and Word Template.

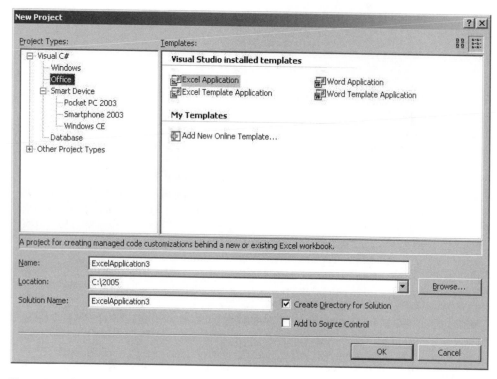

Figure 4-1. *The New Project dialog box with the Office project types*

For example, when you create an Excel project, Visual Studio loads an Excel designer within Visual Studio, as shown in Figure 4-2. As you can see, the Excel designer is hosted within Visual Studio and looks very similar to how you might see Excel if you launched it independently. When you click within the Excel spreadsheet, Visual Studio loads menus that appear when you work within Excel.

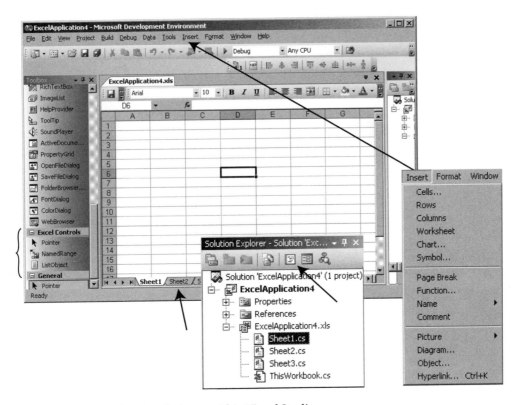

Figure 4-2. *Excel application designer within Visual Studio*

Here are some of the features available when you build an Excel project:

WinForms and Excel controls: When you create an Excel project, the toolbox contains Excel controls and the usual WinForms controls. This means that you can mix and match the two types of controls in your project. For example, you can drop a WinForms button onto the spreadsheet and manipulate it.

Access to properties and events: If you click from sheet to sheet, you can see the Properties window, which allows you to manipulate the properties of each sheet. This is also true of cells and the entire workbook. You also get access to the events on these objects through the Events button in the Properties window, as you would any other object.

Programmatic access: You can gain programmatic access to these sheets by clicking the View Code button in the Solution Explorer's toolbar or by right-clicking a sheet or workbook and selecting the View Code menu item.

Full technology support: All the technologies you expect to have at your disposal for application development are available to VSTO applications. For example, if you write a WinForms application, you expect to be able to use ADO.NET, web services, .NET security, and so on. These are all available with a VSTO application as well.

With VSTO, developers have a more granular level of programmatic control of the spreadsheet. For example, one of the features that Excel doesn't currently provide is events on named ranges. However, with VSTO, you can create a named range by choosing the Named Range Excel control from the Toolbox, and then access its events from the Properties window, as shown in Figure 4-3.

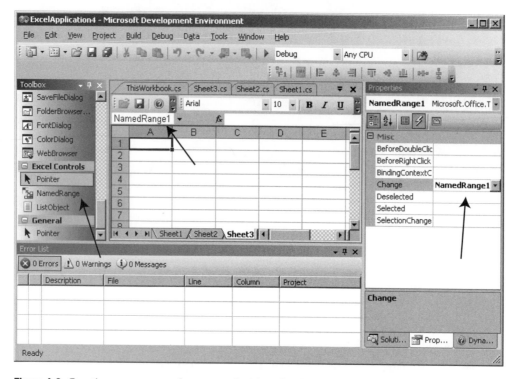

Figure 4-3. *Creating a new named range and wiring the change event*

VSTO 2005 has some powerful features that make building smart client applications based on VSTO a reality. In the next few sections, we'll look at architecture of VSTO and some of the newest features added to VSTO 2005.

VSTO Architecture

VSTO applications are composed of two files: the Word or Excel document and the .NET assembly (the project assembly). Although these are separate files, they are linked together.

■Note The Office document can be linked to only one project assembly, but more than one Office document can point to the same assembly.

The association between the Office document and its .NET assembly is created within the Office document using an *application manifest*. The application manifest is stored within an ActiveX control called the Runtime Storage control. This is an invisible control that is embedded within the Office document.

When the end user opens the Office document, the VSTO runtime gets the Runtime Storage control and reads the application manifest. The runtime then finds the location of the *deployment manifest*, which contains all the necessary details related to the .NET assembly and the current version of the deployment. The runtime reads the deployment manifest, downloads the project assembly along with all of its dependent assemblies, and runs the Office application. Figure 4-4 illustrates the VSTO deployment architecture.

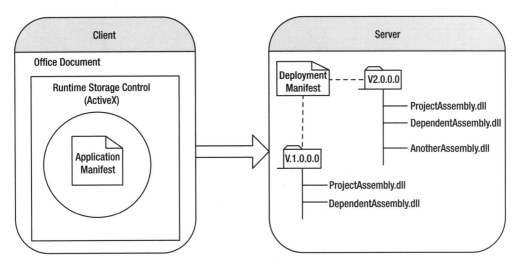

Figure 4-4. *Typical VSTO deployment architecture*

The application manifest is generated and embedded within the Office document when you build the application. The deployment manifest is generated when you deploy the .NET portion to the server. To deploy the .NET portion, Visual Studio provides the Publish Wizard, as shown in Figure 4-5. We will talk about deploying smart clients in great detail in Chapter 6.

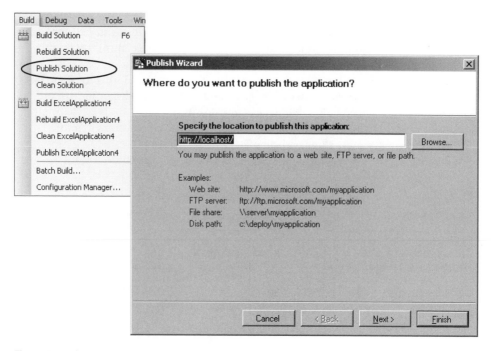

Figure 4-5. *The Publish Wizard in Visual Studio 2005*

Data Binding and Data Caching

WinForms developers have used data binding extensively because this feature is built into a host of WinForms controls. VSTO also provides several Excel and Word controls that support data binding: the NamedRange and ListObject controls in Excel, and the Bookmark control in Word.

Data caching is also supported by Excel and Word applications. VSTO supports data caching by serializing cacheable items directly within the document. Let's see how data binding and data caching work by walking through a simple Excel example.

In this example, we will create an Excel ListObject and bind a dataset to it. We will also cache the dataset to demonstrate caching.

1. In Visual Studio 2005, create a new Excel project by selecting Office, then Excel Application in the New Project dialog box.

2. When the Excel designer loads into the IDE, drag a ListObject from the Toolbox (you'll find this control in the Excel Controls group) and drop it onto the spreadsheet. Then use the Properties window to give the ListObject a name.

3. Build the solution and run it to make sure everything works.

4. To demonstrate data binding, we need some data. For sake of this example, we'll pull the Employees table from the Northwind database into a dataset and bind the dataset to the ListObject. Simultaneously, we'll demonstrate data caching by caching the dataset. Go to the code-behind of Sheet1 of the workbook, and add the `Initialize()` method shown in Listing 4-1.

Listing 4-1. *The Initialize() Method for Sheet1*

```
[Cached]
private DataSet empDs=null;
private void Sheet1_Initialize(object sender, System.EventArgs e)
{
    if (empDs == null)
    {
  mpDs = DataHelper.GetAllEmployee();
      StartCaching("empDs");
    }
    empListObj.SetDataBinding(empDs, empDs.Tables[0].TableName);
}
```

The binding aspects of this example all come down to the last line in Listing 4-1. The SetDataBinding() method takes a data source and a member name to determine what to bind to. In this case, the data source is a dataset, and the first table in the Tables collection is the binding table. Most developers have seen data binding done this way.

Data caching, however, is more interesting. Strictly speaking, there are two requirements to caching something in a VSTO application:

- All cache items must be marked as cacheable, which you can do in two ways. One is to programmatically decorate declarations with the [Cached] attribute. Alternatively, via the designer, you can set the CacheInDocument property. In our example, we are applying the [Cached] attribute.

- You must call StartCaching() with the name of the cache item. This allows you to programmatically enable caching on an item-by-item basis. As you would expect, you can programmatically stop caching an item by calling StopCaching().

Items are cached directly in the document (in the Runtime Storage control) when the user saves the document. When a Word or Excel document is opened, the VSTO loader loads the .NET assembly, rehydrates any cache items, and then calls startup events. So, in our example, the Employees dataset is re-created prior to the Initialize() method being called, which is why we check for null prior to making a call to the database. Figure 4-6 shows the Employees dataset bound to a ListObject.

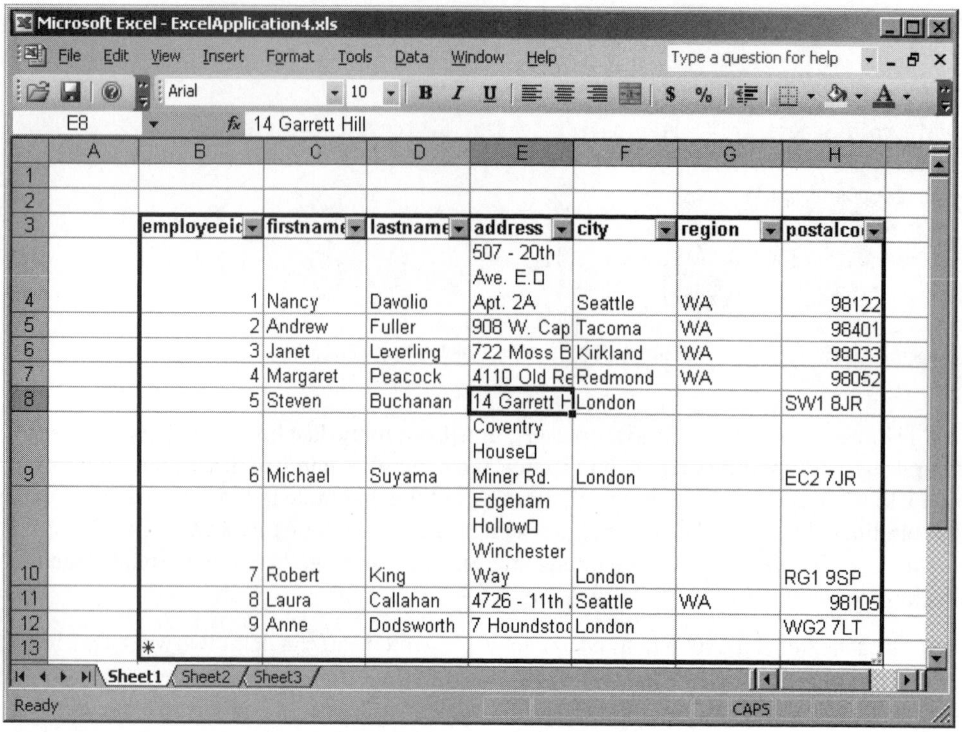

Figure 4-6. *An Excel ListObject bound to a dataset*

Custom Actions Panes

Microsoft introduced the Actions pane in Office XP. Word and Excel users have seen and used the Actions pane, but they may not know that is what it is called. The Actions pane in Word provides links to recently opened documents, a search facility, and a few other links to online resources, as shown in Figure 4-7.

Now VSTO developers can build custom Actions panes for their VSTO applications. Surprisingly, building a custom Actions pane is quite easy in both Word and Excel. The ActionsPane object is a WinForms control, so you can access the Controls collection of the ActionsPane and add controls specific to your application. The workbook in Excel applications has a property called ActionsPane that developers use to refer to the ActionsPane object.

There is one "gotcha," however: the ActionsPane itself does not have designer, so you cannot, for example, open the ActionsPane in the designer and drag-and-drop controls on it. Instead, the recommendation is to use a UserControl as the single child of the ActionsPane and add all of your controls to the UserControl. Since UserControls have designers, you can take advantage of the designer as well as the ActionsPane.

Figure 4-7. *The Actions pane in Word 2003*

To see how easy it is to use the ActionsPane in your projects, create a new Excel application and add a UserControl to your project. Use the designer to add a few controls to the UserControl. Go to the code-behind of the workbook, and in the `Initialize()` method of the workbook, add the following code to access the ActionsPane and add the UserControl to the `Controls` collection:

```
private void ThisWorkbook_Initialize(object sender, System.EventArgs e)
{
    this.ActionsPane.Controls.Add(new UserControl1());
}
```

When you run your application, you should see something similar to Figure 4-8.

Another advantage of the ActionsPane is that you can easily implement interaction with the actual Office document. For example, to handle the click event and iterate over the controls on the first sheet in the workbook, use the following:

```
private void button1_Click(object sender, EventArgs e)
{
    IEnumerator en = Globals.Sheet1.Controls.GetEnumerator();
    while (en.MoveNext())
    {
    Console.WriteLine(en.Current.ToString());
    }
}
```

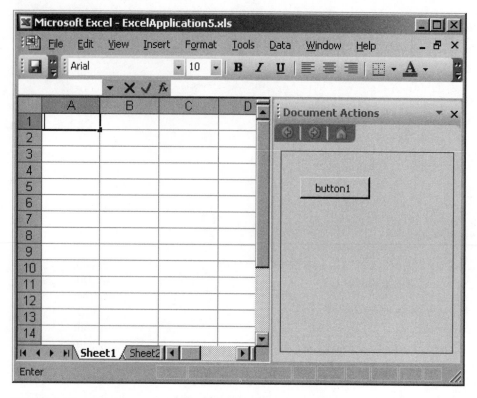

Figure 4-8. *The Actions pane in an Excel application*

VSTO Wrap-Up

As you've seen, the major attraction of VSTO is that it tightly integrates with Visual Studio and .NET. For example, there is really no difference between creating WinForms applications and creating an Office application when it comes to the availability of supported technologies. You have access to the same WinForms controls. This provides the framework for creating powerful smart client applications based on Excel or Word. Moreover, with the granular event model now available, application developers can even extend the functionality provided by Excel itself.

Microsoft has made radical improvements in both Office and Visual Studio to enable developers to build sophisticated Office-based applications. Now, with these two technologies "joined at the hip," you can build smart client applications that are strictly Office-based. Rather than needing to build complex integration layers, you can write your business logic in C# or VB .NET. Moreover, because of the deployment and architectural improvements in VSTO and Visual Studio, you can build true enterprise systems and know that you will be able to deploy them within your enterprise with the full balance of functionality and security.

Information Bridge Framework (IBF) Applications

IBF is a middleware technology that allows organizations to further exploit their investment in their line-of-business (LOB) applications and Microsoft Office. Organizations currently have LOB applications but have no visibility to these applications from Office products. IBF provides the mechanism to connect these applications to your Office products.

IBF is best suited for organizations that have employees who spend a considerable amount of time in one or more of the Office products (Word, Excel, Outlook, and so on). These users currently use Office in a very static way; they use Office as a container to hold static information. IBF provides the ability to transform these static documents to live and actionable creatures, by adding context-based functionality to the content contained in Office documents.

For example, imagine that a doctor working at a local hospital receives an e-mail message concerning a patient. To respond, the doctor must leave Outlook, go to an LOB application to view the patient's medical records, and then return to Outlook. It would be nice if the information concerning the patient were available directly from the e-mail message. Suppose the patient's name is a hyperlink in the e-mail, and when the doctor clicks the link, Outlook gathers the medical records for the patient and presents the information to the doctor within Outlook. The doctor quickly gathers her thoughts and writes her response. This example illustrates the benefit of adding context to content. Outlook was able to look at the content in the e-mail, identify relevant information, and provide the links to these items (the patient's name in this example).

As another example, suppose that a director of a debt-collection company receives a weekly report in an Excel spreadsheet showing which accounts have been closed and which are still outstanding. The spreadsheet shows a list of accounts, how much has been collected, and how much is still owed. It is not unusual for the director to be concerned about a few of the bigger accounts, and so he may investigate these. To do so, he must launch a few of the company's LOB applications to find out more information about these accounts. The director may need to perform repetitive research on each account, spending hours trying to understand the accounts in order to establish a plan of action to collect the debts. What's worse is that the director will need to repeat this process the following week when he gets the report again. It would be nice if the director could find out the details of these accounts directly within the Excel report. IBF is a technology that can deliver this. IBF allows the director to click on accounts within the Excel spreadsheet to find the information about these accounts.

That's the sales pitch for IBF. Now let's see how IBF works.

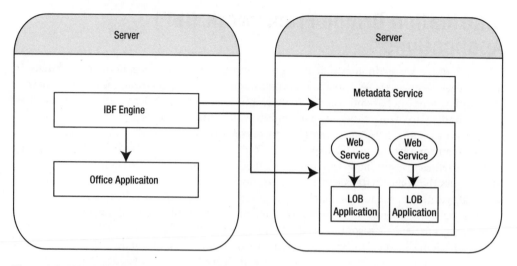

Figure 4-9. *IBF architecture*

IBF Architecture

IBF is a middleware solution that sits in between Office and the web services that provide the visibility to the LOB applications. The architecture of IBF is shown in Figure 4-9.

IBF is initiated by *interaction points,* which are the links in an Office document. When someone clicks one of the links, Office launches IBF, and the IBF engine calls the metadata service to get metadata associated with the request. The engine then queries the web services in the metadata, calls the web services, and paints a view with the data returned from the web services. In addition to the data painted within the Office document, IBF also enables operations to be performed from within these views. Here's a summary of these steps:

1. A user clicks a link in an Office document, and that link is recognized by Office to be an interaction point.

2. Office launches the IBF engine.

3. The IBF engine queries the metadata service, and then calls relevant web services.

4. The IBF engine paints a few views with the data returned from the web services and enables some operations via the data views.

Architecturally, IBF is composed of both server-side and client-side components. The server-side components are the web services and the metadata service. The web services are services that provide the visibility to the LOB applications. These are the services that developers write to expose the data held within the LOB applications. The metadata service is an IBF built-in web service, which provides web methods to read and write metadata. The metadata service stores metadata in a SQL Server database. On the client side, IBF defines only one component: the IBF engine. The IBF engine is an add-in component to Office. The IBF engine undertakes all of the client-side responsibilities, including the following:

- Calling the metadata service to get metadata

- Processing metadata

- Calling the web services to get data

- Rendering the user interface for the IBF solution and reacting to action requests

That's the high-level architecture of IBF. Now, let's see what's involved in building an IBF solution.

IBF Solution Construction

To build an IBF solution, you need to develop or define four components:

- Create the LOB web services, which are the services that expose LOB applications.

- Create the metadata for the web service and solution. The web service metadata describes the web services, and the solution metadata describes the IBF solution. In the usual Microsoft style, IBF comes with several tools that plug in to Visual Studio to assist developers in rapidly developing metadata.

- Add the user interface elements.

- Create an Office document with interaction points. Interaction points are constructed from smart tags and attached schema documents.

To demonstrate these steps, we'll build a sample IBF application. Figure 4-10 shows the overall solution architecture for our example. Note that these elements directly correspond to the preceding steps.

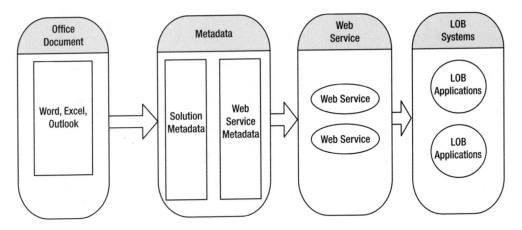

Figure 4-10. *IBF solution architecture*

Before continuing, take a look at Table 4-1, which defines some common IBF terms and their definitions.

Table 4-1. *IBF Terminology*

Term	Definition
Metadata	Data that describes either the web services or the IBF solution.
Service metadata	Metadata associated with a service (for example, a web service or a .NET assembly).
Solution metadata	Metadata that describes the visual portion of your application.
Entity	An item specific to your business. Examples include Customer, Order, Account, Employee, Teacher, Doctor, and Nurse.
View	How you see an entity. There may be several views of an entity. For example, if you have an entity called an Employee, you might have views called EmployeeProfileView and EmployeeWorkHistoryView.
View locator	A way to find a particular view.
Relationship	Defines a mapping between an entity and a view.
Port	A channel for data.
Scope	A high-level grouping of entities.

Note IBF is very XML-centric, so you should be comfortable with the XML platform of technologies before you attempt to build an IBF application. Specifically, you need to understand the basics of XML schemas, SOAP, and XML serialization in .NET. (See MSDN for more information about these technologies.)

Creating "IBF-Friendly" Web Services

To build an IBF solution, you first need to have the web services that expose the LOB applications. Technically, IBF can work with any Web Services Interoperability (WS-I)-compliant web service. However, it works best with web services that have been built following the IBF web service guidelines recommended by Microsoft:

- Write web service methods around an entity. An *entity* is something that is meaningful from a business perspective—Account, Employee, Customer, Order, and so on.

- Write Get, Put, and Act methods for views of the entity. The Get method retrieves an entity view, the Put method writes or updates an entity view, and the Act method performs some other operation on an entity view.

- Use references to uniquely identify entities. A *reference* in this context is an XML schema of an entity that represents a unique instance of an entity, such as <Employee id=123/>. This will become clear when we look at a sample web service.

As you can see, you just need to keep in mind three recommendations when you write IBF web services. The difference between writing IBF web services and some of the web services that you may have written in the past is that you should write IBF web services with specific entities in mind. You should provide Get, Put, and Act methods when appropriate, and use references to uniquely identify an instance of an entity.

To write a web service for an IBF application, follow these steps:

1. Define the entities of the web service.

2. Define the views of each of the entities.

3. Define the operations that will render the views.

In a nutshell, you write web services for specific entities, and each of these entities can have one or more views exposed. To expose a view of an entity, you write operations that satisfy the view. For example, you might have an entity called Employee and want to expose a view called EmployeeContactView. To get this view of the Employee, define a Get method called GetEmployeeContact. Similarly, you may have an entity called Order and define a view called OrderDetail. To satisfy this view, you may need two operations: GetOrder and GetOrderParts.

Listing 4-2 shows our implementation of the EmployeeWS web service, written around an Employee entity. For the example, we assume this information is in some LOB application and a Word document will expose the contact information for this entity. We define a view to expose the contact information for some of these employees. To do that, we define an operation called GetEmployeeContactInfo.

Listing 4-2. *The EmployeeWS Web Service*

```
[WebService(Namespace="http://IBFWS/")]
public class EmployeeWS : System.Web.Services.WebService
{
 WebMethod]
    public Employee GetEmployeeContactInfo(EmployeeReferenceId employeeId)
    {
       Employee emp = DataHelper.GetEmployee(employeeId.EmployeeId);
       return emp;
    }
}
```

The EmployeeWS web service uses several other classes: Employee, EmployeeReferenceId, and DataHelper. The Employee and EmployeeReferenceId classes are shown in Listing 4-3. The DataHelper class is just a database utility class, and its implementation is not shown for brevity.

Listing 4-3. *The Employee and EmployeeReferenceId Classes*

```
[XmlRoot("Employee",Namespace="urn-LobApp")]
public class Employee
{
 XmlElement]
    public string EmployeeId;
    [XmlElement]
    public string FirstName;
```

```
    [XmlElement]
    public string LastName;
    [XmlElement]
    public string Address;
    [XmlElement]
    public string City;
    [XmlElement]
    public string State;
    [XmlElement]
    public string Zipcode;
}
[XmlRoot("EmployeeReferenceId",Namespace="urn-LobApp")]
public class EmployeeReferenceId
{
    [XmlAttribute]
    public string EmployeeId;
}
```

The `EmployeeWS` web service defines one web method: an IBF `Get` method. We have one view and have defined one operation to satisfy that view. Each view in an IBF solution must have an XML schema. In this case, our view has the following schema:

```
<Employee xmlns="urn-LobApp">
 EmployeeId>string</EmployeeId>
    <FirstName>string</FirstName>
    <LastName>string</LastName>
    <Address>string</Address>
    <City>string</City>
    <State>string</State>
    <Zipcode>string</Zipcode>
</Employee>
```

Our `Get` method takes an `EmployeeReferenceId`. This is the "reference" we alluded to earlier. IBF defines references as pointers to unique instances of a view. `Get`, `Put`, and `Act` methods generally take references as input parameters to uniquely identify the instance of the view they need. These references also need to have an XML schema defined. Our `EmployeeReferenceId` class has the following schema:

```
<EmployeeReferenceId EmployeeId="string" xmlns="urn-LobApp" />
```

Each schema must have an associated class. In our case, we have the `Employee` and `EmployeeReferenceId` classes. These two classes have been decorated with XML attributes to ensure that they are serialized to match the preceding schemas.

You may have already noticed that the XML snippets both have an XML namespace defined. It is a good idea to tag all data going into and out of web services with an appropriate namespace. Moreover, the namespace should be one that is indicative of the LOB application. For example, if you write a web service that exposes customer contact information from a customer relationship management (CRM) system, you may use `urn-CRMCustomerContactDetails` as a namespace.

In addition to tagging all input and output data with an XML namespace, the web service also has a namespace assigned. This namespace is different from the namespace given to the input and output parameters. It turns out that IBF prefers to have different namespaces defined for the data elements and for the web service getting the data; the different namespaces differentiate between the data and the thing getting the data.

Now you have seen what it takes to build an IBF-compliant web service. IBF is not very strict in how you write your web service, and the recommendations are fairly straightforward. You'll get a better understanding of why IBF recommends these guidelines for web services in the next section, where we talk about creating the metadata for the web service. We will first create the web service metadata, and then create the solution metadata.

Creating Web Service Metadata

The IBF tool set includes a Visual Studio plug-in that allows developers to rapidly build web service metadata and solution metadata. This tool is called the Metadata Designer and comes with the IBF download package. The Metadata Designer has several components: the Metadata Explorer and the Metadata Guidance tool. The Metadata Guidance tool contains a few wizards that help you to quickly create metadata and some documentation. The Metadata Explorer tool allows you to view the metadata and perform context-sensitive operations on the elements of the metadata (entities, views, actions, and so on). These two tools are automatically loaded into Visual Studio when you create or open an IBF Metadata project, as shown in Figure 4-11.

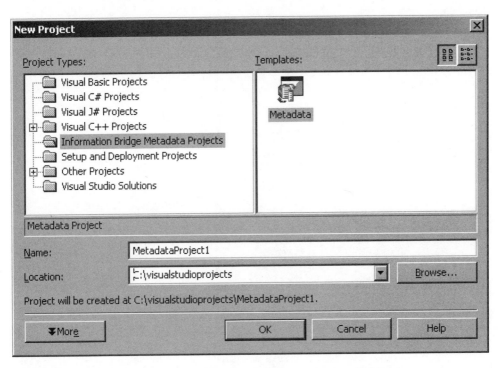

Figure 4-11. *An IBF Metadata project in Visual Studio's New Project dialog box*

When a metadata project is loaded into Visual Studio, by default, the Metadata Guidance tool is loaded into the IDE. The Metadata Guidance tool, as the name suggests, guides developers in creating web service and solution metadata. You create metadata by using the tool's wizards, and each wizard generates base metadata that can be customized and expanded to fully describe the web service and solution. The Metadata Guidance tool has two parts: one for creating web service metadata guidance and another for creating the solution metadata. Figure 4-12 shows the Create Service Metadata section.

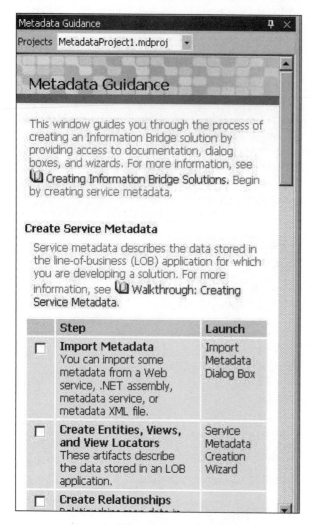

Figure 4-12. *The Metadata Guidance tool*

The wizard can build metadata from several sources: an existing metadata file, the metadata service, a web service, or a .NET assembly. In our example, we'll build metadata from our web service. To import the web service metadata for our EmployeeWS web service, launch the Import Metadata wizard from the Metadata Guidance tool, as shown in Figure 4-13.

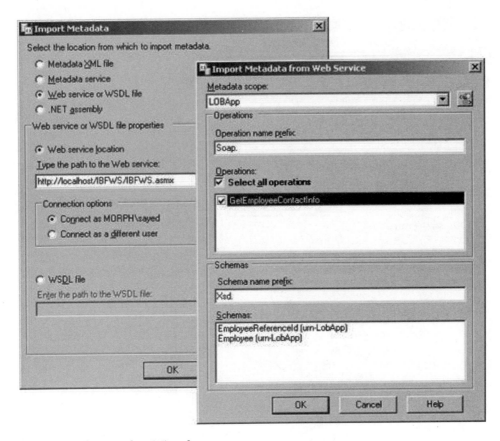

Figure 4-13. *The Metadata Wizard*

When you select to import metadata from a web service, the wizard will detect the operations defined in the web service and allow you to select which operations to import. In this case, we have just one operation. Thus, the first step is to import the metadata from the web service. When you complete the import, the wizard generates the base metadata from the web service, and you can view the metadata using the Metadata Explorer, as shown in Figure 4-14.

Notice that the Metadata Explorer shows the GetEmployeeContactInfo operation we defined in our web service. In addition, the Metadata Explorer shows that the wizard imported the schemas we defined for our input and output classes. But the Employee entity that we've been talking about is not shown in Figure 4-14. That's because the web service doesn't contain this information.

To establish entities, you need to go the second step in the Metadata Guidance tool: Create Entities, Views, and View Locators. When you choose this step, the tool runs the Service Metadata Creation Wizard, as shown in Figure 4-15. This wizard allows you to describe the entities, views, and view locators in your IBF solution by running through a few dialog boxes. Recall that we designed our web service around the Employee entity. We also decided to create one view of this entity and defined just one operation to satisfy the view. So, now we need to describe this using the Service Metadata Creation Wizard. We do this by creating entities and views and linking them to operations in the web service.

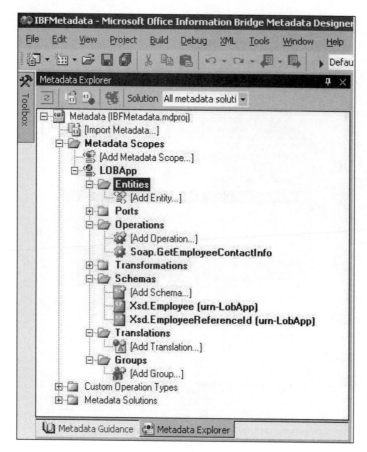

Figure 4-14. *The Metadata Explorer*

As shown in Figure 4-15, the wizard allows you to define or select an entity and associate a view with that entity (either by creating a new view or choosing from an existing view). In this example, we have an Employee entity and an EmployeeContactInfo view. When we create a view, we need to associate the view with a particular schema. In our case, we designed the view to have the Employee schema.

After you create the view, the wizard automatically looks at the web service metadata to see if there is a method that returns that schema; if so, it allows you to choose that operation as a way to locate that view (view locator). After running through this wizard for the EmployeeWS web service, the Metadata Explorer shows our new entity and view, as shown in Figure 4-16.

Note The Service Creation Metadata Wizard allows you to create only one entity at a time. Therefore, if a web service is centered on more than one entity, you will need to run the wizard as many times as there are entities. However, the wizard does allow you to create more than one view on an entity during the last step in the wizard (without needing to rerun the wizard).

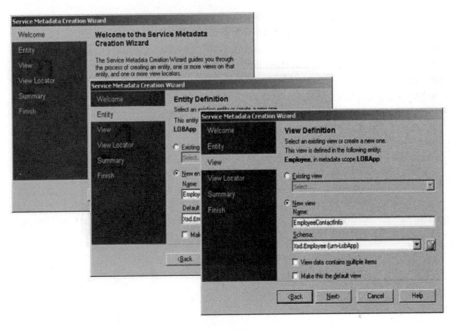

Figure 4-15. *The Service Metadata Creation Wizard*

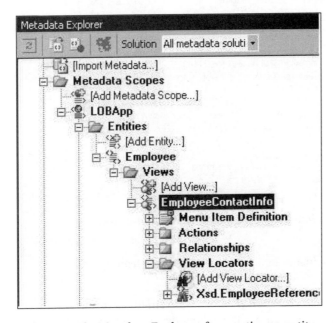

Figure 4-16. *The Metadata Explorer after creating an entity*

Notice that the Metadata Explorer shows that we have an entity called `Employee` and a single view of that entity called `EmployeeContactInfo`. Moreover, the view can be retrieved with the `EmployeeReferenceId` view locator. Also notice that a view can have *relationships*. A relationship is a way to navigate from one view to another. For example, if we had a `Customer` entity and an `Account` entity, we could establish views and relationships to navigate from the customer to his accounts. The Metadata Explorer also shows that views can have *actions*. Actions are operations that appear as menu items to the end user. You'll learn more about actions shortly.

So far, we have created a web service and the metadata for that web service. Our next step is to create the solution metadata.

Creating Solution Metadata

The solution metadata defines the client side of an IBF solution. You create the solution metadata through the Create Solution Metadata section of the Metadata Guidance tool, as shown in Figure 4-17.

Create Solution Metadata

Solution metadata defines how to display or act on data described by service metadata. To create solution metadata, you can complete one or more of the items below. For more information, see 🕮 Walkthrough: Creating Solution Metadata.

	Step	Launch
☐	**Create a Windows Forms-Based or HTML-Based Region** Regions are used to display data in the information window. For more information, see 🕮 Walkthrough: Creating a Windows Forms-Based or HTML-Based Region.	Region Creation Wizard
☐	**Create a Reference List Region** This is a specific type of region that displays lists of data defined by a view. For more information, see 🕮 Walkthrough: Creating a Reference List Region.	Reference List Region Creation Wizard
☐	**Define Menu Items** You can use menu items to execute actions in the information window. For more information, see 🕮 Walkthrough: Defining Menu Items.	Menu Item Definition Wizard
☐	**Implement Search for the Information Window** The Search pane allows users to search LOB applications. For more information, see 🕮 Walkthrough: Implementing Search for the Information Window.	Search Definition Wizard

Figure 4-17. *The Create Solution Metadata section of the Metadata Guidance tool*

As you can see, the Metadata Guidance tool defines four steps to creating and finalizing the solution metadata:

- The first step launches the Region Creation Wizard. A *region* in IBF is an area within the IBF window to display data to end users. IBF defines two types of regions: Windows Forms regions and HTML regions.

- The second step launches the Reference List Region Creation Wizard. A reference list is a way to display lists of data and allow end users to page through the list. An example of a reference list is shown in Figure 4-18.

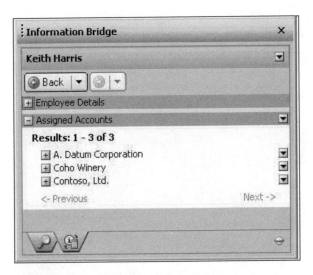

Figure 4-18. *A reference list within the IBF window*

- The third step launches the Menu Item Creation Wizard. This step allows you to create menu items for actions and relationships.

- The final step launches the Search Definition Wizard. IBF provides the facilities to build intelligent queries as a way to quickly find LOB data, rather than needing to rely solely on navigation.

Each of these steps is optional, so you do not need to walk through each wizard unless your solution demands it. In this example, we need to perform only the first step.

Creating a Region

First, we'll create a Windows Forms region by running the Region Creation Wizard. Here are the steps:

1. Create a new metadata solution. We do this by giving the wizard a name for the solution, as shown in Figure 4-19.

2. Define our schema, as shown in Figure 4-20. Windows Forms regions are essentially user controls, and the schema defines what our user control is going to look like. In our simple scenario, we have just two schemas to choose from: the Employee schema and the EmployeeReferenceId schema. Because references are used as inputs to our web methods, and because we want to show employees in our user interface, the Employee schema is the only one that makes sense.

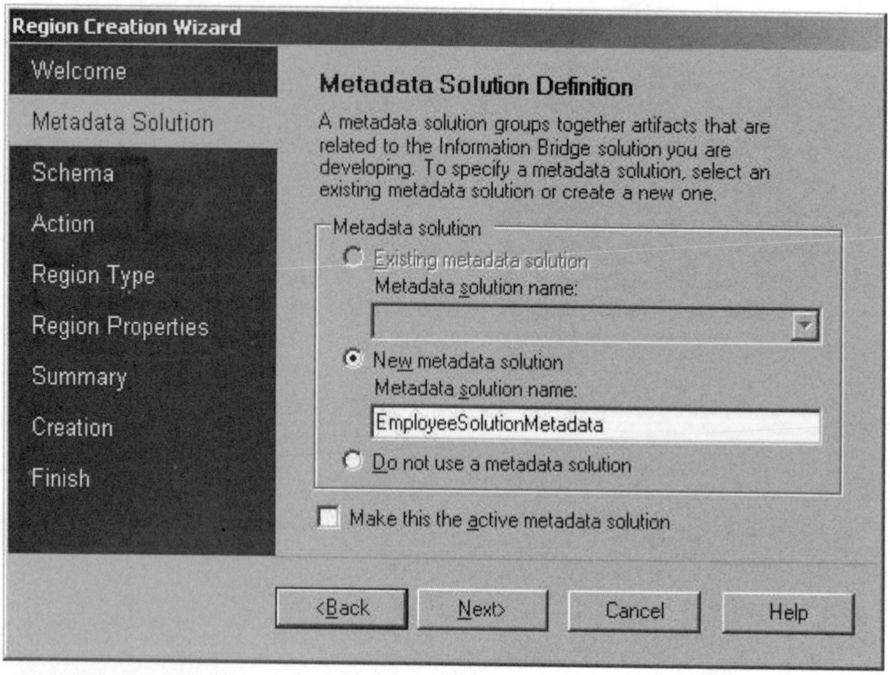

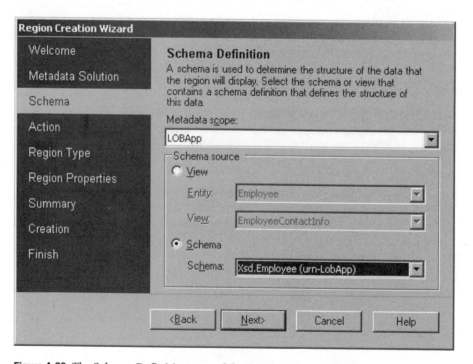

Figure 4-19. *The Metadata Solution Definition step of the Region Creation Wizard*

Figure 4-20. *The Schema Definition step of the Region Creation Wizard*

3. Choose the type of region, as shown in Figure 4-21. There are two types of regions: HTML-based and Windows Forms-based.

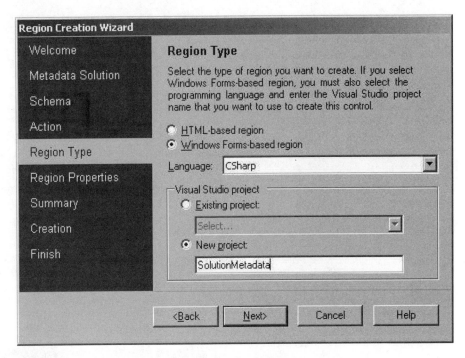

Figure 4-21. *The Region Type step of the Region Creation Wizard*

4. Define the region properties, as shown in Figure 4-22. Here, we give the region a class name. Because Windows Forms regions are user controls, this is the name of the user control class. In the case of the Employee schema, it makes sense to use the name EmployeeUserControl. We also supply a caption and a description for the region. The caption is not the user control caption, but the caption that is displayed in the IBF task pane (see Figure 4-18). The entry in the Description field is actually not shown anywhere in the IBF task pane, but can be used internally. The Show As property defines how the region will be shown in the IBF task pane. Figure 4-22 shows that we choose ExpandedRegion, which tells the IBF runtime to show the region expanded. You can also show the region as collapsed or noncollapsible.

After you finish, the wizard creates a Visual Studio project, as shown in Figure 4-23.

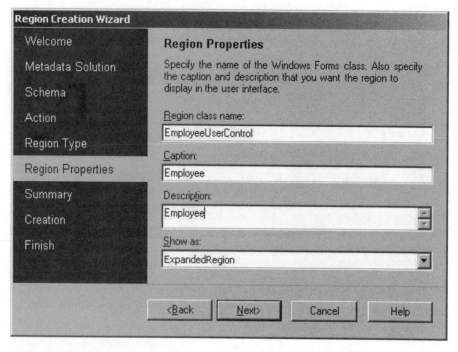

Figure 4-22. *The Region Properties step of the Region Creation Wizard*

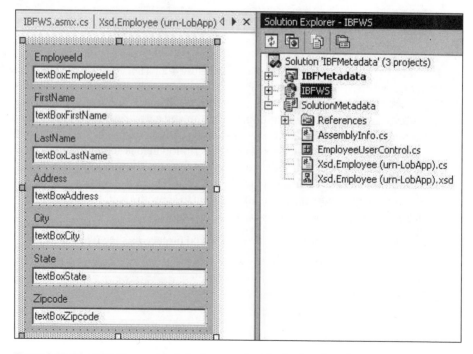

Figure 4-23. *The Solution generated after running the Region Creation Wizard*

As you can see, the wizard created the user control, a C# class, and imported the Employee schema. Let's look at the generated Employee class, shown in Listing 4-4.

Listing 4-4. *The Employee Class*

```
[System.Xml.Serialization.XmlTypeAttribute(Namespace="urn-LobApp")]
[System.Xml.Serialization.XmlRootAttribute(Namespace="urn-LobApp", IsNullable=true)]
public class Employee
{
    public string EmployeeId;
    public string FirstName;
    public string LastName;
    public string Address;
    public string City;
    public string State;
    public string Zipcode;
}
```

This class is used to handle serialization back and forth from the web service. Because we are going to display an employee in our user control, and because we are going to receive XML from the web service, the wizard generated a class to handle the serialization and binding to the user control. Notice also that the user control the wizard created has text boxes that map to the fields of the Employee class.

Now let's look at the generated user control class, shown in Listing 4-5.

Listing 4-5. *The EmployeeUserControl Class*

```
public class EmployeeUserControl :
System.Windows.Forms.UserControl, IRegion
{
    //..

    private IRegionFrameProxy regionFrameProxy;
    private FrameType hostType;
    private IVisualStyles visualStyles;

    public XmlNode Data
    {
        set
        {
            this.SetXmlData(value);
        }
    }
    public IRegionFrameProxy HostProxy
    {
        set
        {
            this.regionFrameProxy = value;
        }
```

```
    }
    public FrameType HostType
    {
        set
        {
            this.hostType = value;
        }
    }
    public IVisualStyles VisualStyle
    {
        set
        {
            if (null != value)
            {
                this.visualStyles = value;
                UpdateStyles(null, null);
                this.visualStyles.UserPreferencesChanged += new
Microsoft.Win32.UserPreferenceChangedEventHandler(this.UpdateStyles);
            }
        }
    }
    private void UpdateStyles(object sender,
    Microsoft.Win32.UserPreferenceChangedEventArgs e)
    {
        if (null != this.visualStyles)
        {
            // Set back colors...
            Color newBackColor = this.visualStyles.
GetColor(Colors.RegionBackColor);
            Color newForeColor = this.visualStyles.GetColor(
Colors.RegionHeaderText);
System.Drawing.Font newBoldFont =
this.visualStyles.GetFont(Fonts.DefaultFontBold);
System.Drawing.Font newFont =
this.visualStyles.GetFont(Fonts.DefaultFont);
this.BackColor = newBackColor;
            foreach (Control c in this.Controls)
            {
                c.BackColor = newBackColor;
                c.ForeColor = newForeColor;

                if (c.GetType() == typeof(Label))
                {
                    c.Font = newBoldFont;
                }
            }
        }
    }
```

```csharp
private Employee controlData = null;

private void SetXmlData(XmlNode data)
{
XmlSerializer xmlSerializer = new System.Xml.Serialization.XmlSerializer(
typeof(Employee));
XmlReader xmlReader = new XmlNodeReader(data);

this.controlData = (Employee) xmlSerializer.Deserialize(xmlReader);


this.textBoxEmployeeId.Text = (this.controlData.EmployeeId != null)?
this.controlData.EmployeeId.ToString():string.Empty;
this.textBoxFirstName.Text = (this.controlData.FirstName != null)?
this.controlData.FirstName.ToString():string.Empty;
this.textBoxLastName.Text = (this.controlData.LastName != null)?
this.controlData.LastName.ToString():string.Empty;
this.textBoxAddress.Text =
(this.controlData.Address != null)?
this.controlData.Address.ToString():string.Empty;
this.textBoxCity.Text =
(this.controlData.City != null)?
this.controlData.City.ToString():string.Empty;
this.textBoxState.Text =
(this.controlData.State != null)?
this.controlData.State.ToString():string.Empty;
this.textBoxZipcode.Text =
 (this.controlData.Zipcode != null)?
this.controlData.Zipcode.ToString():string.Empty;

}
}
```

As shown in Listing 4-5, the class extends UserControl and implements the IRegion interface. IRegion is an IBF interface in the Microsoft.InformationBridge.Framework.Interfaces namespace. This interface defines a few properties that handle serialization and binding of data to and from the user control. That takes care of the user control. To test it, we need to create an action.

Adding an Action

Actions are created to execute operations. An action is defined in IBF as a group of operations. Actions are attached to views. To create an action for our EmployeeContactInfo view, open the Add Action dialog box, as shown in Figure 4-24.

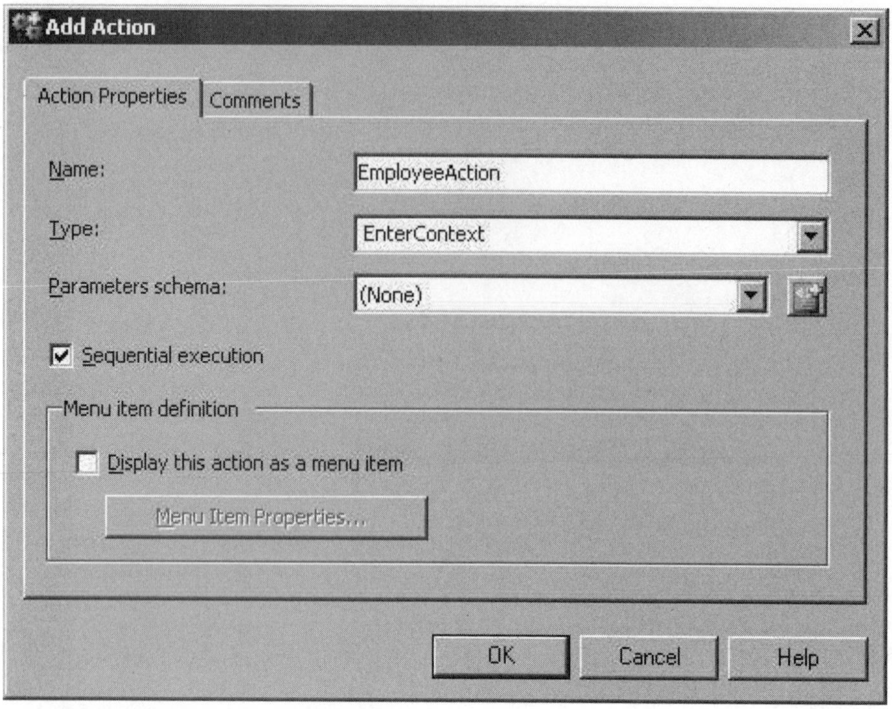

Figure 4-24. *The Add Action dialog box*

To add an action, you need to at least assign the action a name and give it a type. We named our action EmployeeAction. IBF defines two types of actions: EnterContext actions (selected in this example), which derive their data from the context of the document in which they are invoked, and Search actions, which get their input from an IBF search. The Sequential execution check box tells the IBF runtime how to execute the operations of the action. Sequential execution forces all operations to be executed in turn; that is, if an action has three operations, the first is executed, the second will not execute until the first one completes, and the third will not execute until the second completes. This check box is selected in our example. When the Sequential execution check box is not checked, IBF can execute the operations simultaneously.

After you create the action, the next step is to add some operations to the action. When you double-click an action in the Metadata Explorer, Visual Studio shows the action canvas, as shown in Figure 4-25. You can then drag-and-drop operations from the Metadata Explorer to the canvas. When you drop an operation onto the action canvas, you need to create a transformation.

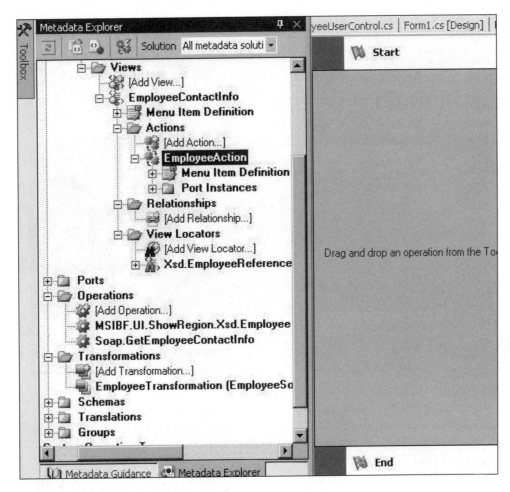

Figure 4-25. *Actions in the Metadata Explorer*

The Transformation Instances dialog box is automatically displayed when you drop an operation on the action canvas, as shown in Figure 4-26.

The data source for an operation defines the input for the operation. As shown in Figure 4-26, data sources can originate from four sources: None, Reference, View Data, and Action Parameters. The most common sources are reference and view data. A reference is the reference schema (for example, EmployeeReferenceId). View data is the data that is passed to the action after the view locator has executed. Operations also have an output data source and a transformation instance. For simple cases, you'll generally leave the defaults.

So far, we have created an entity called Employee and a view called EmployeeContactInfo. We created an action called EmployeeAction and assigned an operation to that action. We defined a transformation for the operation and created a Windows Forms region using the Region Creation Wizard. That almost covers the fundamentals of IBF within Visual Studio. However, we're still missing actually executing actions.

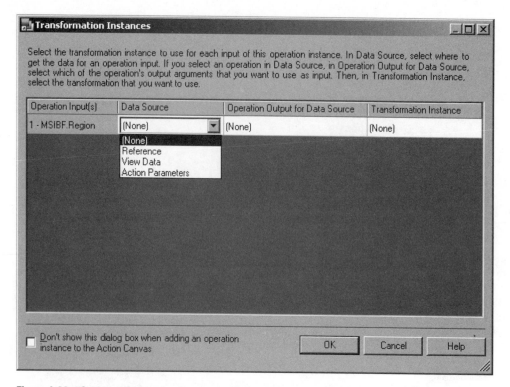

Figure 4-26. *The Transformation Instances dialog box*

Executing Actions

Visual Studio provides a context menu to execute actions within Visual Studio. When you right-click an action in the Metadata Explorer window, the IDE presents the menu shown in Figure 4-27.

To run the action, choose one of the two menus to build and execute the action. When you choose one of these menus, you are presented with a dialog box that allows you to choose the view locator. In our example, we have defined one view locator. When you choose the view locator, the dialog box can automatically insert a template based on the schema. Once the template is inserted, you can modify the template with actual values. As Figure 4-27 shows, we are calling the web service with an EmployeeId=1. When you click the OK button, the IDE should launch the IBF task pane within Visual Studio, and you should see the user control we created displayed within the IBF task pane.

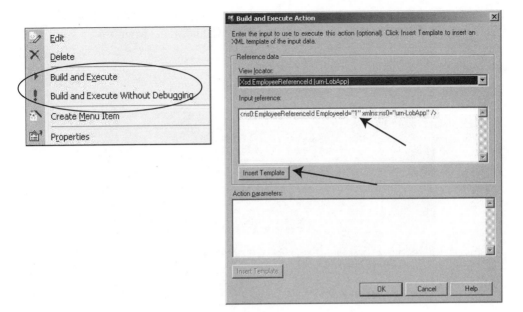

Figure 4-27. *Executing actions within Visual Studio*

Constructing Interaction Points with Smart Tags and Attached Schema Documents

So far, we have talked about aspects of IBF within the Visual Studio environment, but we have not discussed IBF within Office. In this section, we'll discuss smart tags and attached schema documents. These two technologies are the entry into IBF from within Office documents.

Smart tags allow text to be identified as important as the user types into a document. For example, if a Human Resources department representative were typing an e-mail message to his boss concerning a particular employee, the smart tag would identify the employee as contextually important as the representative composed the message. In addition to recognizing important contextual data, smart tags also enable actions and execution of these actions on tagged data, and provide the facility to launch IBF.

Interestingly, there are two types of smart tags: Office smart tags (introduced with Office XP) and IBF smart tags. Both of these are conceptually the same; however, Office smart tags have some deployment restrictions that do not apply to IBF smart tags. Therefore, the discussion of smart tags here is devoted to IBF smart tags.

To build smart tags, you need to do two things:

- Create a .NET assembly that implements the `IRecognizers` interface.

- Create metadata to tell IBF about the smart tag and how to invoke the recognizers when a user types within an Office document.

Classes that implement `IRecognizers` are called smart tag *recognizers*. To implement a recognizer, you need to reference the two IBF assemblies `Microsoft.InformationBridge.Framework.Interfaces` and `Microsoft.InformationBridge.Framework.UI.Interop`, and the

Microsoft Smart Tag 2.0 Type Library. IRecognizer defines two methods: Initialize() and Recognize(). An empty implementation of the interface is shown in Listing 4-6.

Listing 4-6. *The SmartTagImplRecognizer Class*

```
public class SmartTagImpl:IRecognizer
{
    public SmartTagImpl()
    {
    }
    public void Initialize(XmlElement initializationData)
    {
    ///...
    }

    public void Recognize(string text, IF_TYPE dataType,
 int localeID, ISmartTagRecognizerSite recognizerSite)
    {
    ///...
    }
}
```

The important method is obviously Recognize(). This method is called from within the Office document as the user is typing. When the user presses the spacebar, Office calls the registered recognizers with the typed text. The recognizer's job is then to tag the text with zero or more smart tags. If the recognizer finds text that needs to be tagged, it tags the text by calling · the CommitSmartTag() method of the recognizerSite parameter. That's step one.

Step two requires that you write some metadata to inform IBF of the smart tag recognizer(s). The metadata part is still somewhat in its infancy, in that you need to create some predefined elements. To hook the recognizer into the metadata you need to follow this procedure:

1. Create a predefined metadata scope called InformationBridge.

2. Within InformationBridge, create an entity called GenericSmartTags.

3. Create a view for the GenericSmartTags entity called GenericRecognizers.

4. Create an action for the GenericRecognizers and call it EnterContext. The type of this action also needs to be EnterContext.

5. Create two operations to load and activate the recognizers. These must be named LoadRecognizer and ActivateRecognizer. LoadRecognizer must use the port that points to the assembly where the recognizers have been implemented.

As you can see, building recognizers is not a simple process. However, over time, this will likely become easier, as Microsoft further develops the technology and supplies tools to simplify the process.

An alternative to using smart tags is to use attached schema documents. For example, Word documents can have zero or more schemas attached to them. When an end user opens a Word document with one or more attached schemas, IBF looks at the namespace of the attached schemas, and if any of them match `InformationBridge`, IBF will launch and execute the `EnterContext` action.

IBF Wrap-Up

IBF is a sophisticated solution. Implementing an IBF application must be justified, because there is a definite learning curve. The justification requirement is straightforward: IBF solutions make sense only when an organization has employees who spend most of their workday using one or more of the Office products and often need to leave Office to view LOB data.

Justifying an IBF solution is only part of the consideration. The other part is that IBF has a demanding set of software requirements:

- *Client-side requirements*: Office Professional 2003 or later, .NET Runtime 1.1 or later, and IBF

- *Server-side requirements*: Windows Server 2003 or later and SQL Server 2000 (Service Pack 3a) or later

- *Developer requirements*: Visual Studio 2003 or later and IBF Metadata Designer

As you can see, the client must have the full installation of Office Professional 2003 or later, and the server side requires Windows Server 2003 or later and an installation of SQL Server. These requirements are very demanding, and hence cannot be overlooked when considering an IBF solution.

Summary

In this chapter, we discussed the two types of Office smart clients: VSTO-based Office smart clients and IBF-based Office smart clients. Both of these smart clients leverage the power of Visual Studio and Office to enable enterprise smart client applications. VSTO-based smart clients are best suited for applications whose core functionality is either Word or Excel (at the moment). These types of smart clients present the core Office product user interface with additional functionality on top of the Office product. IBF-based smart clients connect an Office product to LOB systems. This type of smart client is best suited for organizations that have a large number of employees who spend most of their workday using one (or more) Office product.

Up to this point, we have discussed WinForms and Office smart clients. In the next chapter, we'll discuss mobile smart clients.

CHAPTER 5

■ ■ ■

Mobile Smart Clients

Java gurus love the saying, "write once, run anywhere." Microsoft has a similar saying: "any time, any place, and on any device."

Starting with Visual Studio 2003, Microsoft began supporting rapidly building applications that target the .NET Compact Framework (.NET CF). The .NET CF, as the name suggests, is a subset of the desktop version of .NET. This framework is used as the platform to run applications on smart devices, such as Pocket PCs Smartphones, and PDAs.

In this chapter, we'll discuss building applications for smart devices using the .NET CF and Visual Studio. We'll start with an overview of the Windows mobile platform. We'll then build a simple application for the Pocket PC using Visual Studio. Next, we'll examine FotoVision, a smart client application built for the Pocket PC. We'll also cover deployment options for mobile smart clients. We'll conclude the chapter with a discussion of what's coming in Visual Studio 2005.

Windows Mobile Platform Overview

Microsoft has two devices available in its mobile platform: the Pocket PC and the Smartphone. These two technologies are considerably different, and it is important to understand the differences when building applications that target these devices. The Pocket PC and Smartphone are the hardware family of Windows Mobile products. Microsoft also has two sides to the software family of products: ASP.NET Mobile Controls and the .NET Compact Framework (.NET CF). The ASP.NET Mobile Controls are controls that you can use to build web-based applications for mobile devices. The .NET CF is used to build smart client applications for mobile devices, which is the focus of this chapter.

Mobile Devices

The obvious difference between a Pocket PC and Smartphone is that the Pocket PC device is larger. With this larger size comes more hardware power—a faster processor, more memory, and so on. Since Pocket PCs generally have a comparatively large memory space, they offer a better solution for applications that need to support offline functionality. Smartphones, on the other hand, are not well suited for offline-capable applications because of their lack of drive space.

These two devices also use different file stores. For example, Pocket PC 2002 and earlier versions use a RAM-based file system; Smartphones use a Flash-based technology. RAM-based file stores are much faster than Flash storage, but are considered volatile because of the potential for losing data if the battery dies.

The Pocket PC and Smartphone also have different usage models. For example, Smartphones cannot go into a standby mode when not in use; Pocket PCs can and do go into standby mode.

The .NET Compact Framework

The .NET CF is used to build applications that run on smart devices. Since the .NET CF is installed on a much smaller device than the desktop version of .NET, this version is about one-tenth the size of the desktop version. So, what's missing?

All of what you need is there, but a few nice-to-have facilities are not available. For example, the desktop version supports C#, VB .NET, Visual C++, J#, and other .NET-compliant languages. The compact version supports only C# and a subset of VB .NET. The desktop version supports a lot of different data providers. The compact version supports only SQL Server and SQL Server for Windows CE. The desktop version supports .NET Remoting and web services as a means of Remote Method Invocation (RMI), but the compact version supports only web services. The desktop version supports a wide range of WinForms controls; the compact version supports a subset of those controls. The point is that you don't have all of the choices you have with the desktop version, but you do have what you need to build real-world smart device applications.

Table 5-1 shows a summary of the facilities in the .NET CF that shipped with Visual Studio 2003. At the end of this chapter, we'll take a look at what you can expect to be added in Visual Studio 2005.

Table 5-1. *Facilities in the .NET Compact Framework*

Facility	Support
Languages	All of C# and a subset of VB .NET
Data	SQL Server and SQL Server for Windows CE
XML	DOM and SAX parsing via XmlDocument and XmlTextReader; writing XML via XmlTextWriter (no support for XPath and XSLT)
WinForms	A subset of the WinForms controls
Graphical Device Interface (GDI)	A subset of GDI classes
Printing	None
RMI and networking	Web services and System.Net namespace
ASP.NET	None

■Note The .NET CF does not provide support for building web applications and hosting them on a smart device. The ASP.NET Mobile Controls are controls that you can use to build web-based applications for mobile devices.

As you can see in Table 5-1, the essentials are included. What is not there falls into two categories: not relevant for smart device development (such as printing) or nice to have but not mandatory (such as .NET Remoting).

Visual Studio 2005 Smart Device Projects

Visual Studio 2005[1] comes with a new project type that simplifies building smart device applications for C# and VB .NET. Under the Smart Device project type in the New Project dialog box, you'll see Pocket PC, Smartphone, and Windows CE choices. To support the widest range of devices, choose Windows CE. If you know definitely that your application will run on a Pocket PC or Smartphone, and you want to use specific functionality for that device, choose the corresponding project type in Visual Studio.

The easiest way to get a feel for smart device development is to create an application. In this section, we are going to build a simple "Hello World" application for the Pocket PC 2003. To begin, start Visual Studio 2005 and choose File ➤ New Project. In the New Project dialog box, choose Pocket PC 2003 under the Smart Device type, and then choose Device Application as the template, as shown in Figure 5-1.

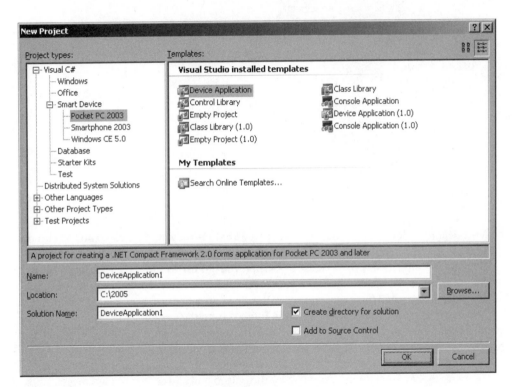

Figure 5-1. *Creating a Smart Device application in Visual Studio*

When you create the application, Visual Studio 2005 opens the Form Designer, just as when you create a desktop Windows application. The Toolbox, however, looks a bit different. The Toolbox contains several groups:

---

1. This example was built with Visual Studio 2005 Beta 2.

- The Device Controls group contains some of the WinForms controls, as shown in Figure 5-2.

- The Device Components contains some components (such as the Timer).

- The General category doesn't have any items in it by default and serves as a container.

Figure 5-2. *The Device Controls group in the Toolbox*

Visual Studio allows you to choose where you want to run the application. You can run the application on the device, if connected, or use an emulator. For our example, choose Pocket PC 2003 SE Emulator, as shown in Figure 5-3. When you choose to run the application using the emulator, Visual Studio emulates the Pocket PC 2003. The Form Designer displays an emulator in place of the usual form that you see in Windows applications, as shown in Figure 5-3.

You can drag-and-drop controls from the Toolbox onto the designer emulator and use the Properties window to set object properties. You can use the same shortcuts to build and run the application as you would when building Windows applications.

To build our simple application, drop a Button control on the design surface and set the Text property to "Say Something." Double-click the button and add code to show a message box that says "Hello World!" Then build and deploy the application. The emulator loads and runs your application. Note that, by default, the Pocket PC 2002, does not come with the .NET CF, so Visual Studio 2003 must first install the .NET CF prior to installing your application. Figure 5-4 shows the process for building and running the sample application.

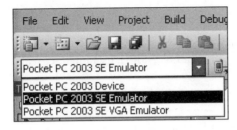
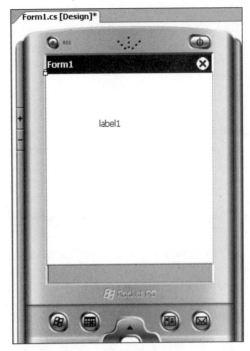

Figure 5-3. *The Visual Studio Form Designer with a Pocket PC emulator*

Figure 5-4. *Running the sample application using the Pocket PC emulator*

Building an application for a smart device using Visual Studio 2005 takes less than five minutes. You use similar construction techniques, whether the target is for a Pocket PC, Smartphone, or another smart device. The real challenge with smart device development using the .NET CF lies in dealing with the device's lack of resources—memory, power, user interface real estate, and so on.

Note For details on developing mobile applications with the .NET CF, see *The Definitive Guide to the .NET Compact Framework*, by Dan Fergus and Larry Roof (Apress, 2003).

WHAT'S THE DIFFICULTY IN WRITING SMART DEVICE APPLICATIONS?

In a way, the challenges we face today with smart device development are similar to what we faced over a decade ago with desktop application development. For example, the developers of desktop applications of the past had to pay attention to how they allocated objects, because memory was expensive and desktops didn't have a lot of it. Similarly, smart devices are small and don't have a lot of memory, so developers need to efficiently manage memory. Power and user interface real estate are other important issues that need special attention when writing smart device applications.

From an application development perspective, power and performance go hand in hand, because CPU cycles consume power. Writing desktop applications for the business world can lead you to forget about algorithms and performance. Moreover, the nature of desktop applications is different from that of smart device applications, because desktop applications try to use local resources and handle background tasks. In other words, desktop applications are very active. Smart device applications cannot afford to actively pursue tasks. Here are some guidelines for developing smart device applications:

- *Delay CPU cycle consumption*: You want to delay CPU cycle consumption as long as possible and spend as little CPU time as possible. The idea is to be passive and not active. For example, an e-mail client running on a desktop would have background threads checking for e-mail every few minutes. A similar e-mail client running on a smart device must be passive and wait for the user to request a check for new e-mail.

- *Choose optimum algorithms*: You also must be very meticulous with algorithms to ensure that you are spending the least amount of CPU time for a given task. For example, in a desktop application it's not uncommon to sort a collection. Usually, you might just look up an API, and if it works, then great. With smart device applications, you need to carefully choose the optimum algorithm for the task to ensure you are not wasting CPU cycles.

- *Design communication channel use carefully*: Pay special attention to how you work with the device's accessories. For example, if you have to do USB or infrared communication, pay special attention to opening and closing these communication channels. Be frugal about how much data you send back and forth, because it costs power to push data to and get data from these channels. Establish a good design for when you open these connections and how long you keep them open.

- *Consider the battery supply.* Needing to worry about the battery supply is one of the biggest changes you encounter when going from desktop development to smart device development. Smart devices, such as Smartphones, have a battery life that can go from hours to days, so how efficiently you use the battery can greatly affect the usefulness of the device. A poorly written application can take a device from potentially operating for days to working for only a few hours.

From a storage technology perspective, two primary factors can affect your application's performance: read throughput and write throughput. In other words, how fast you can read data and how fast you can write data from the storage technology can greatly affect your application's performance. Two types of storage technologies are used by smart devices: RAM and Flash. RAM storage technology is considerably faster than Flash storage. If you are know for sure that your application is going to run on a device that uses RAM-based storage, your job is easier. Unfortunately, all too often, an application designed for one device ends up running on a different device. Because of this, you should try to be careful about the assumptions you make when it comes to storage. The safest approach is to expect to have poor storage performance and design around it.

A Pocket PC Smart Client: FotoVision

FotoVision is a photo-sharing application that has been implemented to demonstrate a desktop smart client and a Pocket PC smart client. In this section, we will explore the Pocket PC version. As is the case with most smart device versions of desktop applications, the FotoVision Pocket PC version supports only a subset of the functionality supported by the desktop version. Its main use is for viewing photos offline.

FotoVision Installation

The FotoVision suite can be downloaded from MSDN at `http://www.microsoft.com/downloads/details.aspx?FamilyId=D4738DCA-E95C-4D4F-BF32-00A865006C73&displaylang=en`. The download is an executable that bundles three MSI files: `FotoVision Desktop.msi`, `FotoVision Web.msi`, and `FotoVision Pocket.msi`. The Desktop MSI contains the desktop smart client, and the Pocket MSI contains the Pocket PC-based solution. The Web MSI is a web application that is used by the two smart client implementations to retrieve photos.

■**Note** FotoVision is not available in C#.

To demonstrate some smart client concepts, the web application comes bundled with some photos that smart clients can download and then access offline. Therefore, the first step in getting the application up and running is to install the FotoVision web application.

Installing and Running the FotoVision Web Application

The FotoVision web application is installed by running the `FotoVision Web.msi` file. During installation, the Windows installer does the following:

- It creates a virtual directory for the web application and copies the VB .NET solution into the virtual directory.

- It sets read/write permissions on the photos directory inside the web application directory.

The installation is depicted in Figure 5-5.

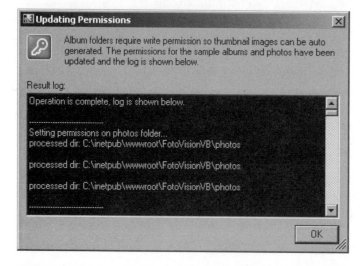

Figure 5-5. *After you select an installation address for the FotoVision web application (top), the installer updates permissions on the photo directory (bottom).*

After the web application is successfully installed, the installer opens Internet Explorer with the application's home page, as shown in Figure 5-6.

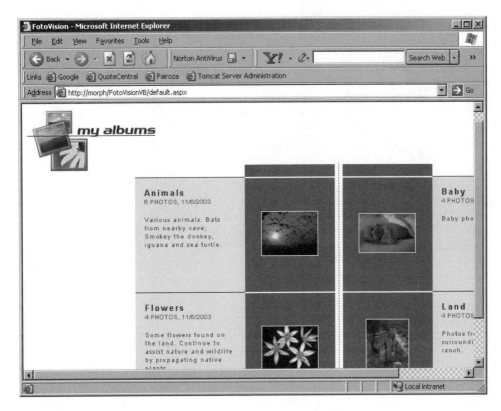

Figure 5-6. *The FotoVision web application*

We'll discuss the web application a bit later when we talk about the FotoVision implementation.

Installing and Running the FotoVision Pocket PC Smart Client

To install the smart client, run the FotoVision Pocket.msi file. This installer creates a directory structure under the Program Files folder and copies the VB .NET solution in one of the folders (along with several other components). The installer also creates shortcuts for the components of the installation, as shown in Figure 5-7.

Figure 5-7. *FotoVision shortcuts*

Browse to the FotoVision Pocket PC smart client shortcut via the Start menu, and click the shortcut to open the solution in Visual Studio 2003. (If you are using Visual Studio 2005, see the next section for information about migrating FotoVision to Visual Studio 2005.) Compile it and run the application using the Pocket PC emulator.

When the application starts up, you need to provide the path to the web application you installed in the previous section, as shown in Figure 5-8. If you are new to smart device development, you may be tempted to type something like `http://localhost/FotoVisionVB`, assuming that since you installed the application on your development machine, it should be available using localhost. The problem, however, is that when you publish the application to the emulator, the device thinks that localhost is the emulator, not the development machine. The easiest solution is to ensure that you have a network connection and type the actual IP address of the development machine (for example, `http://11.11.11.11/FotoVisionVB/`).

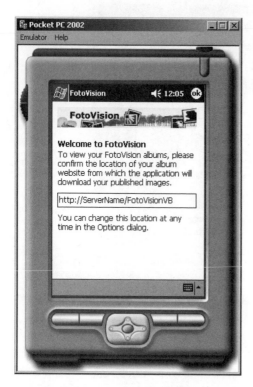

Figure 5-8. *Starting the FotoVision Pocket PC application*

The primary function of the Pocket PC version of the FotoVision is to allow offline viewing of photos. Figure 5-9 shows that when you click the Download Photos button, FotoVision displays a form with a list of albums and thumbnail views of the photos in the album. Notice that each thumbnail has a check box at its bottom-left corner. To a view photo offline, check the thumbnail's check box.

Figure 5-9. *FotoVision in action*

■Note If you want to download photos from more than one album, you can check photos from one album, and then change albums. The application keeps track of the photos you selected in the previous albums.

After you select some photos, you can have FotoVision download them by clicking the OK button. FotoVision starts to download the photos one by one. Because the operation can be time-consuming, FotoVision displays a form showing the progress of download, as shown in Figure 5-10. The figure also shows that after photos have been downloaded, the application displays the local photo cache rather than a view of the photos available for download. After you download photos, the Photos menu at the bottom-left corner of the form allows you to return to the download form and download additional photos.

 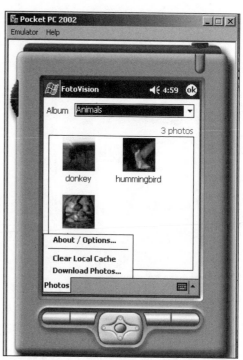

Figure 5-10. *After FotoVision downloads photos to the local cache (left), the Photos menu at the bottom-left corner of the form allows you to download more photos (right).*

Migrating FotoVision to Visual Studio 2005

The FotoVision solution was written for Visual Studio 2003. To migrate the solution to Visual Studio 2005, you'll need to convert the web application and the Pocket PC smart client. Converting the web application is very painless—just open the solution using Visual Studio 2005, and the Visual Studio Conversion Wizard takes care of everything for you.

Converting the Pocket PC smart client requires a bit of work. In fact, if you have Visual Studio 2003, we suggest that you don't bother migrating this project to Visual Studio 2005, because it does not migrate well. If you can live with the solution running under Visual Studio 2003, skip this section.

The Pocket PC smart client project does not convert well when you open the solution using Visual Studio 2005. If you load the application into Visual Studio 2005, you'll get a lot of compiler errors, which don't give a clear indication of the underlying problem. The best alternative is to create an empty project, copy the project files into the new project one by one, and resolve compiler errors incrementally. Here are the steps:

1. Start Visual Studio 2005 and create a new Pocket PC project using VB .NET.

2. Add the following references: `System.XML`, `mscorlib`, `Microsoft.WindowsCE.Forms`, `System.Data`, `System.Drawing`, `System.Web.Services`.

3. As shown in Figure 5-11, add this conditional compilation constant to the project build configuration: `COMPACT_FRAMEWORK=True`.

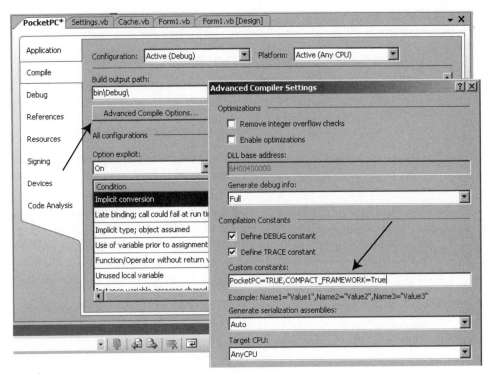

Figure 5-11. *Setting compile-time constants in Project Properties*

4. Add a web reference to the Photos web service, as shown in Figure 5-12.

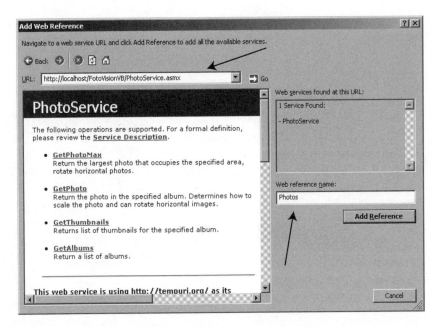

Figure 5-12. *Adding a web reference to the Photos web service*

5. Create two folders within the project: `images` and `util`. Copy the contents of these folders from the old FotoVision application into the new one.

6. Copy the contents of the `AssemblyInfo.cs` file from the old FotoVision application into the new one.

7. The FotoVision application has a class named `Global`, which needs to be renamed in the new FotoVision application because `Global` is a new keyword in VB .NET. Therefore, create a class called `AppGlobals` and copy the contents of `Global` into this new class.

8. Create a class named `PhotoControl` and copy the contents of this class from the old FotoVision application. After copying the class, find all references to `Global` and change them to `AppGlobals`.

9. The FotoVision application has five forms, which you'll need to re-create. First create a new windows form called `WelcomeForm`. After you create the form, open the `WelcomeForm.Designer.vb` file and delete the contents of this file. Visual Studio 2005 uses partial classes to separate designer-generated code from the code-behind code, but this causes a problem because the existing FotoVision application has everything in one file. For simplicity, we'll just put things in one file. After you delete the contents of the designer file, open the form's code-behind file and copy-and-paste the `WelcomeForm` code-behind from the old FotoVision application into it. After that, change the references from `Global` to `AppGlobals`.

10. Repeat step 9 again for the following forms: `OptionsForm`, `DownloadForm`, `SelectForm`, and `MainForm`. Note that if the form has images (for example, an image list), you'll need to create the images manually.

11. When you created the application, Visual Studio 2005 created a form named `Form1`. Delete this form.

12. Open the Project Properties dialog box (Project ➤ Properties), and set the Startup Object value to `MainForm`, as shown in Figure 5-13.

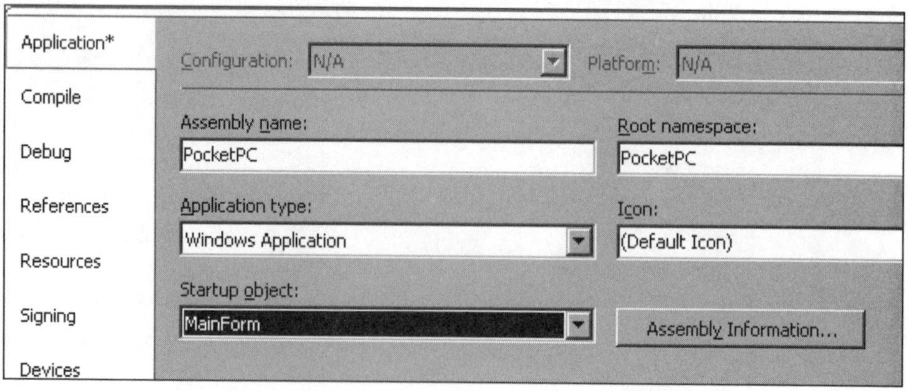

Figure 5-13. *Setting the project startup object*

■**Note** If you have problems or additional questions regarding migrating FotoVision to Visual Studio 2005, visit the FotoVision forum at http://www.windowsforms.net/Forums/Search/default.aspx?➥ tabIndex=1&tabId=41.

Web Application Implementation

The Pocket PC smart client version of FotoVision downloads photos by using a web service implemented in the web application. The web service is named PhotoService and has four web methods defined, as summarized in Table 5-2.

Table 5-2. *Web Methods Defined in PhotoService*

Method	Description
GetAlbums	Returns the list of available albums
GetThumbnails	Returns a list of thumbnails given an album
GetPhoto	Returns an image (byte array) given the album name and photo name; can also scale and rotate horizontal photos
GetPhotoMax	Returns a scaled/rotated version of photo to ensure that the photo sufficiently occupies the region in which it will be displayed

■**Note** The web application actually has other web methods that are not critical to its construction; however, these don't apply to the Pocket PC version of the application so we will not discuss that here.

Smart Client Implementation

The FotoVision smart client solution is composed of five forms, a WinForms control, and a few utility classes. The solution is shown in Figure 5-14.

We mentioned earlier that the primary function of this version of FotoVision is to allow users to view photos while offline. To do this, the application first downloads photos from a web server to a local cache and then uses the MainForm class to show its contents; that is, the MainForm class shows offline stored photos, while the other forms provide support services. For example, the DownloadForm class displays the download log shown earlier in Figure 5-10. Let's take a look at the MainForm class, and then review the utility classes.

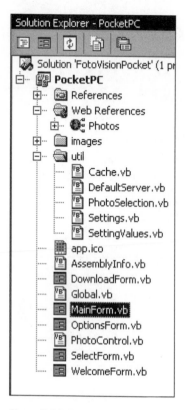

Figure 5-14. *FotoVision smart client Solution in Visual Studio 2003*

MainForm Class

The contents of the photo cache are stored within a folder, and each subdirectory of the cache is considered to be an album. Each album contains a list of photos. To show this arrangement, the MainForm class displays a combo box representing the albums and a list view to display thumbnails of the photos in the album.

When a user clicks a photo, a custom WinForms control, named PhotoControl, is used to display the photo. The PhotoControl class has two properties: PhotoFile and PenColor. PhotoFile indicates the path of the photo, and PenColor is used when users want to annotate the photo (when the photo is shown, users can use the mouse to annotate the photo). PhotoControl extends System.Windows.Forms.Control and overrides the OnPaint() method to draw the photo.

Within the OnPaint() method, the control calls LoadPhoto() to do the actual drawing, as shown in Listing 5-1.

Listing 5-1. *The OnPaint() Method*

```
Private Sub LoadPhoto(ByVal g As Graphics)
Try
    ' first paint entire area color of parent
    g.Clear(Parent.BackColor)

    ' load photo image
    Dim photo As New Bitmap(PhotoFile)

    ' calculate entire bounding area around photo with border and shadow
    Dim width As Integer =
photo.Width + Consts.ShadowSize + Consts.BorderSize * 2
    Dim height As Integer =
photo.Height + Consts.ShadowSize + Consts.BorderSize * 2
    Dim x As Integer = ((Me.Width - width) \ 2) + 1
    Dim y As Integer = ((Me.Height - height) \ 2) + 1

    ' make sure there is enough room to display border
    If x < 0 OrElse y < 0 Then
        ' there is not enough room to display a border,
        ' just draw the photo
        g.DrawImage(photo, _
          (Me.Width - photo.Width) \ 2, _
          (Me.Height - photo.Height) \ 2)
        Else
            ' horz shadow
            g.DrawImage(_shadowHorz, _
 New Rectangle(x + Consts.ShadowSize, y +
height - Consts.ShadowSize,
width - Consts.ShadowSize, _shadowHorz.Height), _
New Rectangle(0, 0,
 _shadowHorz.Width, _shadowHorz.Height), GraphicsUnit.Pixel)

' vert shadow
g.DrawImage(_shadowVert, _
New Rectangle(x + width - Consts.ShadowSize, y +
Consts.ShadowSize, _shadowVert.Width, height - Consts.ShadowSize), _
 New Rectangle(0, 0, _shadowVert.Width,
 _shadowVert.Height), GraphicsUnit.Pixel)

' corner shadow
g.DrawImage(_shadowCorner, x +
 width - _shadowCorner.Width, y + height - _shadowCorner.Height)
```

```
' frame
Dim rcFrame As New Rectangle(x, y,
width - Consts.ShadowSize - 1, height - Consts.ShadowSize - 1)
g.FillRectangle(_brushBorder, rcFrame)
      g.DrawRectangle(_penFrame, rcFrame)

      ' photo
      g.DrawImage(photo, x + Consts.BorderSize, y + Consts.BorderSize)
End If

  ' don't want the photo to hang around in memory
      photo.Dispose()
  Catch ex As Exception
    ' log the error for debug, but continue for release
    Debug.WriteLine(ex.Message)
  End Try
End Sub
```

As shown in Listing 5-1, the LoadPhoto() method creates a bitmap using the path to the photo, and then draws the photo within the display area.

The MainForm class also uses the Cache class to access the contents of the local photo cache. The Cache class is a custom implementation that provides utility methods to access the photo cache. For example, the class provides a static property to get the number of albums in the cache:

```
Public Shared ReadOnly Property AlbumCount() As Integer
  Get
    ' return right away is cache folder has not been created
    If Directory.Exists(_folder) = False Then Return 0

    ' count number of albums (folders)
    Dim folders As String() = Directory.GetDirectories(_folder)
    Return CInt(IIf(folders Is Nothing, 0, folders.Length))
  End Get
End Property
```

SelectForm Class

The SelectForm class is responsible for displaying the contents of the photo repository (albums and thumbnails) on the web server. The form does this by first getting a list of albums from the web server and displays them using a combo box. When the user chooses an album, the control makes another web service call to get a list of thumbnails for the album and displays that list using a ListView control that has its CheckBoxes property set to True.

Listing 5-2 shows the selection-changed event handler of the combo box, along with the UpdateThumbnails() method, which calls the web service to get the thumbnails for a given album, and then binds the new list to the thumbnail's ListView control.

Listing 5-2. *The Selection-Changed Event Handler*

```
Private Sub listAlbums_SelectedIndexChanged(
ByVal sender As System.Object, ByVal e As System.EventArgs)
 Handles listAlbums.SelectedIndexChanged
    ' make sure the user changed the selection and
    ' not from populating the droplist
      If Not _updatingAlbums Then
          ' save current checked thumbnails
          UpdateSelections()

          ' update thumbnails for the selected album
          _curAlbum = listAlbums.Text
          UpdateThumbnails()
      End If
End Sub


' update the thumbnails based on the selected album,
' use web service to download thumbnail information
Private Sub UpdateThumbnails()
    Cursor.Current = Cursors.WaitCursor
    ShowStatus("Retrieving photo thumbnails...")

    ' clear current thumbnail list
    listThumbnails.Items.Clear()

    Try
        ' always get thumbnails from the web service, this could be
        ' improved by caching the images on the device or in the
        ' hashtable, however, have to consider the storage / memory
        ' requirement if there are a lot of albums and thumbnails
        Dim thumbnails As Photos.Thumbnail() = _
        _service.GetThumbnails(_curAlbum, Cache.ThumbnailSize)

        If Not (thumbnails Is Nothing) Then
            ' use an imagelist to display the thumbnails, go
            ' through the list and create an image for each thumbnail,
            ' depending on the memory available, this can fail if there
            ' are a lot of thumbnails
            imageList.Images.Clear()
            For i As Integer = 0 To thumbnails.Length - 1
                ' make sure have thumbnail image, service could
                ' return null if there was a problem on the server
                ' end (like a bad jpg or something)
                If Not (thumbnails(i).Image Is Nothing) Then
                    imageList.Images.Add(GetThumbnailImage(thumbnails(i)))
                End If
            Next
```

```
' now go through and populate the listview control
For i As Integer = 0 To thumbnails.Length - 1
    ' make sure have thumbnail image
    If Not (thumbnails(i).Image Is Nothing) Then
        Dim item As New ListViewItem(thumbnails(i).Name)
            listThumbnails.Items.Add(item)
            item.ImageIndex = item.Index
    End If
Next


    ' the user might have checked some of items before, look
    ' at the hashtable and check any items that have been
    ' previously selected
    RestoreSelections()
End If
Catch ex As Exception
    ' trouble using the web service or populating the
    ' listview with thumbnail images (ran out of memory)
    HandleError(ex)
End Try

' always update the thumbnail count (the album might
' be empty and not contain any photos)
UpdateThumbnailCount()

HideStatus()
Cursor.Current = Cursors.Default
End Sub
```

The SelectForm class is also responsible for tracking the users selection of thumbnails. Internally, the class does this by keeping a dictionary of albums to selected photos.

DownloadForm Class

SelectForm captures what the user wants to download to the local cache, and DownloadForm downloads the actual photos to the cache. When the user clicks the OK button after checking a few thumbnails in SelectForm, SelectForm creates a new instance of DownloadForm and passes to its constructor the PhotoService and the hashtable that contains the list of albums and their thumbnails. DownloadForm stores the reference to the web service and the hashtable, and then waits for the OnLoad() event to fire, as shown in Listing 5-3.

Listing 5-3. *The New() and OnLoad() Methods*

```
Public Sub New(ByVal service As Photos.PhotoService, ByVal list As Hashtable)
    MyBase.New()

    ' save info passed in from caller, use service to download
    ' photos, the list contains the selected photos to download
    _service = service
    _list = list

    InitializeComponent()
End Sub
Protected Overrides Sub OnLoad(ByVal e As System.EventArgs)
    MyBase.OnLoad(e)

    ' see if should download standard or full-screen photos
    _fullScreenPhotos = Global.Settings.GetBool(SettingKey.DownloadMode)

    ' update UI right away
    Me.Show()
    Me.Update()

    ' download photos and store on local device, this is
    ' executed in the current thread (synchronously), the
    ' listview control and progress bar control are updated
    ' after each photo is downloaded
        DownloadPhotos()

    ' done downloading, close the form
    CloseForm()
End Sub
```

When the form's OnLoad() method fires, the method shows the user interface, and then calls the DownloadPhotos() method to download the selected photos, as shown in Listing 5-4.

Listing 5-4. *The DownloadPhotos() Method*

```
Private Sub DownloadPhotos()
    Cursor.Current = Cursors.WaitCursor

    Try
        ' calculate number of ticks in progress, include all
        ' of the photos in the list (if selected or not)
        Dim count As Integer = GetListCount()
        progressBar.Maximum = count
```

```
    ' make sure the user selected some photos before
    ' the current cache is deleted
    If count > 0 Then Cache.Delete()

    ' loop through the hashtable and process each item,
    ' each item is an album
    Dim enumerator As IDictionaryEnumerator = _list.GetEnumerator()
    While enumerator.MoveNext()
        DownloadAlbum(CStr(enumerator.Key), _
        CType(enumerator.Value, PhotoSelection()))
        End While

  Catch ex As Exception
     HandleError(ex)
  End Try

    ' store setting how the photos were downloaded
    ' so they can be displayed correctly
    Global.Settings.SetValue(SettingKey.LocalMode, _fullScreenPhotos)

    Cursor.Current = Cursors.Default
End Sub
```

The DownloadPhotos() method iterates over the list of albums and calls the DownloadAlbum() method, giving it the album name and the selections list, as shown in Listing 5-5.

Listing 5-5. *The DownloadAlbum() Method*

```
Private Sub DownloadAlbum(
ByVal album As String, ByVal selections() As PhotoSelection)
    ' make sure this album has some selected photos
   If GetCheckedCount(selections) = 0 Then Return

    ' add log entry that an album is being downloaded
    AddLogEntry(String.Format(" {0}", album), LogIcon.Album)

    ' loop through each item, download photos and write to the cache
   For Each selection As PhotoSelection In selections
      If selection.Checked Then
          ' update log that starting to download a new photo
          Dim logRow As Integer = AddLogEntry(String.Format( _
          "  {0} ...", selection.Name), LogIcon.Photo)

          ' download photo, call different service methods depending if
          ' user wants to display photos in standard or full-screen mode
          Dim bitsPhoto As Byte()
```

```
    If _fullScreenPhotos Then
        itsPhoto = _service.GetPhotoMax(album, selection.Name, _
        e.ClientRectangle.Width, Me.ClientRectangle.Height)
    Else
    ......bitsPhoto = _service.GetPhoto(album, selection.Name, _
    ......Cache.PhotoSize, False)
    End If


    ' download the thumbnail image
    Dim bitsThumbnail As Byte() = _service.GetPhoto( _
    album, selection.Name, Cache.ThumbnailSize, False)


    ' add photo to the local cache
    If Not (bitsPhoto Is Nothing) AndAlso Not (bitsThumbnail Is Nothing) Then
        ' store photo and thumbnail on the device
        Cache.AddPhoto(album, selection.Name, bitsPhoto)
        Cache.AddThumbnail(album, selection.Name, bitsThumbnail)

        ' update status
        _downloadCount += 1
        UpdateLogEntry(logRow, True)
    Else
        ' could not download the photo or thumbnail,
        ' don't add to the local cache and update log
        ' showing the photo could not be downloaded
        UpdateLogEntry(logRow, False)
    End If
    End If


    ' move to next tick in the progress bar
    progressBar.Value += 1
    progressBar.Update()
    Next selection
End Sub
```

The DownloadAlbum() method iterates over the thumbnails in the album and checks to see if the check box for the thumbnail is checked. If so, the photo is downloaded and added to the cache. After the photo is downloaded, the UpdateLogEntry() method is called to add an appropriate icon to the user interface to indicate that the photo was downloaded successfully. The method also shows a progress bar to indicate the overall progress of the download.

OptionsForm Class

OptionsForm provides a user interface to communicate device and application information to the user. The form contains a tab control that has two tabs: About and Options. The About tab shows who developed the application and system-level information concerning the device (for example, the operating system version). The Options tab allows the user to configure the application's configurable settings (for example, the URL to the web service).

The application can also be configured manually via the application's configuration file, as shown in Listing 5-6.

Listing 5-6. *The FotoVision Configuration File*

```
<configuration>
  <appSettings>
    <add key="ServiceName" value="PhotoService.asmx" />
    <add key="ServiceTimeout" value="60" />
    <add key="ServiceLocation" value="http://www.myserver.com" />
    <add key="ServiceLastLocation" value="http://11.11.11.11/FotoVisionVB" />
    <add key="DownloadMode" value="True" />
    <add key="LocalMode" value="False" />
    <add key="PenColor" value="-256" />
  </appSettings>
</configuration>
```

WelcomeForm Class

The last form of interest is WelcomeForm, which displays a welcome message and the URL to the web application. Users are allowed to change this setting prior to moving on to view photos.

This completes our exploration of the FotoVision smart client. This should give you a good idea of what is required to develop your own mobile smart clients. Next, we will discuss deploying smart device applications.

Smart Device Application Deployment

Applications built with the .NET CF are generally packaged into a CAB file and deployed using one of several approaches: over the air (OTA), MSI deployment, or remote deployment. Here, we'll first describe how smart device applications are packaged, and then cover the different deployment methods.

Smart Device Application Packaging

Smart device applications are packaged into cabinet (CAB) files. CAB files are then executed on the smart device during installation. CAB files contain several elements: the application files, an *.INF file, and an optional setup.dll. The .INF file describes the list of files included in the application and some installation instructions. For example, the .INF file might contain instructions to create shortcuts. The setup.dll file is sometimes used to customize the installation.

Because smart device applications built with the .NET CF are packaged as CAB files, Visual Studio automates this process. In Visual Studio 2003, you can create a CAB file for your application by choosing Build ➤ Build Cab File. When you select this option, Visual Studio creates several CAB files specific to processors available on CE devices, an .INF file that describes the installation, and a batch file to rebuild the CABs and INF file when necessary (BuildCab.bat).

Visual Studio 2005 extends the CAB facilities provided by Visual Studio 2003 by providing an entire project type where developers can customize CAB contents and functionality. As shown in Figure 5-15, Visual Studio 2005 has a new project type, under Setup and Deployment in the New Project dialog box, that supports building and customizing CAB files for smart device applications.

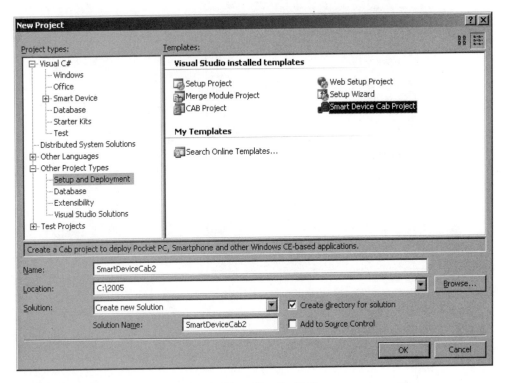

Figure 5-15. *Smart Device CAB Project in Visual Studio 2005*

■**Note** The CAB Project you see in Visual Studio 2005's New Project dialog box (Figure 5-15) is meant for desktop applications.

As shown in Figure 5-16, the user interface for building CAB files for smart devices is very similar to the setup projects for normal Windows and web applications. To build the CAB, you create a CAB project for the smart device solution and define the output that goes into the CAB. You can also create shortcuts, Registry entries, and so on, just as you can with the usual setup projects. If you have built installers for web or Windows applications, creating CAB files for smart devices will be a friendly experience, because the user interfaces look the same.

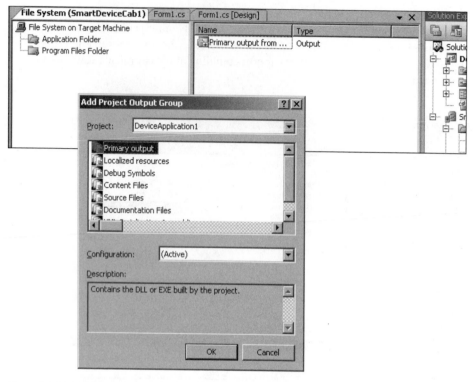

Figure 5-16. *The Smart Device CAB Project user interface*

Building the CAB file is the first step to deploying the smart device applications. The next step is to choose a deployment strategy.

Over the Air (OTA) Deployment

OTA deployment works similar to how client/server applications were deployed in the past. Essentially, you deploy your application and a version manifest to a deployment server. You then distribute a link to the application to your users. When your users have a network connection, they download and install the application. When they run the application, the application compares the local manifest file against the server to see if an update is available. If a new version is available, the new version can be downloaded and installed. OTA deployment is depicted in Figure 5-17.

Using the OTA approach, the initial download and subsequent updates are automated, so you can reach a large user base fairly easily. Moreover, the downloaded application can be stored in RAM or using Flash-based technology. The disadvantages of this approach are that the user must have a network connection and sufficient battery power to download the application or any updates. In addition, applying updates is generally left up to the user. When the user launches the application, the application compares the version stored locally against the version on the server. If the version on the server is later than the local version, the user is prompted to download and install the new version.

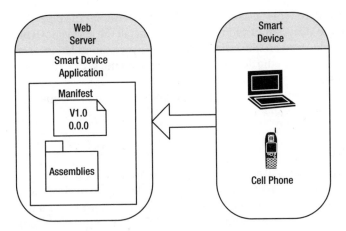

Figure 5-17. *OTA deployment*

Note It is not good practice to force a download on users, because they could be using a dial-up connection or may not have sufficient battery supply.

MSI Deployment

MSI deployment works by deploying a Windows installer (MSI) file to the user's desktop. The user then runs the MSI file to install the application on the smart device. MSI deployment is depicted in Figure 5-18.

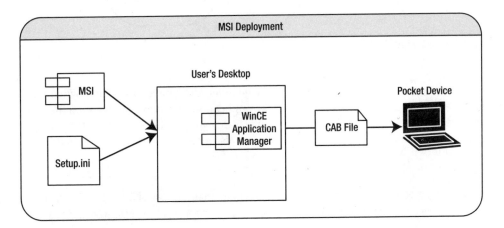

Figure 5-18. *MSI deployment*

As shown, the user runs the MSI from his desktop. The MSI then determines the type of the smart device and works with the WinCE Application Manager to install the correct CAB file on the device (based on the processor type on the device). The WinCE Application Manager is responsible for installing the application on the device. The manager uses the setup.ini file to determine what needs to be installed.

With this approach, users can also uninstall the application from the desktop, via the WinCE Application Manager, or directly from the device.

Sneakernet Deployment

Sneakernet deployment is something that is used fairly often with smart device applications. The term *sneakernet* has been around for a long time. It means you walk around to all of the machines and install the application. With smart devices however, you don't need to literally have access to all the devices. Instead, you can place images of the application onto a Flash card and distribute the card to individual users. Sneakernet deployment is depicted in Figure 5-19.

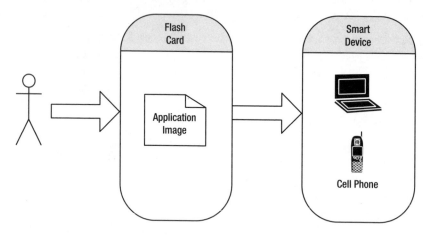

Figure 5-19. *Sneakernet deployment*

The advantages of this approach are that you generally don't have a lot of deployment problems because you can create an image of the application, and this includes all of the configuration requirements. The obvious disadvantage is that you need to get the card to your users so they can install the application. Updates are also a problem with this approach.

■**Note** .NET CF-based applications are generally deployed with more than one of the deployment methods. For example, it's not uncommon to use sneakernet for the initial deployment of an application, and then use OTA for subsequent updates.

What's Coming in Visual Studio 2005

Visual Studio 2005 offers a lot of additions to the .NET CF and the IDE related to mobile development. The sections below outline the additions and improvements categorically.

Smartphone and Emulator Improvements

One of the first things you'll notice when moving to Visual Studio 2005 is that the IDE supports building Smartphone projects, along with Pocket PC 2003 projects, as shown in Figure 5-20. The emulators used to build and test applications are much improved in Visual Studio 2005. Notable features include the following:

- *Save and restore multiple emulator states:* You can save the state of more than one emulator to facilitate testing and debugging.

- *Landscape and portrait support:* Support for portrait and landscape view of the emulator.

- *ActiveSync support:* With Visual Studio 2003, if your application integrated with an ActiveSync, the emulator could not emulate this. Visual Studio 2005 can.

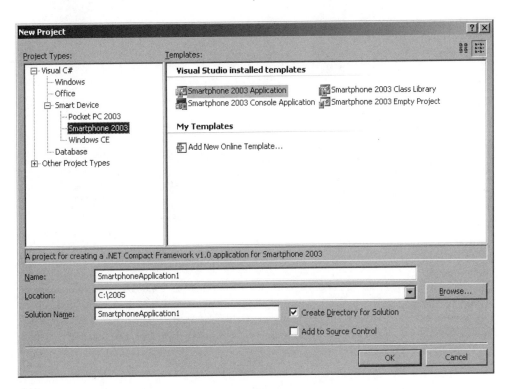

Figure 5-20. *Smartphone projects in Visual Studio 2005*

IDE, RAD Development, and Debugging Improvements

A lot of effort has gone into improving the development experience within the IDE. Visual Studio 2005 adds a host of additional WinForms controls and a richer design-time environment for the .NET CF. Notable WinForms controls include the Web Browser, RichInk, DateTimePicker, and MonthCalendar controls. Design-time features worth noting include designers for the emulators, shown in Figure 5-21, which allow you to drag-and-drop controls onto the device. You can also add event handlers by clicking buttons on the emulator in the designer. There is also an extensibility model that allows you to add skins.

Figure 5-21. *Visual Studio 2005 designers for emulators*

With Visual Studio 2003, you needed to use the eMbedded VC++ 4.0 IDE to build unmanaged projects. With Visual Studio 2005, you can create solutions that contain unmanaged and managed projects. Moreover, you can debug from managed to unmanaged code, and vice versa. You can even attach to a running application on a smart device. Visual Studio 2003 could debug an application only if it launched the application.

Language/Runtime, Managed APIs, and Deployment Improvements

.NET CF 2.0 supports the latest additions to C# language (such as iterators, generics, partial classes, and anonymous methods) and adds to its support for VB .NET (adds the My.* namespace). It also supports C++ (MFC 8.0 and ATL 8.0)

.NET CF 2.0 also adds managed APIs for Bluetooth, Telephony, Pocket Outlook (POOM), the Message Application Programming Interface (MAPI), and Short Message Service (SMS). Moreover, some managed APIs allow you to access some operating system features.

You can also do COM Interop with Visual Studio 2005 and .NET CF 2.0. Figure 5-22 shows the Add Reference dialog box, which allows you to browse to a file that contains COM components.

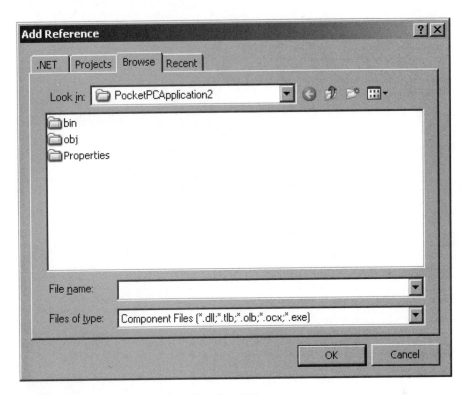

Figure 5-22. *COM Interop in Visual Studio 2005*

Service Pack 2 of .NET CF 1.0 made enormous performance improvements. The .NET CF in Visual Studio 2005 has additional performance benefits in its core execution engine and the ADO.NET and XML APIs. The Just-in-Time (JIT) compiling engine has also been improved.

Visual Studio 2005 also includes improvements in the CAB building facility. Now, you don't build CAB files through the Build menu. Instead, you use the new Smart Device CAB Project type under Setup and Deployment.

Summary

In this chapter, we introduced the Windows mobile platform for smart device development, including the .NET CF. Then we looked at the tools for developing smart device applications in Visual Studio. As an example, we dissected the Pocket PC version of the FotoVision smart client application.

We also discussed deploying smart device applications, including the OTA, MSI, and sneak-ernet approaches. Often, you need to use a variety of deployment approaches. For example, you may need to use sneakernet for the initial deployment, and then use OTA for updates. Finally, we introduced some of the up-and-coming features in Visual Studio 2005.

In the next chapter, we'll discuss a feature that is common to all of the various types of smart clients: offline support.

CHAPTER 6

■ ■ ■

Offline Support

All of the types of smart clients we explored in the previous chapters are intelligent enough to function while offline. This means that you need to store data both on the client and the server. The more data you put on the client, the more difficult it becomes to manage. Therefore, you need to carefully consider the functionality that must be supported when the application loses its network connection and the data associated with it. This can vary from application to application.

Additionally, working in a "sometimes connected" environment means that you need to deal with data synchronization and consistency issues. If you don't have a connection, should you allow your application data to be modified on the client? If you allow the data to be modified, then how do you go about synchronizing the modified data with the back-end data store? If you are going to use possibly stale data, then what policy should you use to renew the data? If you need to renew the data, should this be initiated by the front-end or the back-end? These types of questions make offline support a bit complex. Just how complex depends on your application.

In this chapter, we'll address the various ways to handle offline support for smart clients. We'll start with strategies for client-side caching, including identifying data you can store on the client, refreshing data, and synchronizing this information with the back-end data store. Then we'll explore two handy tools for smart application developers: the Offline Application Block and the Caching Application Block. Next, we'll talk about how to maintain data consistency when you allow changes to be made on the client. Finally, we'll consider some ways to deal with sensitive data that must be protected on the client and during transport.

Designing a Client-Side Cache or Data Store

Smart clients employ a client-side data store for several reasons: to increase availability, improve performance, decrease server load, and increase scalability. Of these reasons for storing data locally on a client, the primary one is to increase availability, or to provide offline support.

■**Note** A cache is not necessarily the same thing as a data store. A data store generally stores large amounts of data and can contain transient data. A cache usually holds nontransient data (for example, a few lookup tables). Moreover, data stores may provide complex querying facilities; caches generally don't. Having said that, in the context of smart clients, we use the two terms interchangeably, because the primary goal of both a cache and a data store (on the client side) is to provide offline support.

A local data store, unfortunately, is not something that you can write once and reuse in other applications, because every application has its own data requirements. Caching sometimes applies, sometimes doesn't apply, and sometimes applies for just a finite amount of time. The scenarios go on and on, but for most applications, you can cache some data on the client.

In this section, we will address the issues that you need to consider when designing a client-side caching strategy for smart clients. We'll start by identifying what data to store on the client, and then go into refreshing this data with the back-end data store. We'll conclude by talking about ways to persist the state of stored data.

Identifying Locally Storable Data

Identifying the data to store on the client is an important decision. The following are some guidelines for deciding which data to keep on the client:

Identify the nontransient data used by the application. If the data doesn't change often, putting this information on the client for long periods is perfectly okay. Type tables, or lookup tables, are good examples of nontransient data. As an example, suppose you have a mapping application that requires zip codes and state abbreviations. These two are great candidates for client-side caching because they don't change very often.

Identify the portion of the application's functionality to be supported while offline. For example, if you plan to provide read-only views of only a few use cases, you may not need to cache a lot of data. You will cache only the data you need to populate some views and do data validation. If you decide to support more than this, however, you need to carefully analyze what use cases you can support while offline, and to what extent, and the data associated with these use cases. All of the data required by these use cases may not be cacheable, so you might need to support a variation of the use case. As another example, consider a smart client that serves auto insurance quotes. This smart client may serve rate quotes while offline, but not generate bindable proposals because census factors may change while the client is disconnected. In this scenario, you would keep all of the data required to calculate a rate on the client, but not store any information concerning proposals.

Identify data associated with functionality that is time-consuming. As we mentioned earlier, one of the reasons for caching is performance. When deciding on what to cache, identify the data associated with functionality that is time-consuming and see what portion of this data can be cached; the closer the data is to the client, the better the performance.

Consider the sensitivity of the data. Some applications must protect the data they use. For example, if you are writing a smart client that allows users to manage medical claims information or bank account information, you must look very closely at what can and cannot be cached on the client. Privacy laws may not allow you to push this data to the client unless you can guarantee that it is going to be protected. We'll talk about handling sensitive data in more detail in the final section of this chapter.

Identify minimum system requirements. Smart clients are smart because they make intelligent use of the client's resources. In deciding what and how much to cache, you need to carefully consider the smart client target machine/device.

Refreshing Local Data

When you put some data on the client and some on the server, at some point, the client data needs to be refreshed with the server-side data store. Depending on the application, accomplishing this can be as simple as a server call or as complex as a push algorithm from the server to registered clients. As an example, consider a smart client application that allows users to place stock trades and do stock analysis. This smart client may store data locally to allow users to do research and view historical statistics. In addition, because not all stocks are extremely time-sensitive (some may take hours before their value changes), some stocks can be cached locally for extended periods.

The following are the three main approaches to refreshing data:

Pull: In a pull scenario, clients pull data from the server and set up a timer to refresh the data. For example, a client may pull mapping data and set up to be notified in a few hours. The pull approach is the simplest because the server doesn't get involved directly; clients pull data whenever they see fit.

Push: In a push scenario, clients pull initial reference data, and then register for changes giving the server a push policy (for example, every time data changes or only when changes deviate by more than one percent). Pushing data to clients can be difficult because it introduces several additional unknowns to the equation.

Pull/push: Using a combination of pull and push may be necessary for some applications depending on the granularity of data requirements. Generally, clients pull data and register for updates. When updates become available, servers push data to the clients.

There are several difficulties with a push approach:

- The server must implement a method of detecting changes to the data, or the data store needs to notify the server of changes. Either way, some effort is required to detect changes. Note that this has the side effect of putting additional load on the database server as well.

- Servers push data to registered clients, and as the number of clients increases, this may introduce a scalability concern. The server may not be able to get the information the clients need in a timely manner due to the number of registered clients. As a result, proper benchmarking and sizing must be done.

- Clients need to remember to unregister.

- Not all data needs to be pushed every time a change occurs. For example, a client may be interested in updates only when a change deviates by a certain percentage from the original value. Therefore, an intelligent registration policy may need to be implemented.

- Depending on the application, the registration policy may need to be updatable at runtime.

- The server needs to store the list of registered clients to some form of persisted medium to guard against outages. Since the server maintains a list of registered clients, it must protect the list against failures in order to guarantee an acceptable level of service. Otherwise, clients will need to constantly ping the server for availability.

- For mission-critical systems, all communication between client and server will likely need to be implemented with reliable delivery methods to meet quality of service requirements.

Although these difficulties must be considered, the data requirements of an application will dictate whether a pull, push, or combination pull/push approach is used for refreshing data.

Implementing Local Data Storage

When you store application data on the client, it must be in a persisted form to allow users to exit the application and then come back and continue their work. Consider a logistics application that captures truck driver status updates as the drivers make their rounds. As a driver goes from stop to stop, he uses a handheld running a smart client to enter stop details (location, time, load, and so on). When the driver goes back to the warehouse, he establishes a network connection and synchronizes with the running application on the server. Because the driver may take hours, days, or weeks to complete his route, the application obviously cannot assume it will have a network connection, but it must be operating at all times. Therefore, when the user chooses to work offline, the application stores the application's required offline state to a local data store and uses that until the application reestablishes online status.

One way to persist state locally in a smart client is to store state in some form of a file structure, particularly XML. Another way is to use a local database. Let's look at both methods, first considering how to use an XML file.

Storing Application State in XML

The TaskVision smart client application we discussed in Chapter 3 used XML documents to store application state during offline use. As shown in Listing 6-1, when users choose the Work Offline toolbar button, TaskVision internally calls the SwitchOnlineMode() method of the MainForm class.

Listing 6-1. *The SwitchOnlineMode() Method in TaskVision's MainForm*

```
private void SwitchOnlineMode()
{
  if (m_IsOnline)
  {
     OfflineSelectionForm oForm = new
     OfflineSelectionForm(m_DataLayer, m_ProjectID);
     DialogResult oFormResult = oForm.ShowDialog();

     if (oFormResult != DialogResult.Cancel)
     {
       try
       {
         m_DataLayer.DsProjects.WriteXml
                (m_MyDocumentsPath + c_OfflineProjectsFile,
                 XmlWriteMode.WriteSchema);
```

```
m_DataLayer.DsTasks.WriteXml
        (m_MyDocumentsPath + c_OfflineTasksFile, XmlWriteMode.WriteSchema);
m_DataLayer.DsLookupTables.WriteXml
        (m_MyDocumentsPath + c_OfflineLookUpTablesFile,
         XmlWriteMode.WriteSchema);

try
{
  File.Delete(m_MyDocumentsPath + c_OfflineTaskChangesFile);
}
catch
{}

ChangeOnlineStatus(false);

}
catch (Exception ex)
   {
      LogError.Write(ex.Message + "\n" + ex.StackTrace);
      MessageBox.Show(m_ResourceManager.GetString
                              ("MessageBox.Show_Unable_to_write_files"));
      GetProjects();
        }
      }
    }
else
{
  if (DisplayLoginForm() != DialogResult.Cancel)
  {
    ChangeOnlineStatus(true);
    LockControls(true);
    GetProjects();
    LockControls(false);

    if (m_DataLayer.DsProjects.Projects.Rows.Count > 0)
    {
      if (m_DataLayer.DsProjects.Projects.
        Rows.Find(m_ProjectID) == null)
        m_ProjectID = (int) m_DataLayer.DsProjects.Projects.Rows[0]["ProjectID"];
    }
    else
    {
      m_ProjectID = -1;
    }
```

```
cbProjects.SelectedValue = m_ProjectID;
if (m_DataLayer.DsTasks.HasChanges())
{
    foreach (DataRow dr in m_DataLayer.DsTasks.Tasks.Rows)
    {
      if ((int) dr["ModifiedBy"] == -1)
        dr["ModifiedBy"] = m_DataLayer.CurrentUserInformation.UserID;
    }
    UpdateTasks();
}
else
{
    GetTasks(m_ProjectID, true);
}

GetLookUpTables();
    DeleteOfflineFiles();
      }
  }
}
```

This method checks the online flag, and if it finds offline mode, it creates several documents locally and uses these documents for offline operations. If the user closes the application and later starts it again, the client looks for the XML documents and realizes it was working offline and didn't attempt a network connection. The process is described in more detail in Chapter 3. Here, we would like to point out the following considerations regarding persistence through XML files:

- .NET has excellent support for XML and datasets throughout the .NET Framework.

- The DataSet class supports reading and writing XML structures.

- TaskVision's application state is fairly small—less than 40KB.

- TaskVision put the XML files in the My Documents folder under the logged-in user.

So, when is it a good idea to store application state in XML? The general rule is to look at how much data needs to be persisted. If the amount of data is fairly small (less than 2MB), then it makes sense to store the file locally and expect to get acceptable performance. If it turns out that the state is too large, then it makes sense to persist the state in a local database because databases are optimized to store and retrieve data.

Storing files locally has some security implications as well. You may need to encrypt the files you store locally depending on your application requirements. Also, files must be stored somewhere on the system. As noted, TaskVision stores its files under the My Documents folder for the logged-in user. A better place to put application-specific files is to use `Environment.GetFolderPath(Environment.SpecialFolder.LocalApplicationData)`.

The local application folder is the recommended folder for application-specific files, from a security perspective. In fact, IssueVision, the other application discussed in Chapter 3, uses this folder to store its serialized files.

Using MSDE to Maintain Application State

Using an XML file or some other file structure is not feasible in all situations. For example, if you have a mapping application and need to store mapping data to support some offline use cases, you may not be able to put this information in XML files and deliver the user experience your users expect. In situations where smart client applications need to handle large sets of data, it makes sense to consider using a client-side database.

Years ago, Microsoft released Microsoft SQL Server Desktop Engine (MSDE) for thick clients that were deployed with a local database. MSDE is essentially SQL Server without the administrative tools (for example, Enterprise Manager).

The good news is that MSDE can be distributed royalty-free, and you get all the SQL capabilities that you get with the real SQL Server. In addition, several free administrative tools, similar to Enterprise Manager, are available for download.

The bad news is that this arrangement may create a deployment problem for smart clients. As you'll learn in Chapter 7, a deployment option for smart clients is No-Touch deployment. With No-Touch deployment, you simply copy your smart clients to a server and distribute a link, and Internet Explorer takes it from there. Using MSDE may force you to distribute an MSI (Windows installer) instead of using No-Touch deployment, because you need to distribute, and run, an executable to install MSDE. However, you can still use No-Touch deployment if you can guarantee that MSDE will be on the client machine. This is quite possible, because MSDE is automatically installed with a host of Microsoft products, including the following:

- Application Center 2000

- BizTalk Server 2002 Partner Edition

- Microsoft Encarta Class Server 1.0

- Host Integration Server 2000

- Microsoft Operations Manager 2000

- Project Server 2002 and 2003

- Retail Management System 1.0

- SharePoint Team Services

- Small Business Manager 6.2 and 6.3

- Stress Tools version 1.2

- Visio 2000 Enterprise Edition

- Visio Enterprise Network Tools (VENT)

- Windows XP Embedded Build Tool

Also note that MSDE is distributed, but not installed, with several Microsoft products. You may be able to have your clients install MSDE prior to downloading your application if they have any of the following products:

- Access 2002

- ASP.NET Web Matrix Tool

- MSDN Universal and Enterprise subscriptions

- Office XP (Developer and Professional Editions)

- Visual FoxPro 7.0

- Visual Studio .NET (Architect, Developer, and Professional Editions)

MSDE is not suitable for every application, and neither is XML, but more than likely, one of these two options will work for most applications. Usually, you either have a lot of data and need to use MSDE (or another database engine) or you have a smaller amount of data and can use XML documents.

Using Smart Client Tools: Application Blocks

A few years ago, Microsoft created the Platform Architecture Guidance (PAG) group and made that group responsible for distributing best practices, books, application blocks, and so on for some of Microsoft's .NET-related technologies.

Recall that application blocks are reusable and extensible code written to solve specific problems. For example, the Data Access Application Block we discussed in Chapter 3 was one of the first application blocks released by PAG to relieve .NET developers of having to write ADO.NET-specific code (for SQL Server). Developers can use the Data Access Application Block to make data access calls without needing to deal with and remember ADO.NET techniques. Similarly, another dozen or so blocks solve other recurring problems for developers.

Here, we will discuss two application blocks that are very useful for smart client developers: the Offline Application Block, which provides smart client applications with offline facilities, and the Caching Application Block, which offers some caching APIs. We will start with the Offline Application Block.

Adding Offline Capabilities with the Offline Application Block

You can download the Offline Application Block from the following site:

```
http://www.microsoft.com/downloads/details.aspx?FamilyID=
bd864eb5-56b3-43a5-a964-6f23566df0ab&DisplayLang=en
```

The Offline Application Block encapsulates common offline capabilities. For example, smart clients often need to determine whether a network connection is available. The Offline Application Block provides a facility to determine network connectivity. In addition, smart clients need to have a facility to queue up requests (or work) while they use the client offline. They also need a mechanism to synchronize their work when they resume online status. The Offline Application Block provides these facilities out of the box. In this section, we'll take an in-depth look at this application block.

Offline Application Block Subsystems

As illustrated in Figure 6-1, the offline application block is made up of four subsystems: Connection State Management, Reference Data Management, Message Data Management, and Service Agent Management.

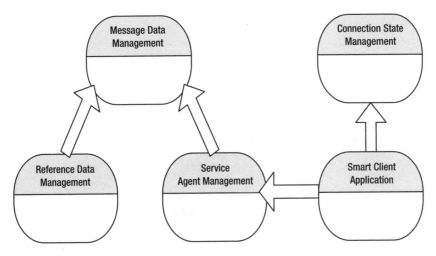

Figure 6-1. *Subsystem view of the Offline Application Block*

From a collaboration perspective, the Connection State Management subsystem is used by only the smart client application and is self-contained. The Reference Data Management subsystem collaborates with the Message Data Management subsystem when it needs to refresh the local cache. The Message Data Management subsystem collaborates with the Service Agent Management subsystem and vice versa. The Service Agent subsystem also collaborates with the Reference Data Management subsystem.

Each of the subsystems in the Offline Application Block has specific responsibilities. The subsystems are composed of one or more classes and interfaces that work together to accomplish specific tasks. For example, the Connection State Management subsystem is made up of a few core classes and one interface that work together to provide connectivity detection capabilities. The responsibilities and core classes/interfaces of each subsystem are discussed in the following sections.

Connection State Management

The Connection State Management subsystem is responsible for detecting changes to the network connectivity of the system and informing registered listeners of these changes. In other words, this subsystem knows when changes occur to the network connection and provides an API to communicate these changes to the application using the Offline Application Block. Its core classes and interface are as follows:

- `ConnectionManager`: A factory class that is responsible for discovering and creating the connection-detection strategy implementation.

- `ConnectionDetector`: A class that knows how to detect physical network connectivity.

- `IConnectionDetectionStrategy`: An interface to hide how network connectivity is detected.

Reference Data Management

Reference data is cached data that is stored locally on the client. This is the data that the client needs to function while offline. The Reference Data Management subsystem provides the facilities to download this data and refresh it when necessary. It has two core classes:

- `DataLoaderManager`: Responsible for refreshing the local cache.

- `ReferenceDataCache`: Represents the local cache. This class uses the Caching Application Block to manage most of the caching.

Message Data Management

The Message Data Management subsystem defines message data as the data that was generated while the application was offline. This is the data that needs to be synchronized with the server when the application goes online. The Message Data Management subsystem provides the means to carry out this synchronization. Note that this subsystem requires a network connection. It has the following core classes:

- `QueueManager`: Used to store service requests in a queue. Note that the Offline Application Block implements configurable queues.

- `Executor`: Takes requests from the queue and executes them using the `OnlineProxy` class.

Service Agent Management

The Service Agent Management subsystem manages service agents and returns the results of executing service requests to the application using the Offline Application Block. It has the following core classes:

- `ServiceAgent`: A base class for all service agents. It provides base-level service agent functionality (for example, handles registering itself with the `ServiceAgentManager`).

- `ServiceAgentManager`: Responsible for creating and managing all service agents.

- `ApplicationServiceAgent`: Responsible for creating service messages and queuing requests so that they can be executed later if the application does not have network connectivity. Note that this class must be implemented by the smart client application.

- `OnlineProxy`: A proxy class that handles direct communication with services over the network. This class can also cache request results for offline use.

Offline Application Block Design Patterns

The Offline Application Block has implemented several design patterns. One of these is the Strategy design pattern. The Strategy design pattern defines an interface and allows variations of the implementation to be plugged into the system. For example, the application block implements a Strategy pattern to detect network connectivity. The application block provides a default implementation of this and allows smart clients to plug in their implementation, too. A similar strategy is implemented for queuing service requests. The Offline Application Block also uses the Observer, Builder, and Factory patterns in its design.

Offline Application Block Demo Application

The Offline Application Block is released with a sample application that demonstrates how a smart client application might use it. The sample application is an insurance claims application where agents take the application offline to complete claims forms, and then return to the office to upload, or synchronize, the claims with back-end servers. The user interface of this application is shown in Figure 6-2.

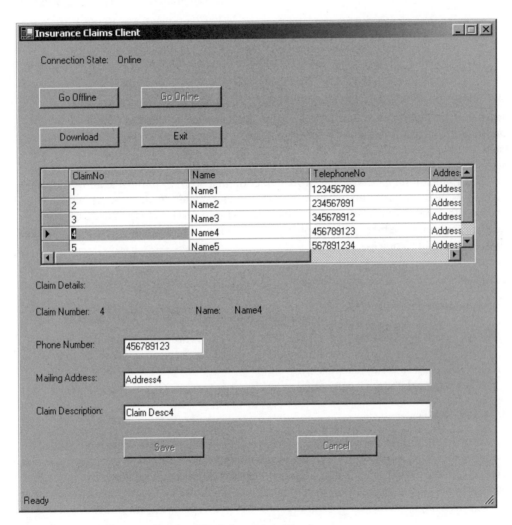

Figure 6-2. *The Offline Application Block demo user interface*

The scenario is that an insurance agent will start at her office and download necessary data, such as customer details, to her machine prior to going offline. Once she has the reference data needed by the application, she goes offline to do some work. In this case, the agent goes to a customer's location to take a few claims. While offline, the agent queues work in the form of claims. Obviously, nothing gets processed because the application is not online. When the agent returns to the office, she connects to the network and starts the application. The application realizes that there are work items that were queued, and that it has network connectivity, so it processes the work items.

The Offline Application Block offers several key facilities that support working offline:

- Automatic detection of a network connection

- Seamless download of reference data—a few simple lookup tables or an entire database

- Ability to queue work items for later processing; if the application is offline, work items are processed when the connection comes back

It is instructive to look at how these facilities are implemented in the sample application.

Automatically Detecting a Network Connection

Recall that the TaskVision and IssueVision applications we talked about in Chapter 3 did not automatically detect network connectivity. Instead, users had to click a button from the toolbar to work online or offline. Refreshingly, the Offline Application Block supports automatic network detection.

The application block wraps network detection in a Strategy pattern to allow for smart clients to substitute variations of network-detection strategies. By default, the Offline Application Block detects network connectivity using interop services to the Win32 function `InternetGetConnectedState()`. The implementation of this is in the `WinINetDetectionStrategy` class, as shown in Listing 6-2.

Listing 6-2. *Detecting Network Connectivity*

```
<ConnectionManagerProviders>
  <provider name="connectionDetectionStrategy" enabled="true"
type="Microsoft.ApplicationBlocks.SmartClient.Offline.WinINetDetectionStrategy,
Microsoft.ApplicationBlocks.SmartClient.Offline.Providers,Version=1.0.0.0,
Culture=neutral,PublicKeyToken=null">
    <pollingInterval>2</pollingInterval>
  </provider>
</ConnectionManagerProviders>
```

Note that this implementation can determine only whether an Ethernet connection or a modem connection is available; it cannot tell whether the smart client can communicate with a specific host, such as the back-end web service. Smart clients can configure the connection strategy by modifying the application configuration file to point to another network-detection strategy (possibly one that can determine connectivity to a specific host).

Downloading Application Reference Data

When the application is online, the reference data that is needed to run the application offline can be downloaded. The application service agent (`InsuranceClaimsClientServiceAgent` class) is responsible for downloading this information, and it does this by calling the `DataLoader`➡ `Manager`'s `LoadData()` method:

```
offlineBlockBuilderInstance.DataLoaderManager.LoadData(this.Guid,
specificServiceAgentContext, refDataDefination);
```

The LoadData() method calls the QueueManager to queue the request for processing:

```
public void LoadData(ReferenceDataDefinition dataDefinition, Guid serviceAgentGuid){
  ReferenceCacheDataPayload payload = new ReferenceCacheDataPayload
       (dataDefinition.RefreshMethod, serviceAgentGuid, dataDefinition);
  queueManager.Enqueue(payload);
}
```

If the application is online, the Executor class gets the request and calls the OnlineProxy class to process it, as shown in Listing 6-3.

Listing 6-3. *Processing the Reference Data Request*

```
// Executor's WorkerThread() method.
private void WorkerThread(){
  if(AreMessagesAvailable() == false)
  {
    Thread.Sleep(QueuePollDelayInMilliseconds);
    return;
  }
  QueueMessage message = messageProvider.Dequeue();
  executor.ExecuteMessage(message);
}
// SimpleCommandProcessor's ExecuteMessage() method.
virtual public void ExecuteMessage(QueueMessage message){
  Payload payload = message.MessagePayload;
  OnlineProxyContext methodToExecute = payload.MethodToExecute;
  methodToExecute.InvokeMethodThroughReflection(payload);
  ServiceAgentContext resultCallbackTarget = payload.ResultCallbackTarget;
  resultConsumer.ReturnDataToCaller(payload);
}
```

Note that the Executor class has a processor that it uses to process requests. The ExecuteMessage() method of the processor (SimpleCommandProcessor) handles this by calling the online proxy. After the request is executed by the proxy, the Executor tells the ServiceAgentManager to return the results to the application service agent. Requests are executed asynchronously, so the application service agent gets notified by the ServiceAgentManager, via a callback, after the request comes back from the online proxy, as shown in Listing 6-4.

Listing 6-4. *Returning the Reference Data*

```
// see ServiceAgentManager class
public void ReturnDataToCaller(Payload payload)
{
  ServiceAgent serviceAgent = agentRegistry.Find(payload.ServiceAgentGuid);
  if(serviceAgent != null)
  {
    ThreadPoolInvoker invoker = new ThreadPoolInvoker(serviceAgent, payload);
    if(payload.Success)
    {
      invoker.ReturnResults();
    }
    else
    {
      invoker.ReturnFailure();
    }
  }
}
```

Queuing Work Items

Smart clients create requests and have them executed using the application service agent. The application service agent encapsulates work items in a Payload object, and Payload objects are wrapped in QueueMessage objects. A QueueMessage object can be put onto a queue for processing, and processing of queues is done with the Executor class. The important aspect of using queues and processing asynchronous requests is that it lets smart clients push requests onto queues and go back to managing the user interface, allowing seamless operation while working either online or offline.

The Offline Application Block abstracts the queue backing store in *queue storage providers.* The application block has several implementations of queue storage providers (out of the box):

- The InMemoryQueueStorageProvider uses a memory block to store queue data.

- The MSDEQueueStorageProvider stores queue data to an MSDE.

- The MSMQQueueStorageProvider storage provider stores queue data in a message queue.

- The IsolatedStorageQueueStorageProvider stores queue data in an isolated storage, on a user-by-user basis (prevents a user from seeing queue data for someone else).

All of the storage providers extend QueueStorageProvider (which implements IQueueStorageProvider). Storage providers are strategized and can be configured via the application configuration file (similar to how you can configure a connection-detection strategy).

Offline Application Block Wrap-Up

The Offline Application Block addresses some of the fundamental requirements placed on smart client applications. To use the application block, however, you must design the application to operate in an offline mode from the start; making an application offline-capable after the fact requires significant effort.

The Offline Application Block offers three key facilities that are useful to Windows Forms-based smart clients:

- Provides the framework to enable an application to work offline

- Provides the framework to execute requests asynchronously; allows user interface to be responsive while the client communicates with the server

- Provides the framework to automatically download offline reference data

Caching Data with the Caching Application Block

You can find the Caching Application Block in the 2005 release of the Enterprise Library, at the following site:

```
http://www.microsoft.com/downloads/details.aspx?FamilyID=
0325b97a-9534-4349-8038-d56b38ec394c&DisplayLang=en
```

The Caching Application Block is a general-purpose caching utility that can be used in any application, not just smart clients. The level of sophistication in caching can vary from application to application. For example, some applications need a simple name value dictionary; others need complex expiration policies and encryption techniques associated with cache items. The Caching Application Block is very easy to use, yet offers a great deal of extensibility that can meet multifaceted caching requirements. Some of the features of the Caching Application Block include proactive or reactive loading of the cache, custom cache policies, and custom security policies.

Caching Application Block Components

The Caching Application Block is composed of three high-level components:

- The Cache Manager is the interface applications use to interact with the Caching Application Block. The Cache Manager provides the APIs to manage cache items (for example, add an item to the cache).

- The Cache Service is responsible for managing cache-item lifetime; this class monitors the cache items for expiration.

- The Cache Storage component defines various caching repositories (such as SQL Server).

The collaboration among these components and the client application using the Caching Application Block is shown in Figure 6-3.

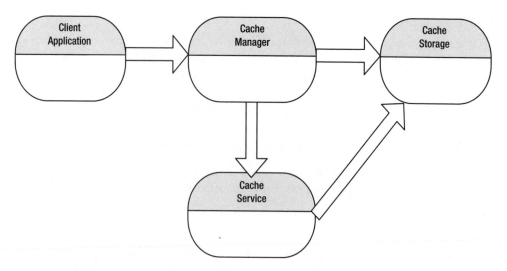

Figure 6-3. *Caching Application Block collaboration*

Figure 6-3 shows that clients of the Caching Application Block interact with the caching block via the Cache Manager. The Cache Manager is implemented as a singleton class (CacheManager) in the caching block. This class also interacts with the cache repository.

Storage Implementation

Cache repositories are the ultimate persistence locations of the cache. Since the repository can vary from application to application, the Caching Application Block comes with several storage facilities out of the box. These include SQL Server storage, memory-mapped files, and singleton cache storage. The Caching Application Block uses a storage implementation to store cache items. Storage implementations use the ICacheStorage interface. Listing 6-5 shows the CacheManager class and ICacheStorage interface.

Listing 6-5. *The CacheManager Class and ICacheStorage Interface*

```
public sealed class CacheManager
{
    private CacheService manageCacheService;
    private static ICacheStorage manageCacheStorage;
    public static ICacheStorage CacheStorage
    {
      get{return manageCacheStorage;}
    }
    // Creating a static instance
    private static CacheManager cachManager = new CacheManager();
    private CacheManager()
    {
      ...
    }
```

```
  public object this[ string key ]
  {
    get{return this.GetData(key);}
  }
  public static CacheManager GetCacheManager()
  {
    return cachManager;
  }
  public void Add ( string key, object keyData)
  {

    ...
  }
  public void Add ( string key,
   object keyData,
   ICacheItemExpiration[] expirations,
   CacheItemPriority priority,
   CacheItemRemovedCallback onRemoveCallback )
  {
   ...
  }
  public object GetData ( string key )
  {

    ...
  }
  public CacheItem GetItem ( string key )
  {

  }
  public void Remove ( string key )
  {

    ...
  }
  public void Flush()
  {

    ...
  }
}
public interface ICacheStorage
{
    void Init( XmlNode config );
    void Add ( string key, object keyData);
    void Flush ();
    object GetData ( string key);
    void Remove( string key);
    void Update( string key, object keyData);
    int Size{ get; }
}
```

The repository implementation can also add data protection to cached items. The `SqlServerCacheStorage` implementation of `ICacheStorage`, for example, can be configured to apply data protection to all cached items. When this flag is turned on, `SqlServerCacheStorage` encrypts cache items prior to storing them in the database, and then decrypts them when they are retrieved from the repository. The Caching Application Block uses an interop call to a Win32 function to do data protection of cache items (via the Data Protection API). However, this is also configurable because the application block hides the actual implementation of the protection scheme behind the `IDataProtection` interface, as shown in Listing 6-6.

Listing 6-6. *The IDataProtection Interface*

```
public interface IDataProtection
{
   void Init( XmlNode config );
   byte[] Encrypt( byte[] plainValue );
   byte[] Decrypt( byte[] cipherValue );
   byte[] ComputeHash(byte[] plainValue );
}
```

Cache Item Expiration

The Cache Manager initializes the Cache Service in its constructor. The Cache Service then monitors cache items that are placed in the cache (through the Cache Manager). The Cache Service uses a scavenging algorithm to find items that have expired (to monitor memory). By default, the Caching Application Block uses a last recently used algorithm. This algorithm is implemented by the `LruScavenging` class. The scavenging algorithm is configurable, and the Cache Service reads the scavenging implementation in its constructor. The Cache Service internally operates against an `IScavengingAlgorithm` interface, as shown in Listing 6-7.

Listing 6-7. *The IScavengingAlgorithm Interface*

```
public interface IScavengingAlgorithm
{
   void Init ( CacheService cacheService,
   ICacheStorage cacheStorage,
   ICacheMetadata cacheMetadata,
   XmlNode config );

   void Notify( string key );
   void Execute ();
   void Add ( string key, CacheItemPriority priority );
   void Remove ( string key );
   void Flush ();
}
```

The Cache Service uses a configurable algorithm to find expired cache items. The Caching Application Block allows cache items to have various expirations through an expiration interface. Internally, the Cache Service works with an `ICacheItemExpiration` interface, shown in

Listing 6-8, so clients (users of the Caching Application Block) can plug in any expiration that best describes the expiration of the cache item.

Listing 6-8. *The ICacheItemExpiration Interface*

```
public interface ICacheItemExpiration
{
   bool HasExpired();
   void Notify();
   void Key(string keyVal);
   event ItemDependencyChangeEventHandler Change;
}
```

The Caching Application Block has four implementations of this interface:

- AbsoluteTime: Allows you to invalidate a cache item giving a specific or relative time.

- SlidingTime: Allows you to define a policy where a cache item can be removed if it has not been touched over a specific time period. For example, if the item is not used within ten minutes, then the cache item can be removed.

- ExtendedTimeFormat: Allows you to expire a cache item giving it a custom time format. For example, an item can be expired every day at 12:00 AM.

- FileDependency: Allows you to expire a cache item based on a file dependency. For example, a cache item can be expired when a file is deleted.

■**Note** Caching itself can become a recipe for disaster if not used properly (for very large applications). For example, with long-running distributed applications that store a lot of items in the cache, some care must be given to the expiration of cache items. If you mindlessly store items in the cache without regard to expirations, then eventually, the memory footprint of the cache is going to grow to an unmanageable size and may introduce performance problems. Using expirations with cache items can circumvent this problem and allow even very large applications to scale and perform well.

Caching Application Block Modes

The Caching Application Block can be deployed in either of two modes of operation: in-process and out-of-process.

The in-process mode is the simplest and most commonly used option. Using this option allows clients to choose from any of the three storage methods mentioned earlier: SQL Server, memory-mapped file, or singleton.

The out-of-process option is an advanced option. It allows the Caching Application Block to run within multiple application domains on a single machine or multiple application domains on multiple machines. For more information about this mode, see the Caching Application Block documentation on MSDN.

Caching Application Block Wrap-Up

The Caching Application Block is a general-purpose caching framework that offers significant rewards. This application block is very easy to configure and use.

The Caching Application Block can be used with virtually any type of application; however, it is useful to smart clients because it provides various types of cache repositories. This caching block is valuable not only on the client side, but can also be used to cache queries, large datasets, lookup tables, and other data on the server side as well.

Maintaining Data Consistency

If cached data is not going to be read-only, then you need to decide how you are going to support modifications to the cache and how changes will be synchronized with the back-end data store. Updating the back-end data store with the changes to the cache poses several data consistency issues. For example, what happens if when you attempt to synchronize with the back-end, you realize that after you retrieved data into your cache, someone else modified the data? Now you must decide whether to override the other user's changes and keep yours, throw away your changes and leave the other user's, or just have the application throw an exception. Depending on your situation, any of these choices may apply. The point is that you have a data consistency issue, and how you handle it has consequences.

Fortunately, data consistency issues come up often enough that there are some guidelines you can follow. The bottom line is that when you're working in an environment where multiple users have access to the same data, you need to have support at the database level or at the application level for ensuring that more than one user does not modify the same data.

Choosing a Data Concurrency Approach

You need to consider several factors when choosing a mechanism to ensure data concurrency. These include application requirements, load on the database server, development ease, and number of users that need to access the data. The two main approaches are pessimistic locking and optimistic locking. You can also take a simple approach called blind updates.

Pessimistic Locking

With pessimistic locking, a client locks a row on data retrieval, expecting to do an update, and releases the lock afterwards. Pessimistic locking must be supported at the database server level because a lock needs to be placed on the rows that may be modified. This approach is very constraining because it can even prevent other users from reading the data while you have the lock. This can pose obvious problems, unless the data is really meant for only one person at a time. Pessimistic locking has other issues as well.

Notoriously, the biggest problem with a pessimistic locking approach is that clients open connections expecting to quickly do updates, but the connections hang for extended periods and others are prevented from accessing the data. Pessimistic locking is very intrusive and does not work well for most situations, because you need to maintain a connection to the database. This is especially true for smart clients, because a smart client cannot expect to maintain a connection to the database.

You can, however, implement an expiration feature with your updates if you need to implement pessimistic locking in smart clients. To demonstrate this, consider an airline reservation smart client where travel agencies book airline reservations for travelers. This smart client might support views where agents can choose seats and then pay for them after the traveler specifies all travel details. With this application, you need to reserve the seats first and book them after the traveler decides on all travel details and purchases the travel package. Unfortunately, it is possible for the buyer to change his mind after the seats are reserved but before they are purchased. Similarly, it doesn't make sense for you to promise seats to the traveler but then inform him that someone else booked them during the conversation. The better approach is to implement a pessimistic lock with expiration. With this approach, when the traveler chooses his seats, you place an update lock on the records with an expiration date and time (such as 15 minutes). If a second agent starts looking for seats, the seats appear to be booked, and so this agent can't propose them to her client. Ultimately, the seats will either get booked or the traveler will decide not to purchase them, and the seats will become available after the timeout expires or the agent cancels the reservation.

Blind Updates

A simple approach to handling data consistency issues is called *last wins* or *blind update*. Blind update is the easiest method, because it doesn't care if someone else modified the data while it was using it; it simply does the update. That's why it's sometimes called last wins—the last person doing the update will have her changes override the previous person's updates.

Optimistic Locking

Another approach to handling data concurrency is optimistic locking. In optimistic locking, the assumption is that the client using the data will check to see if the data has changed when attempting an update. With this method, no lock is maintained on the records fetched, and it's up to the application using the data to ensure that the data was not modified during the time period when the application was using it. The optimistic locking method works this way:

- Application A fetches some data from the data store and disconnects.
- Some short time later, Application B fetches the same data and also disconnects.
- Application A then modifies the data and goes to the back-end for an update. It checks to see if the data was modified. If the data was not modified, the update is executed; otherwise, an exception is thrown.

So, if Application B had modified the data after Application A got it, then Application A would have detected this while attempting an update and would have thrown an exception.

In most situations, you'll choose optimistic locking because you expect to modify the data with the assumption that others are not doing the same. This works for most application scenarios, and is easy to implement. In some cases, particularly small applications, you can get away with doing a blind update, too. However, you're better off implementing optimistic locking, since it doesn't really require much more work, will satisfy most application requirements, and is the recommended approach.

One reason why optimistic locking is generally recommended is because of short locking times. With pessimistic locking, applications need to lock records for extended periods, which creates concurrency problems and places more stress on the database server. Optimistic locking, however, starts with the assumption that the update can fail, and the lock is placed only during the actual update operation. This locking approach dramatically reduces concurrency problems, offers better performance, and avoids deadlocks. Therefore, we'll now look at how to implement optimistic concurrency.

Implementing Optimistic Concurrency

Implementing optimistic locking is fairly easy. The following are the two main approaches, which both rely on a comparison to detect violations:

Use a timestamp: The idea with this approach is that all the tables in the database have a column that might be named LastUpdated. This column's SQL type is set to DATETIME and is used to indicate the last updated date and time of the row. When doing an update, the update query adds a WHERE clause to compare the LastUpdated column's value to the value pulled when the row was fetched. If the two values are identical, then the update is executed. Otherwise, an optimistic concurrency violation has occurred.

Compare existing column values: The second approach is similar to the first. With this method, you don't add a new column to the database, but compare the existing column values to the fetched values. Again, if the values match, the row was not modified and the update query executes. This option has the advantage of not having an additional column added to the row, but requires many comparisons when doing updates.

The recommended approach is to use a timestamp column, rather than comparing the values of all the columns. It is fairly common practice to have one or more timestamp columns to track changes to tables for auditing purposes, and so one of these columns can be used without needing to add yet another column. Doing a comparison of all the columns can create a maintenance nightmare because new columns are added frequently to tables, and every time a new column is added to a table, the update query must be modified to account for the new column. Additionally, it is not uncommon to have tables of 20 to 30 columns, and doing a comparison of all of these columns is not practical. This can also cause difficult-to-track bugs when updates fail.

Synchronizing Data

We talked earlier in this chapter about persisting data on the client using either an XML data structure or a local database with MSDE. With XML documents, the choice comes down to doing synchronization with the dataset and data adapter.

When we discussed TaskVision in Chapter 3, we talked in detail about updating the back-end SQL Server with updates from the client. Server-side updates, in a nutshell, came down to calling the Update() method of the SqlDataAdapter. Using an MSDE, however, may require more complex synchronization because of the sheer volume of data that may need to be updated. Fortunately, MSDE is the same engine used by SQL Server, so the replication facilities are available to manage the complexities associated with synchronization. Refer to MSDN sources for more information about synchronization with MSDE.

Handling Sensitive Data

There are three areas of concern with regard to protecting sensitive data when building smart client applications:

- Securing data from the server to the client and vice versa.

- Applying authentication and authorization with client/server communication.

- Protecting data that is placed on the client for offline use.

We'll look at each of these aspects in the following sections.

Securing Data Transportation

The first concern is preventing the unwanted disclosure of and tampering with sensitive data while in transit between the client and server. This is usually addressed by using Secure Sockets Layer (SSL), Internet Protocol Security (IPSec), or both. Generally, an SSL can be applied from the client to the web server channel, and then from the web server to the application server and/or database server, as illustrated in Figure 6-4.

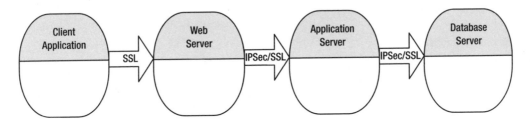

Figure 6-4. *Secure data transport*

Applying Authentication and Authorization

Authorization/authentication is a broad subject and generally spans allowing web servers to manage authentication and authorization to programmatically handling it. With web services and platform-agnostic communication, however, allowing web servers to manage authentication and authorization does not make sense, unless the application is an intranet application and the assumptions are acceptable.

With broad-reaching applications that span the Internet, authentication and authorization must be managed using the web services security model. Web services security is an ongoing initiative, and Microsoft supports this through the Web Service Enhancements (WSE) initiatives. Using web service security to manage authentication and authorization not only offers a fine-grained security solution, but it also allows for a scalable solution in a disparate environment.

Protecting Client-Side Data

Protecting data on the client is something new to developers. Thin clients did not have to deal with this problem, and thick clients didn't either, because security was not at the forefront when thick clients were the clients of choice. Today, however, security is a growing concern, and federal laws dictate protecting confidential information.

Smart clients that place sensitive data on the client have several options to protecting locally stored data: .NET Encryption Services and Data Protection APIs (DPAPI). .NET Encryption Services offers cryptographic services, which include encoding and decoding classes, as well as hashing services. DPAPI is a data protection scheme that is considered virtually irreversible. As mentioned in Chapter 3, DPAPI is used in IssueVision to protect offline files.

An implementation of using DPAPI to encrypt and decrypt data is shown in Listing 6-9. Note that this class is distributed with the Caching Application Block we discussed earlier in this chapter. The class is self-containing and can be used in other applications easily.

Listing 6-9. *The DataProtection Manager Class*

```
class DataProtectionManager
{
  // Private Members
  private static IDataProtection dataProtection;

  [Serializable]
  private struct MACValue
  {
    public byte[] Value;
    public byte[] MAC;
  }

  static DataProtectionManager()
  {
    try
    {
     // Read storage mode from config file
     if( ! Object.Equals(
       CacheConfiguration.Config.DataProtectionInformation, null))
     {
      // Initialize the Data Protection provider
      dataProtection = CacheConfiguration.Config.
      DataProtectionInformation.CreateInstance();
     }
     else
     {
       // Initialize the default DataProtection provider
       dataProtection
       = new DataProtection.DefaultDataProtection();
       dataProtection.Init( null );
     }
    }
```

```
    catch( Exception genException )
    {
      ExceptionManager.Publish( genException );
      throw;
    }
    }

private DataProtectionManager(){}

public static byte[] Encrypt ( byte[] plainValue )
{
    try
    {
      byte[] encryptedData;

      if( Object.Equals(plainValue, null) )
      {
        throw new ArgumentNullException( "plainValue",
        CacheResources.ResourceManager[
        "RES_ExceptionNullPlainValue" ] );
      }
      encryptedData = dataProtection.Encrypt( plainValue );

      return encryptedData;
      }
      catch( Exception genException )
      {
        ExceptionManager.Publish( genException );
        throw;
      }

}
public static byte[] Decrypt ( byte[] cipherValue )
{
    try
    {
      byte[] decryptedData;

      if( Object.Equals(cipherValue, null) )
      {
        throw new ArgumentNullException( "cipherValue",
        CacheResources.ResourceManager[
        "RES_ExceptionNullCipherValue" ] );
      }
      decryptedData = dataProtection.Decrypt( cipherValue );
```

```
      return decryptedData;
    }
    catch( Exception genException )
    {
      ExceptionManager.Publish( genException );
      throw;
    }
}

public static byte[] AppendMAC ( byte[] plainValue )
{
    try
    {
      byte[] hashCode;

      if( Object.Equals(plainValue, null) )
      {
        throw new ArgumentNullException( "plainValue",
        CacheResources.ResourceManager[
        "RES_ExceptionNullPlainValue" ] );
      }
      MACValue macVal = new MACValue();
      macVal.Value = plainValue;
      macVal.MAC = dataProtection.ComputeHash( plainValue );

      MemoryStream memStream = new MemoryStream();
      new BinaryFormatter().Serialize( memStream, macVal );

      hashCode = memStream.ToArray();
      memStream.Close();

      return hashCode;
    }
    catch( Exception genException )
    {
      ExceptionManager.Publish( genException );
      throw;
    }
}
public static byte[] RemoveMAC ( byte[] binaryMacValue )
{
    try
    {
      byte[] hashCode;
```

```
    if( Object.Equals(binaryMacValue, null) )
    {
      throw new ArgumentNullException( "binaryMacValue",
      CacheResources.ResourceManager[
       "RES_ExceptionNullBinaryMACValue" ] );
    }
    MemoryStream memStream = new MemoryStream( binaryMacValue );
    MACValue macVal =
    (MACValue)new BinaryFormatter().Deserialize( memStream );
     memStream.Close();

     byte[] hash = dataProtection.ComputeHash( macVal.Value );

     // Compares the original hash with the new hash
     for( int index = 0; index < hash.Length; index++ )
       if( hash[index] != macVal.MAC[index] )
         throw new Exception(
           CacheResources.ResourceManager[
           "RES_ExceptionDataValidation" ] );

          hashCode = macVal.Value;

       return hashCode;
    }
    catch( Exception genException )
    {
      ExceptionManager.Publish( genException );
      throw;
    }
  }
}
}
```

Summary

In this chapter, we discussed some of the issues in supporting offline functionality. We said that the biggest challenge smart client developers face is having to manage two different data stores and synchronizing the two. Moreover, we said that the key to reducing the complexity associated with implementing offline support is to identify what functionality will be supported while offline and the data associated with it, and to do so early in the design of the application as presented in the section "Identifying Locally Storable Data."

We also discussed the Offline Application Block and the Caching Application Blocks, which are reusable blocks that can help you to implement offline facilities with your own smart client applications. Next, we covered ways to maintain data consistency. We concluded with an introduction to managing sensitive data.

In the next chapter, we'll move on to the topic of deployment and explain the various techniques available for deploying and updating smart clients.

CHAPTER 7

■ ■ ■

WinForms Smart Client Deployment

In Chapter 1, we reviewed some of the problems developers have faced in deploying applications, including the infamous DLL Hell. Microsoft has been working toward an effective solution to deploying rich clients for over a decade. With the release of .NET in 2000, Microsoft developers introduced their initial cut at solving the problem, which they called No-Touch deployment. This solution, as you'll see, has some shortfalls and must be supplemented to be effective.

In this chapter, we will discuss the various approaches to deploying WinForms smart clients. We'll start with No-Touch deployment and end with Microsoft's next-generation deployment approach, called ClickOnce deployment. Finally, we'll examine two tools for updating smart clients: the Application Updater component and the Updater Application Block.

No-Touch Deployment

No-Touch deployment (NTD) is a technology that enables Windows Forms applications to be deployed in a manner that is very similar to how thin clients are deployed. Thin clients are deployed by copying the application to a web server, and then users can access the application via a URL. Similarly, you can deploy smart clients by copying the application to a virtual directory on a web server, and then distributing a link that points to the executable. When the user clicks the link, Internet Explorer (IE) downloads the application to the user's machine, and then tells a special executable (IEExec.exe) to run the application.

The beauty of NTD is that it does not require application authors to touch the client machine in order to deploy the application (hence, the *no-touch*). This is also true for updates. To do an update, you simply copy the new version of the application onto the server, and the next time the application is launched, IE checks for a newer version. If a new version of the application is available, it is downloaded, and then the new version is launched.

NTD Architecture

Figure 7-1 illustrates how NTD works. A client makes a request to a web server for an executable, and the web server sends the response with a particular MIME type that IE (versions 5.01 and later) knows about. This particular MIME type indicates to IE that the requested executable is a .NET assembly. When it sees this, IE downloads the application and runs IEExec.exe to launch it.

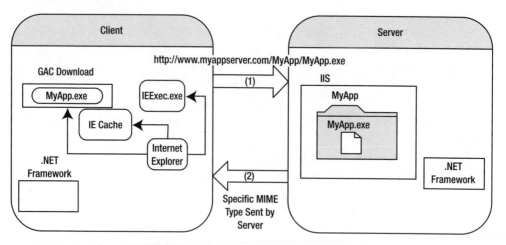

Figure 7-1. *No-Touch deployment architecture*

Figure 7-1 also shows that the application is potentially downloaded to several places: the Global Assembly Cache (GAC) download cache and the browser cache (temporary Internet files). Note also that for NTD to work, the client must have the .NET Framework installed.

■**Note** You can check the contents of the GAC download cache by running the GAC utility with a specific command-line switch (GACUTIL /LDL). For more information about the GAC, see http:// msdn.microsoft.com/library/default.asp?url=/library/en-us/cpguide/html/ cpconglobalassemblycache.asp.

NTD Example

As an example, let's write a simple Windows Forms application and deploy it with NTD. Follow these steps to run through this exercise:

1. Open Visual Studio and create a new Windows Application. Name it NoTouch.

2. Use the Form Designer to drag a label on to the form. Set the Text property of the label to "Hello World!".

3. Compile the application.

4. To deploy the application with NTD, you need to put the executable in a virtual directory. The easiest approach is to just go to the bin\Debug folder where the executable was generated and enable Web Sharing on the folder. In Windows Explorer, right-click the Debug folder, choose Sharing and Security, and then choose the Web Sharing tab. In the Web Sharing tab, enable web sharing and set the alias to NoTouch.

5. Start IE and go to http://localhost/NoTouch/NoTouch.exe. You should see something similar to Figure 7-2.

Figure 7-2. *A deployed NTD application*

If you went through this exercise, you probably agree that NTD deployment is fairly easy. As with all things that seem to demo well, NTD has considerable drawbacks and is suited only for particular applications. Now, let's take a look at those disadvantages, as well as the advantages of this deployment method.

NTD Advantages and Disadvantages

As you've seen, NTD is easy to implement. The following are the advantages of NTD:

- It's easy to deploy.

- It's easy to update.

- The user does not need to be an administrator to install the application, which is generally the case with thick clients.

Deploying smart clients with NTD has some drawbacks, however. Notably, because the application is downloaded from an unknown source, the application is treated as potentially malicious and must run within the code-access security (CAS) sandbox. This prevents the application from using local resources, and so the application is limited in its functionality. The following are the disadvantages of NTD:

- It requires an IE version later than 5.0 and doesn't work with non-Microsoft-friendly browsers.

- The application runs in the CAS sandbox, so you lose a lot of the advantages of having built a Windows application. For example, the application cannot use the disk or the printer, integrate with the Windows shell (for example, interoperate with Office), and so on. It also requires manual intervention by an administrator to install a policy (if the sandbox needs to be expanded).

Note Applications whose identity cannot be verified run with limited privileges, often referred to as a *sandbox*. For more information about CAS, see `http://msdn.microsoft.com/library/default.asp?url=/library/en-us/cpguide/html/cpconcodeaccesssecurity.asp`.

- The entire application must be downloaded prior to running the application.

- There is no support for install-time actions. For example, you can't create shortcuts at install time.

- NTD deployment requires a network connection; it will not work when the client is offline.

- The user experience is similar to running a web application rather than a traditional Windows application, because users must click a link; there isn't the expected Start menu shortcut. The application resembles a web application because users are clicking a link.

- Client machines must have the .NET runtime installed prior to downloading the application.

- Updates happen just as they do with web applications—just copy the latest version of the application onto the server, and users get the updates the next time they run the application. The disadvantage is that the user always gets the latest update, and there is no possibility of maintaining versions on the clients.

NTD is very restrictive and best suited for applications that do not require interaction with local resources. This removes a lot of the benefits of building smart clients; however, you do get the responsive user interface with ease of deployment.

One-Touch Deployment

Another method of deploying smart clients is called One-Touch deployment (OTD). As you learned in the previous section, two of the primary concerns with NTD are that the application must reside inside the CAS sandbox and that the entire application must be downloaded before it can be run. OTD circumvents these problems by first installing a minimal (stub) version of the application on the user's machine (hence, the *one-touch*), and then downloading the rest of the application on demand. Installing the stub program solves both of the problems associated with NTD.

OTD Architecture

With OTD, the application's author distributes a stub program to the user. The stub program can be distributed a number of ways, including using the File Transfer Protocol (FTP), e-mail, and so on. The stub program is generally just a small executable that users copy onto their desktop, which takes care of installing the stub. After the stub program is installed, the user launches the application by double-clicking the executable. Figure 7-3 illustrates how OTD works.

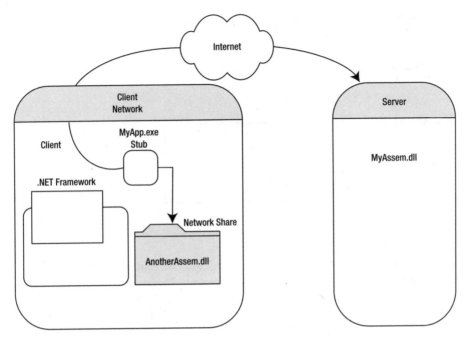

Figure 7-3. *One-Touch deployment architecture*

Because the stub program is not downloaded and launched by IE (as with NTD), the stub runs with the privileges of the logged-in user, just like any other Windows application. The application starts up, and the user begins to work with the application. As the user selects menu items or clicks toolbar buttons, additional assemblies that contain functionality are downloaded on demand. Eventually, either the entire application or only that part of the application that the user requires is downloaded.

The trick with OTD is that everything other than the stub will have limited privileges because it comes from somewhere other than the My Computer Zone (for example, the Local Intranet Zone). Moreover, the stub program carries out any privileged tasks, such as interacting with Office.

OTD Example

Now, let's build a sample application and deploy it with OTD. We'll build a stub application, and to simulate distribution to the end user, we will copy the executable (along with its dependencies) somewhere under the Program Files folder. Next, since the stub program must be designed to pull additional functionality on demand, we'll let the user click a button to download and load an assembly at runtime. This assembly will be a separate project that we will build and deploy on a web server (in this case, locally under IIS). When the user clicks a button, we will download the assembly over HTTP.

The idea here is that the application's functionality could be sitting somewhere on the Web, or perhaps on the local network, and as the user uses the application, various component assemblies are downloaded and loaded at runtime. The user interface of the application is shown in Figure 7-4.

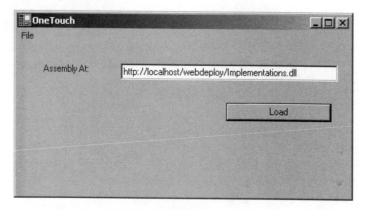

Figure 7-4. *OTD sample application*

It is also helpful to see a component-level view of the solution that we are going to build and deploy. Figure 7-5 shows the three projects in the solution. The smart client application is called OneTouch. The Interfaces project will contain interfaces that will be implemented by the "components" project. The separation between interfaces and implementations is important here. The idea is that the stub program will load assemblies at runtime, and there must be a protocol of communication between the smart client and the assemblies it loads; otherwise, it will become very difficult and time-consuming for the smart client to communicate with those assemblies. The Interfaces project establishes this contract of communication, the components implement the interfaces, and the smart client operates on them.

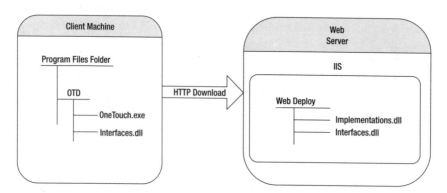

Figure 7-5. *Deployment architecture of the OTD example*

Creating the Sample Application

Follow these steps to create and deploy the application:

1. Start Visual Studio and create a new Windows Application. Name it OneTouch. This will be the stub program.

2. Using the Form Designer, drop a label on the form and name it "Assembly At:".

3. Drag a TextBox onto the form, next to the label. Set its Text property to `http://localhost/webdeploy/Implementations.dll`. This TextBox will contain the location of the component assembly that we will load over HTTP.

4. Place a Button control on the form and name it `loadBtn`. Double-click the Button so you can add some code to load the component assembly. Paste the following into the handler:

```
try
{
    if(this.textBox1.Text==null||textBox1.Text.Trim().Length==0)
    {
        MessageBox.Show("Need to know where and what dll to load.");
    }
    Assembly asm = Assembly.LoadFrom(textBox1.Text.Trim());
    Object obj = asm.CreateInstance("Implementations.MyImpl");
    ISayHello ihi = (ISayHello)obj;
    MessageBox.Show(ihi.SayHi());
}
catch(Exception ex)
{
    MessageBox.Show(ex.Message);
}
```

5. Create a Class Library project and name it `Interfaces`. Add an interface to this project named `ISayHello`, as follows:

```
public interface ISayHello
{
    string SayHi();
}
```

6. In the `OneTouch` project, add a reference to this Class Library project. To do this, right-click the References node, select the Projects tab, choose `Interfaces`, and then click OK.

7. Open `Form1.cs` and add the following `using` statement at the top of the file:

```
using Interfaces;
```

8. Create a new project and name it `Implementations`.

9. Add a new class to this project and name it `MyImpl`.

10. Add a reference to the `Interfaces` project, using the procedure described in step 6.

11. Implement the `ISayHello` interface in `MyImpl`, as follows:

```
public class MyImpl:ISayHello
{
    public MyImpl()
    {
    }
```

```
        public string SayHi()
        {
            return "Hello from MyImpl";
        }
    }
```

12. Build the application.

Deploying the Solution

We now need to deploy the solution, as shown earlier in Figure 7-5. The deployment essentially has two parts: a server-side deployment and a client-side deployment. The server-side deployment is the interface-implementation project, and the client-side deployment is the stub program. Deploy each side as follows:

Client-side deployment: Create a folder under Program Files and name it OTD. Copy OneTouch.exe and Interface.dll into this folder.

Server-side deployment: Create a folder anywhere on the machine and label it WebDeploy. To enable download over HTTP, create a virtual directory that points to this folder. The easiest way to do this is to enable Web Sharing on the folder. Right-click the folder, choose Sharing and Security, choose the Web Sharing tab, and then click the Share This Folder radio button. Copy implementations.dll and interfaces.dll into this folder.

Now, you can run the application by launching the stub program. Double-click OneTouch.exe to launch the application. You should get the user interface shown earlier in Figure 7-4. Click the Load button to see what happens. You should see a message box that displays "Hello from MyImpl."

Now that we've been through the initial deployment of an application with OTD, let's see how updates are done.

OTD Updates

As you've seen, with OTD, assemblies are downloaded at runtime using Assembly.LoadFrom(). Interestingly, loading assemblies using this approach has the side effect of handling updates automatically. The Assembly.LoadFrom() method takes a path to the assembly; however, prior to going to the specified location, the method checks to see if the assembly is in the GAC download cache. If it is, the method checks the version of the assembly in the local cache against the remote version. If the two differ, the newer version is downloaded into the cache, and that version is loaded into the application domain.

Since you ran the sample application in the preceding example, the implementations.dll should be in the GAC download cache. You can verify this by running the GAC utility with the LDL switch: GACUTIL /LDL. Figure 7-6 shows the contents of the download cache on the machine where we ran the sample application. You can see that version 1.0.0.0 of implementations.dll is in the cache.

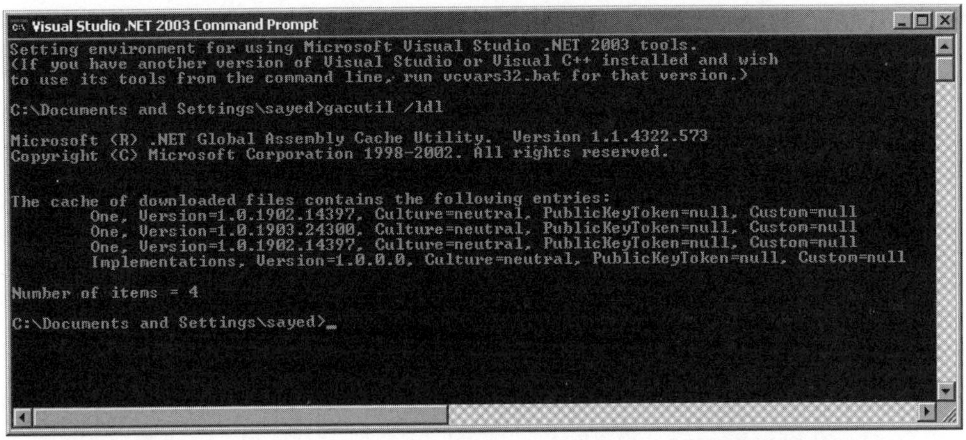

Figure 7-6. *Contents of the GAC download cache after running the sample application*

To verify that updates occur automatically, modify the SayHi() method of the MyImpl class, and then rebuild the assembly. Copy the assembly to the WebDeploy folder again, and rerun the application to verify that the newest version of the assembly was downloaded automatically. Also verify the contents of the GAC download cache. In our case, the contents of the GAC download cache shows that there are two copies of version 1.0.0.0 of implementations.dll in the cache, as shown in Figure 7-7.

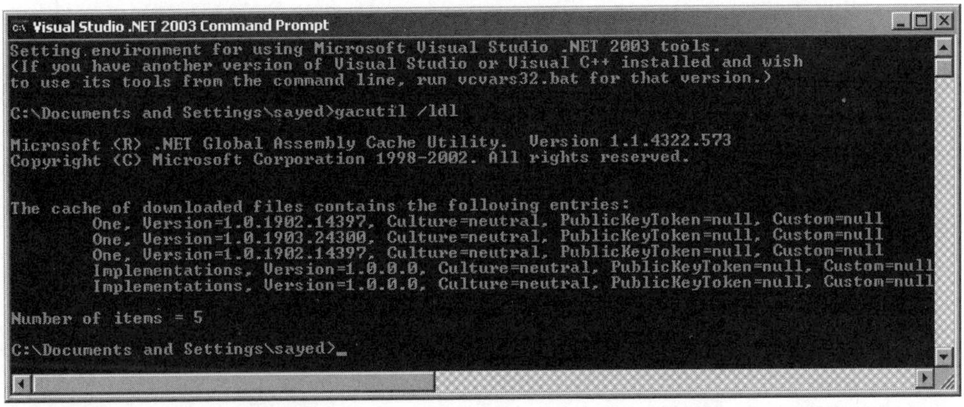

Figure 7-7. *Contents of the GAC download cache after doing an update*

It may seem strange that the cache has two versions of the same assembly loaded. It turns out that the criteria used to compare versions of assemblies when looking for updates is the modified timestamp on the assembly, not the version number. You can, however, bypass this if you use strong-named assemblies. By strong-naming assemblies, you can specify an exact version of the assembly, and the runtime will look for that version in the GAC prior to attempting a download.

OTD Advantages and Disadvantages

OTD is an improvement when compared to NTD; however, it also has some obvious disadvantages.

First, let's review OTD advantages:

- Users don't need to download all of the code at once. You can ask users what they want to download initially, to avoid needing to download code as users play with the application.

- OTD allows you to obtain more privileges by having the code downloaded from a network share rather than from the Web. The stub application has full rights. However, the assemblies that are downloaded get their privileges assigned depending on the location from which they were downloaded.

- Because the application stub is installed on the user's machine, the application can be made accessible from the Start menu. This delivers a more thick client–like user experience and is better than having users click a link to run the application.

- It's easy to deploy updates. As the user interacts with the application, the assembly-loading process can check for new versions of the assembly.

The following are the disadvantages of OTD:

- If the assembly being downloaded is large, requiring the user to download code on demand may give the user the impression that the application is slow, which is not a good first impression.

- Development efforts should not be guided by deployment. To some extent, all applications are developed with some deployment constraints; however, OTD places a lot of restrictions on development. For example, you need to partition the application into assemblies so that it is suitable for OTD. For this reason, it's difficult to deploy an existing application with OTD.

- Because assemblies are downloaded on demand, a network connection is needed to run the application, or considerable development effort is needed to enable appropriate functionality based on the presence or absence of a network connection. This is not a bulletproof solution, since it is virtually impossible to guarantee that a specific host will be reachable.

As you can see, the OTD development constraints and the requirement of a network connection can be imposing. Moreover, for large applications, it may be difficult to justify the initial on-demand download of all of the required assemblies as the user interacts with the application. Thus, this approach is best suited for applications that lend themselves to being partitioned, so as to optimize downloading the application piecemeal.

Microsoft Installer (MSI) Deployment

One of the compromises that developers make when choosing either NTD or OTD is in the area of offline support. With NTD, there are obvious restrictions because code is downloaded from the Web and the application has limited privileges. With OTD, the stub program can handle offline support, but the actual functionality is implemented in assemblies that must be downloaded.

Another possible solution to deploying smart clients is to deploy a full MSI. The beauty behind deploying an MSI is that you can deliver the best user experience. The obvious trade-off, however, is that you must somehow get the MSI to the user. But once the user has the MSI, the installer can do anything it needs to install the application and also gives the application full trust, so it can provide full support while offline. Moreover, the application can implement a self-update feature that relieves the application author of needing to go through the initial deployment cycle again.

In summary, MSI deployment has the following advantages:

- The smart client has full trust on the client side.

- Applications have good performance because the entire application is installed locally (the client does not need to download any assemblies).

- Offline support is available.

- The application can use local resources and integrate with the Windows shell.

- By implementing a self-updating scheme, you just need to distribute the initial version of the application.

- The MSI can create databases, shortcuts, and so on.

MSI deployment has two main disadvantages:

- It requires that you get the MSI to the client somehow.

- The application has a large client-side footprint.

ClickOnce Deployment

All of the deployment approaches we've talked about so far have limitations. For example, with NTD, you need to overcome the security restrictions manually by asking an administrator to modify the security policy. With OTD, you need to design your solution so that it can be easily broken up into parts that can be downloaded piecemeal.

Microsoft recognized these problems and has responded by developing a deployment technology especially for deploying smart clients. This new technology is called ClickOnce, and it will be shipped with the release of Visual Studio 2005. The ClickOnce deployment solution is an extension of NTD, but it solves all the problems of that deployment method (see the "NTD Advantages and Disadvantages" section earlier in this chapter).

The ClickOnce Deployment Manifest

ClickOnce deployment is driven by a *deployment manifest*. This manifest is an XML-based file that describes a ClickOnce deployment. ClickOnce works in a manner similar to NTD, in that users are sent a link; however, with ClickOnce, users are sent a link to the deployment manifest rather than to the executable, as is the case with NTD. Additionally, with ClickOnce, the deployment manifest describes everything about the deployment, rather than relying on the runtime to determine the dependencies of the application (through the assembly manifest). The deployment manifest includes the application's version information; that is, the deployment manifest points to a particular version of the application, which allows you to deploy version 1.0, and then later 1.1, while keeping the two deployments separate. A sample deployment manifest is shown in Figure 7-8.

```
<?xml version="1.0" encoding="utf-8"?>
<asmv1:assembly xsi:schemaLocation="urn:schemas-microsoft-com:asm.v1 assembly.adaptive.xsd" manife
  <assemblyIdentity name="ClickOnceSample.application" version="1.0.0.0" publicKeyToken="b9cc3d5e2
  <description asmv2:publisher="SH" asmv2:product="ClickOnceSample" xmlns="urn:schemas-microsoft-c
  <deployment install="true">
    <subscription>
      <update>
        <beforeApplicationStartup />
      </update>
    </subscription>
    <deploymentProvider codebase="http://morph/ClickOnceSample/ClickOnceSample.application" />
  </deployment>
  <dependency>
    <dependentAssembly codebase="ClickOnceSample_1.0.0.0\ClickOnceSample.exe.manifest" size="3495"
      <assemblyIdentity name="ClickOnceSample.exe" version="1.0.0.0" publicKeyToken="b9cc3d5e2849f
      <hash>
        <dsig:Transforms>
          <dsig:Transform Algorithm="urn:schemas-microsoft-com:HashTransforms.Identity" />
        </dsig:Transforms>
        <dsig:DigestMethod Algorithm="http://www.w3.org/2000/09/xmldsig#sha1" />
        <dsig:DigestValue>EIKBgEbpBcwhXj7y9mK/j4M6qHY=</dsig:DigestValue>
      </hash>
    </dependentAssembly>
  </dependency>

<Signature Id="StrongNameSignature" xmlns="http://www.w3.org/2000/09/xmldsig#"><SignedInfo><Canoni
```

Figure 7-8. *A ClickOnce deployment manifest*

The deployment manifest shown in Figure 7-8 shows five higher-level tags within the assembly tag: `assemblyIdentity`, `description`, `deployment`, `dependency`, and `Signature`. The purpose of each tag is described in the following sections.

The assemblyIdentity Tag

The `assemblyIdentity` tag, which does not have any child elements, determines the application being deployed. In the example shown in Figure 7-8, the deployment manifest was produced with Visual Studio 2005, which generated a default value for this tag. This tag has four required attributes and one optional attribute:

- The `name` attribute is a name for the application being deployed.

- The `version` attribute determines the current deployment version of the application.

- The `publicKeyToken` attribute is used for signing the deployment manifest.

- The `processorArchitecture` attribute determines the application's processor architecture. Valid values for this tag include `msil`, `x86`, `IA64`, and `amd64`.

- The optional `language` attribute determines the language that ClickOnce presents to the user while doing the deployment. Note that this is not the application's preferred language. The value `neutral` tells ClickOnce to refer to the client's machine settings to determine which language to use.

The description Tag

The description tag contains descriptions of the application. The information in this tag is used when the application is deployed in install mode, described next.

The deployment Tag

The deployment tag determines the mode of deployment and identifies the update policy for the application. ClickOnce applications can be deployed in one of two modes: install or online. Install-mode deployed applications can run without a network connection; online-mode deployments cannot run without a network connection. Applications that are deployed in online mode require that their users always run the application by pointing to the deployment manifest; that is, users will always go to a web page and click a link that points to the deployment manifest. Additionally, online mode requires that the client have a network connection while running the application because the application is always run from the deployed location.

Install-mode deployed applications are installed locally and executed via a shortcut from the Start menu. This mode of deployment does not require a network connection because the application, along with the deployment manifest, is cached locally on the client machine. Install-mode deployed applications also are versioned on the client and are available through Add/Remove Programs, just like traditional thick clients. Also, install-mode deployed applications can have various update policies (for example, check for updates at startup) and are installed on a per-user basis, so they do not require an administrator to perform the installation.

The deployment tag has an optional minimumRequiredVersion attribute, which can be used to control the earliest version that can be run by clients. For example, you can use this tag to ensure that all clients run version 1.2.4.5 of the application and nothing earlier.

The subscription tag within the deployment tag is an optional tag that determines the update-check policy for the application. If the tag is not defined in the deployment manifest, ClickOnce does not check for updates for the application. If the application is deployed in online mode, ClickOnce will ignore this tag, because the application will always run the latest version of the application from its deployed location (the web server). When the subscription tag is defined and the application is deployed in the install mode, ClickOnce can be configured to check for updates, either on application startup or based on an interval after startup, by using the required update tag.

The update tag has two optional tags: beforeApplicationStartup and expiration. To check for updates at startup, define the beforeApplicationStartup tag within the update tag. Alternatively, use the expiration tag to construct a finer-grained update-check policy (for example, every two hours after the application starts). When you're using the expiration update policy, ClickOnce checks for updates in the background while the application runs. When an update becomes available, the user is presented with a dialog box to choose to install the newest version the next time the application is launched, rather than immediately.

The deploymentProvider tag defines where the deployment manifest lives. This may seem like overkill, because the user first clicked a link to the application manifest and now the manifest has a link to itself. However, this is useful in situations where the application is deployed outside ClickOnce but will use the update facility provided by ClickOnce. For example, very large applications can be distributed on a DVD and still be updatable via ClickOnce by using the deploymentProvider tag.

The dependency Tag and Application Manifest File

The dependency tag determines the specifics of the application to install, such as its version and actual assemblies. This tag actually points to another manifest file called an *application manifest*. An application manifest file is how ClickOnce enables application authors to deploy and manage versions of an application on the client and the server. Application manifest files are also XML-based files that end with a .manifest extension and contain everything required by the application for a particular version. A sample application manifest file is shown in Figure 7-9.

```xml
<?xml version="1.0" encoding="utf-8"?>
<asmv1:assembly xsi:schemaLocation="urn:schemas-microsoft-com:asm.v1 assembly.adap
  <asmv1:assemblyIdentity name="ClickOnceSample.exe" version="1.0.0.0" publicKeyTo
  <entryPoint>
    <assemblyIdentity name="ClickOnceSample" version="1.0.1906.22742" language="ne
    <commandLine file="ClickOnceSample.exe" parameters="" />
  </entryPoint>
  <trustInfo>
    <security>
      <applicationRequestMinimum>
        <PermissionSet Unrestricted="true" ID="Custom" />
        <defaultAssemblyRequest permissionSetReference="Custom" />
      </applicationRequestMinimum>
    </security>
  </trustInfo>
  <dependency>
    <dependentAssembly codebase="ClickOnceSample.exe" size="16384">
      <assemblyIdentity name="ClickOnceSample" version="1.0.1906.22742" language="
      <hash>
        <dsig:Transforms>
          <dsig:Transform Algorithm="urn:schemas-microsoft-com:HashTransforms.Iden
        </dsig:Transforms>
        <dsig:DigestMethod Algorithm="http://www.w3.org/2000/09/xmldsig#sha1" />
        <dsig:DigestValue>GjRUUCXOLrCfva9nX5igSv9WGxw=</dsig:DigestValue>
      </hash>
    </dependentAssembly>
  </dependency>
  <dependency>
    <dependentAssembly codebase="ComponentsLib.dll" size="16384">
      <assemblyIdentity name="ComponentsLib" version="1.0.1906.22657" language="ne
      <hash>
        <dsig:Transforms>
          <dsig:Transform Algorithm="urn:schemas-microsoft-com:HashTransforms.Iden
        </dsig:Transforms>
        <dsig:DigestMethod Algorithm="http://www.w3.org/2000/09/xmldsig#sha1" />
        <dsig:DigestValue>M1xx7D5ZulxwZPFiw8L+2VfaLrE=</dsig:DigestValue>
      </hash>
    </dependentAssembly>
  </dependency>
```

Figure 7-9. *A sample application manifest file*

Every version of an application has an associated application manifest file. This manifest file defines the version number of the application, the security requirements of the application, the dependent assemblies of the application, and so on. In other words, it tells ClickOnce everything it needs to download and run the application on a client's machine. As shown in Figure 7-9, the entryPoint tag defines the executable that holds the entry point method (the main() method), and there is an entry for every dependent assembly that needs to be downloaded to run the application. The trustInfo tag defines all of the permissions necessary to run the application, from the CAS standpoint.

The Signature Tag

The Signature tag defines a public/private key signature for the deployment. Deployment manifests and application manifests both must be signed with the same signature to tell the

ClickOnce runtime that the publisher that published the application is the same publisher doing updates to the application. If the signatures in the two manifest files don't match, ClickOnce will not allow updates.

ClickOnce Example

Now, we'll walk through an exercise of creating and deploying an application with ClickOnce.[1] To create and deploy the application, follow these steps:

1. Launch Visual Studio 2005.

2. Create a new Windows Application and name it HelloFromClickOnce.

3. Using the Form Designer, place a label on the form.

4. Create a new Class Library project and name it DependentAssm.

5. Create a new class in the DependentAssm and name it SayHelloComp.

6. Add a method to this class named SayHello() and return the string "hello world!".

7. Add DependentAssm as a referenced project to HelloFromClickOnce.

8. In Form1.cs, add a using statement to make SayHelloAssm visible.

9. In the default constructor of Form1.cs, set the label's Text property to the string returned by the method created in SayHelloComp.

10. Open the AssemblyInfo.cs file under the Properties node and set the AssemblyVersion for both projects to 1.0.0.0 (note that this is not the deployment version).

Note The deployment version is not the same thing as the assembly version. The deployment version is the version you set in the deployment manifest, and the assembly version is the version you set in the assemblyInfo.cs file. The deployment version is the version number that ClickOnce is concerned with, and the version number in the assemblyInfo file is the assembly's version number.

---

11. Build the application. At this point, you have a smart client application that has a dependent assembly.

12. To deploy the application using ClickOnce, in Visual Studio 2005, select Build ➤ Publish Solution to start the Publish Wizard, as shown in Figure 7-10.

13. Assuming you have IIS installed locally on your machine, choose the default location for the deployment. ClickOnce will create a virtual directory at the specified location and will copy the application to the directory. Click Next.

---

1. The sample described here was built with Visual Studio 2005 Beta 8.0.60607.16.

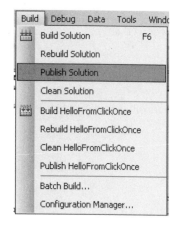

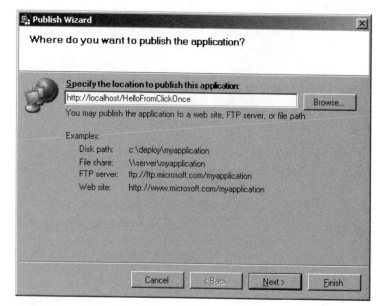

Figure 7-10. *Starting the Publish Wizard*

14. In the next wizard page, choose "Yes, this application is available online or offline" to set the install mode, as shown in Figure 7-11. Click Next to continue.

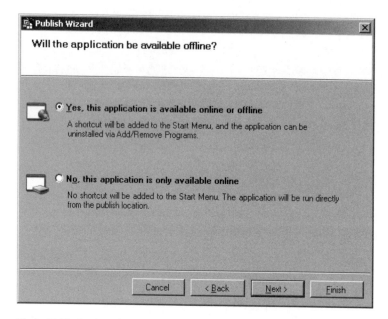

Figure 7-11. *Setting the application to be available online and offline*

15. You are presented with a dialog box to sign the deployment. Leave the default and click Next, and then click Finish to complete the deployment.

At this point, ClickOnce should have published the application under the locally installed IIS and presented you with a web page in IE that looks similar to Figure 7-12.

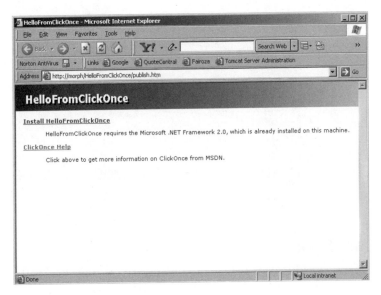

Figure 7-12. *A ClickOnce-generated page to launch the published application*

The first link shown in Figure 7-12 allows you to install the deployed application to your machine, and the second link points to the ClickOnce documentation. Click the Install HelloWorldFromClickOnce link to install the application. After the installation completes, you should have a shortcut under Program Files. Also verify that ClickOnce created entries in Add/Remove Programs.

It is instructive to see what was installed when you published the application with Visual Studio 2005. Again, assuming you have IIS installed locally, browse to c:\Inetpub\wwwroot\. ClickOnce should have created a directory under wwwroot with the name HelloWorldClickOnce, and the contents of the folder should be similar to the example in Figure 7-13. Notice that ClickOnce created the deployment manifest (HelloFromClickOnce.application) and the application manifest (HelloFromClickOnce.exe.manifest). You can also see that ClickOnce created a setup.exe file and a folder that contains the .NET Framework. The setup.exe file is a bootstrapper that can be used to ensure all of the prerequisites of your application are installed on a client's machine prior to installing your application. For example, if your application needs to install the Microsoft SQL Server Data Engine (MSDE), the bootstrapper can be used to ensure that MSDE is installed prior to running your installation. We'll explain how the bootstrapper works in the "The Bootstrapper and Prerequisites" section later in this chapter.

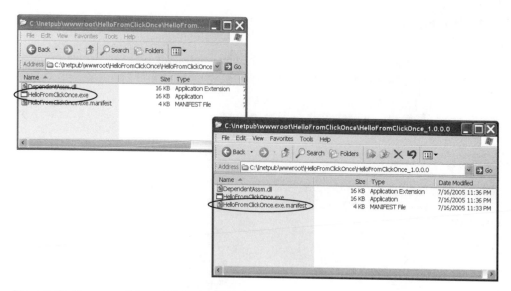

Figure 7-13. *Contents of the published folders*

Automatic ClickOnce Updates

Now, let's see how updates work with ClickOnce. We'll slightly modify our component assembly and deploy the application again with a new deployment version. Our previous version was set to 1.0.0.0, and we'll kick that up to version 2.0.0.0.

Recall that when we deployed our HelloFromClickOnce application, we didn't specify any information specific to doing updates. If you take a peek at the deployment manifest, you'll see that Visual Studio 2005 set the update policy to check for updates before startup (beforeApplicationStartup). Since we have deployed our application once already, we'll modify our sample and publish the new version to the web server, and then run our application again to see if ClickOnce realizes that a new version is available.

To test updating with ClickOnce, modify the SayHelloComp class so that the SayHello() method returns a different string, and then build the solution. Now, you need to modify the version number of the deployment. Recall that when we wrote the initial version of this application, we didn't set a version number. By default, Visual Studio 2005 set the version number to 1.0.0.0. To modify the version number, you need to use Visual Studio 2005's Project Designer. As shown in Figure 7-14, the Project Designer has two tabs specific to ClickOnce: Security and Publish. Figure 7-14 shows the contents of the Publish tab. (We'll look at the Security tab in the next section.)

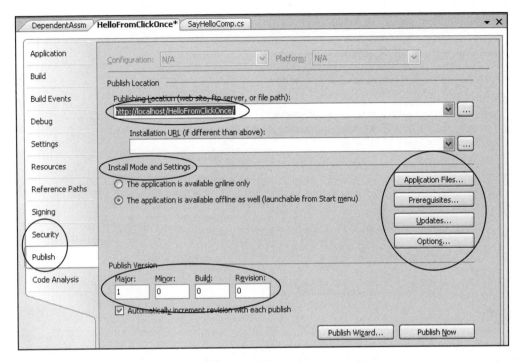

Figure 7-14. *The Publish tab of the Project Designer in Visual Studio 2005*

The Publish tab allows you to customize and manage the contents of the deployment manifest and application manifest. Notice that the Publish Designer allows you to set the initial deployment location, the publish version, and the install mode of the application. The Publish Designer also provides dialog boxes to specify the update policy and the prerequisites for the deployment (for example, the client must have MDAC installed prior to installing your application). You can even customize the language presented to the user during the installation, and whether or not the Publish.htm file should be shown. Figure 7-15 shows the various options available through the Publish tab of the Project Designer.

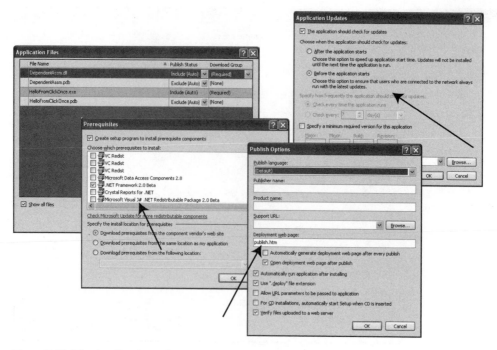

Figure 7-15. *The Application Files, Prerequisites, Application Updates, and Publish Options dialog boxes*

Using the Publish Version option on the Publish tab of the Project Designer, increment the publish version number to 2.0.0.0, and then click the Publish Now button. Visual Studio 2005 will build the solution, and then publish the application to the web server. Since you incremented the version number, Visual Studio 2005 will create another folder on the web server with the newer version and will also update the deployment manifest to point to this new version, as shown in Figure 7-16.

To see if the update is detected by ClickOnce, go to the Start menu and launch the application from the Program Files menu shortcut. ClickOnce detects that there is an update to the application and prompts you to install the latest version. If you choose OK, the new version of the application is downloaded and installed to the machine, and then the new version is launched.

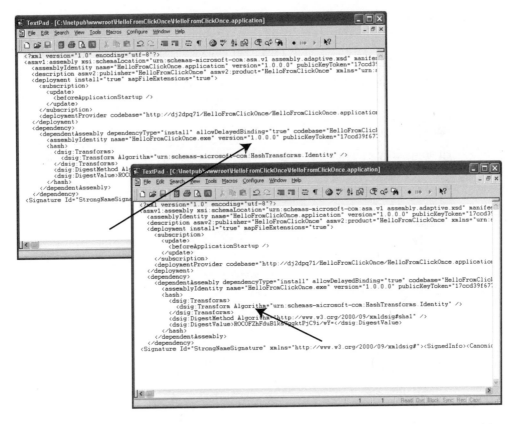

Figure 7-16. *The deployment manifest with the updated version number and the contents of the web server deployment folder after an update*

Application Security with ClickOnce

When you deployed the sample application, you probably noticed that ClickOnce prompted you with a security dialog box prior to installing the application. By default, ClickOnce-deployed applications run within the CAS sandbox. This prevents the application from performing privileged actions on the client. If an application needs additional permissions, you can take one of two approaches:

Use the application manifest: You can declare the permissions your application needs in the application manifest. Visual Studio 2005 helps with this by providing a user interface to customize application security via the Project Designer. With this approach, you identify the permissions you want, and when users install the application, they are presented with a dialog box to choose whether to allow the application to be installed.

Use a trust license: With this method, the application author obtains a trust license from a trust license issuer by submitting his public key. With the trust license in hand, he also signs the two manifests with the same public key and deploys the application. When the client installs the application, ClickOnce compares the keys in the manifest files against the key in the trust license (in the background), and if they match, the permissions requested by the application are granted and the application runs as expected, without prompting the user.

Unfortunately, trust licenses don't work with the Visual Studio 2005 beta version we used, so we'll touch on security with ClickOnce by looking at the security settings in the Security tab of the Project Designer. Figure 7-17 shows the Security tab in Project Designer for the `HelloFromClickOnce` application.

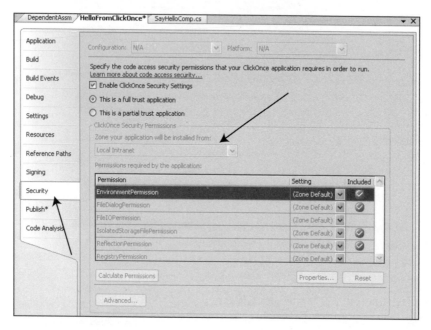

Figure 7-17. *Using the Project Designer's Security tab to configure permissions required by an application*

By default, ClickOnce-deployed applications are set to have full trust on the client machine. With this in place, the application can do whatever it needs on the client. However, the client is prompted with a dialog box to verify the installation of an untrusted application before proceeding.

The ClickOnce APIs

The ClickOnce technology also has a programmatic interface that you can use to customize deployment and updates. For example, if the core of your application is deployed initially, and then users are allowed to choose optional features (plug-ins) and have them installed on demand, the ClickOnce APIs can help.

To demonstrate using the ClickOnce APIs, we'll build an application that has an optional feature, called PluginOne, which the user can install via a menu item. The scenario is depicted in Figure 7-18.

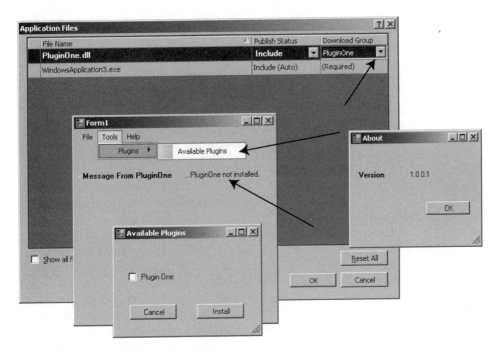

Figure 7-18. *The ClickOnce API in action*

As shown in Figure 7-18, the application has a simple user interface: a form with two labels, a menu bar, and a few dialog boxes. The menu bar has several menu items. The Tools ➤ Plugins ➤ Available Plugins menu item displays the application's optional plug-in and allows the user to install it on demand. The other interesting menu is the About menu. When the user clicks this menu item, it displays a dialog box that shows the application's current deployment version number. The main user interface (Form1) displays a message that says "Message From Plugin One." This label points to a message from PluginOne. When the application starts, it checks to see if the plug-in has been installed, and if so, it loads a class and gets a message from the plug-in. Listing 7-1 shows the Form1() method.

Listing 7-1. *The Form1() Method*

```
public Form1()
{
    InitializeComponent();
    CheckForPluginOne();
}
private void CheckForPluginOne()
```

```
{
    try
    {
        Assembly asm = Assembly.Load("PluginOne");
        if (asm == null)
        {
            throw new Exception("Failed to get reference to PluginOne");
        }
        msgLbl.Text = asm.GetType("PluginOne.Class1").ToString();
    }
    catch (Exception ee)
    {
        msgLbl.Text = "...PluginOne not installed.";
    }
}
```

The ClickOnce technology defines *download groups* (accessed via the Application Files button in the Publish Wizard). Features of a deployment, or solution, can be organized into groups, and these groups can be downloaded on demand or set to download initially with the application. Figure 7-18 shows that the application assembly, WindowsApplication3, is in a group by itself, called Required, and its publish status is set to Include (Auto). This configuration tells the ClickOnce runtime that this assembly needs to be installed every time.

The application also has a dependent assembly called PluginOne. This assembly has been configured in a separate download group named PluginOne, and its publish status is set to Include, rather than Include (Auto). This tells the ClickOnce runtime not to download the assembly at install time. When the user chooses Tools ➤ Plugins ➤ Available Plugins, selects PluginOne, and clicks Install, the application uses the ClickOnce APIs to download and install the group named PluginOne, as shown in Listing 7-2.

Listing 7-2. *Downloading the PluginOne Group*

```
private void availablePluginsToolStripMenuItem_Click(object sender, EventArgs e)
{
    AvailablePluginFrm frm = new AvailablePluginFrm();
    if (frm.ShowDialog() == DialogResult.OK)
    {
        ApplicationDeployment.CurrentDeployment.DownloadFileGroup("PluginOne");
        CheckForPluginOne();
    }
}
```

ClickOnce APIs are packaged in the System.Deployment assembly, and the deployment details of an application are in classes within the System.Deployment.Application namespace. This namespace holds the ApplicationDeployment class shown in Listing 7-2. The ApplicationDeployment class is used to support programmatic updates of an application.

This class defines methods to, for example, download groups synchronously and asynchronously. In our example, the `ApplicationDeployment` class is used to download our `PluginOne` group synchronously. After the download is complete, the application calls the `CheckForPluginOne()` method to instantiate a class from the downloaded plug-in and to call a method on it to update the label shown on the main form.

Figure 7-18 also shows that the menu bar has a Help ➤ About menu item. When the user clicks the About menu item, the application displays a dialog box that shows the current version of the application.

```
ApplicationDeployment ad = ApplicationDeployment.CurrentDeployment;
versionLbl.Text=ad.CurrentVersion.ToString() ;
```

In this example, you saw that you can use the ClickOnce APIs to customize the deployment of your application so that not all of the application's referenced assemblies are downloaded initially. That's just one possible use of the APIs. With the ClickOnce APIs exposed, you can take over the entire deployment process—from the user interface options to what gets downloaded and what doesn't get downloaded. You can also control what and how updates are done.

The Bootstrapper and Prerequisites

We mentioned earlier that when Visual Studio 2005 publishes an application, it can also generate a bootstrapper that can be used to install any prerequisites required by the application. The bootstrapper is an executable (`setup.exe`) application that is published next to the deployment manifest. The job of the bootstrapper is to check for a list of prerequisites on the client's machine, and if any of the prerequisites are missing, ensure that they are installed prior to running the ClickOnce installation.

Visual Studio 2005 provides a user interface, via the Project Designer, to configure the bootstrapper with the prerequisites. As shown in Figure 7-19, you can configure the bootstrapper to install one or more of the components from the list or specify a custom component at a specific location.

To configure the bootstrapper to install a custom component, click the "Download prerequisites from the following location" radio button, and then click the . . . button. This brings up a dialog box that allows you to choose a location from: the local file system, a local web server, an FTP site, or a remote web site, as shown in Figure 7-20.

There is a caveat to using the bootstrapper, however. As we mentioned, the bootstrapper is an executable, and this executable must run prior to running the deployment manifest. The bootstrapper will take care of launching the deployment manifest, but you must have the client run the bootstrapper first. Unfortunately, the bootstrapper is not a managed executable that can be launched from IE, as with NTD applications. Instead, the bootstrapper must be downloaded and launched manually. The good news is that the bootstrapper is a very small application and will take only seconds to download (even over a dial-up connection). Once the bootstrapper is downloaded, the user can run the application to install the entire product.

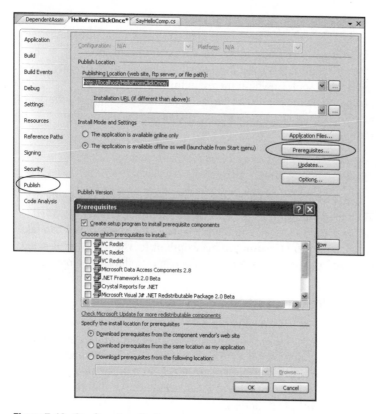

Figure 7-19. *Configuring the bootstrapper with deployment prerequisites*

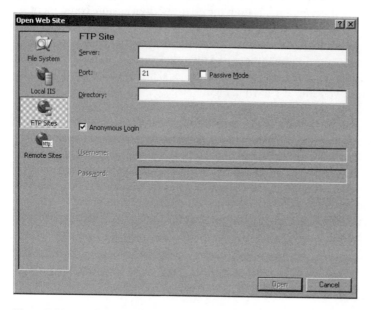

Figure 7-20. *Configuring the bootstrapper to download a custom component from a specific location*

Smart Client Tools: The Application Updater Component and Updater Application Block

Until Visual Studio 2005 is released, smart clients can use one of two technologies to support auto-updating an installed application: the Application Updater component and the Updater Application Block. We'll take a brief look at the component here, and then examine the application block.

The Application Updater Component

The Application Updater component is a small component that supports automatically updating an application by using the concept of a bootstrapper. Essentially, users launch the Application Updater executable rather than launching the smart client, and the executable handles launching the application and managing updates.

We talked about the Application Updater component in Chapter 3, when we discussed the TaskVision sample application. TaskVision uses this component to handle updates. Refer to that discussion for details on using the Application Updater component.

The Updater Application Block

The Updater Application Block (UAB) is an unofficial extension of the Application Updater component. The Application Updater component is easy to use and can meet the basic needs of most applications. However, this component lacks the flexibility and scalability needed by large distributed applications. The UAB, conversely, is easy to use and provides the options needed when deploying such applications. For example, for a large application, it may be necessary to download large binaries and be able to monitor downloads and be notified of progress. The UAB provides this flexibility, while not intruding on smaller applications that need the simplicity of ease of use. You can download the Updater Application Block from the following site:

```
http://www.microsoft.com/downloads/details.aspx?FamilyID=
c6c17f3a-d957-4b17-9b97-296fb4927c30&DisplayLang=en
```

Version 2.0 of the UAB is targeted to easily migrate to ClickOnce. That way, until the final release of Visual Studio 2005, developers can use the UAB. Version 2.0 of the UAB is located at the following URL:

```
http://www.microsoft.com/downloads/details.aspx?FamilyID=
c6c09314-e222-4af2-9395-1e0bd7060786&DisplayLang=en
```

UAB Architecture

A high-level architecture of the UAB is shown in Figure 7-21.

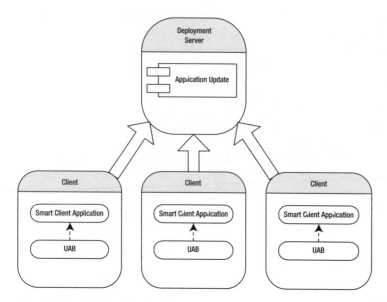

Figure 7-21. *High-level architecture of the UAB*

At a high level, the UAB sits on the client machine and is responsible for detecting, downloading, and installing application updates. Similar to ClickOnce, the UAB is driven by a manifest file that contains an application's dependencies (binaries, resources, and so on). When an application is installed on a client's machine, the UAB manifest is also installed along with the UAB. The UAB looks at the manifest file on the local machine and compares it with the manifest on the server to determine if an update is available. When an update is detected, the UAB can do either of the following:

- Notify the application that an update is available, via an event-based notification system, and subsequently download and install the update.

- Download the update and install it silently. The client will see the new version the next time the application is launched.

Elements of the UAB

The UAB block is made up of some key elements. We have already mentioned that the UAB is driven by a manifest file. This manifest file defines everything that makes up an application. For example, most applications have an executable, some dependent assemblies, and likely some resource files (for example, some icons).

The UAB also defines a *controller* and a *bootstrapper*. The controller is used to manage the update process. This includes starting and stopping the updater and handling events that are raised during the update process. The UAB defines two types of controllers, which are external to the application that is being updated:

Computer-wide controller. An external application that is used to manage the update process for one or more smart client applications on a machine. This controller is implemented as a Windows service and driven by a configuration file that defines the applications that are going to be updated.

Application-launcher controller. A controller used to ensure that clients run only the latest version of an application and nothing else. This type of controller is useful when you want to force clients to run the latest version of an application.

The bootstrapper is also an external application that is used to launch the application being updated. The bootstrapper serves two purposes:

- After an update, the bootstrapper ensures that the correct version of the application is launched.

- The bootstrapper ensures that shortcuts to the application don't break after the installation of an update.

The relationship between the application, the bootstrapper, and the controller is shown in Figure 7-22.

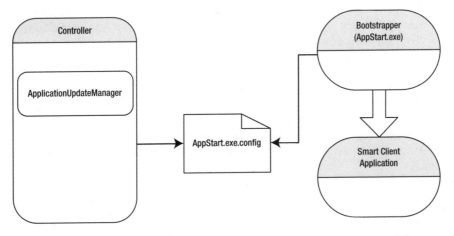

Figure 7-22. *The relationship between the application, the bootstrapper, and the controller*

As shown in Figure 7-22, the controller contains the ApplicationUpdateManager, which is the entity that knows how to detect, download, and install updates. When an update is installed, the controller updates the bootstrapper's configuration file to reflect the new installation. When the user launches the bootstrapper, the bootstrapper looks at the configuration file to determine which application to launch, and then launches the application. As an example, assume that version 1.0.0.0 of an application is installed on a client's machine. In this case, the client would have a shortcut that points to AppStart.exe, and the AppStart.exe.config file would have a reference to the version 1.0.0.0 of the application, as shown in Figure 7-23.

```
<?xml version="1.0" encoding="utf-8" ?>
<configuration>
        <configSections>
                <section name="appStart">
                type="Microsoft.ApplicationBlocks.ApplicationUpdater.A
        </configSections>

        <appStart>
                <ClientApplicationInfo>
                        <appFolderName>D:\ConsultingEngagements\PAG\Ap

                        <appExeName>SampleAssembly.exe</appExeName>

                        <installedVersion>1.0.0.0</installedVersion>

                        <lastUpdated>2003-05-04T14:49:18.4483296-05:00

                </ClientApplicationInfo>
        </appStart>

</configuration>
```

Figure 7-23. *Contents of the AppState.exe.config file*

When the user clicks the shortcut, AppStart.exe launches version 1.0.0.0 of the application. After an update is installed, the AppStart.exe.config file is modified by the controller to reflect the new version (for example, 2.0.0.0), and AppState.exe will launch the new version the next time the user clicks the shortcut.

The UAB also provides a programmatic interface to the UAB and can be used by self-updating applications. Self-updating applications don't rely on a controller to manage the update process. They manage the updates process themselves. but use the UAB facilities to detect, download, and install updates. In this scenario, the UAB provides an event when updates are available directly to the application, and the application can react accordingly. For example, when an update becomes available, the application can prompt the user to install the update.

UAB QuickStart—Service Demo Application

When you installed the UAB, the Windows Installer created a folder under Program Files\ Microsoft Application Blocks for .NET\Updater. In that folder are several sample applications in C# and VB. NET. One of the samples is called QuickStart—Service. This sample implements a computer-wide controller and handles updates for several applications. In this section, we'll walk through how to update an application using the UAB by dissecting this demo.

Recall that the idea behind the computer-wide controller is that you have one or more applications installed on a client that require updating, and rather than create several individual controllers to manage each one, you configure a computer-wide controller to manage the update process for all applications. The computer-wide controller works by creating an ApplicationUpdateManager. This manager handles the entire process for the controller; truthfully, the only purpose of the controller is to be a container for the ApplicationUpdateManager. The code for the controller is shown in Listing 7-3.

Listing 7-3. *The UpdaterApplicationBlockService Class*

```
public class UpdaterApplicationBlockService : System.ServiceProcess.ServiceBase
{
    private System.ComponentModel.Container components = null;

    private ApplicationUpdateManager _updater = null;

    public UpdaterApplicationBlockService()
    {
        InitializeComponent();
    }
    static void Main()
    {
        System.ServiceProcess.ServiceBase[] ServicesToRun;

        ServicesToRun = new System.ServiceProcess.ServiceBase[]
          { new UpdaterApplicationBlockService() };

            System.ServiceProcess.ServiceBase.Run(ServicesToRun);
        }
      private void InitializeComponent()
    {
        this.CanShutdown = true;
        this.ServiceName = "UpdaterApplicationBlock";
    }
    protected override void Dispose( bool isDisposing )
    {
        if( isDisposing )
        {
            if (components != null)
                {
                    components.Dispose();
                }
            }
            base.Dispose( isDisposing );
        }
        protected override void OnStart(string[] args)
        {
            if( _updater == null )
            {
                _updater = new ApplicationUpdateManager();
            }
            _updater.StartUpdater();
        }
        protected override void OnStop()
        {
            _updater.StopUpdater();
        }
}
```

As shown in Listing 7-3, the controller simply instantiates the manager when the service is started, and then stops the manager when the service is stopped. The key to the controller and manager, however, is the service's configuration file. The configuration file is the key because it contains specific information about the applications that are being managed by the controller. Figure 7-24 shows the service's configuration file.

```
<?xml version="1.0" encoding="utf-8" ?>
<configuration>
    <configSections>
        <section name="appStart">
            type="Microsoft.ApplicationBlocks.ApplicationUpdater.Ap
    </configSections>
    <appUpdater>
        <UpdaterConfiguration>
            <polling type="Seconds" value="120"
            <logListener logPath="C:\Program Files\Microsoft Application Blocks fo
            <!-- *************** BITS DOWNLOADER  **************** -->
            <downloader type="Microsoft.ApplicationBlocks.ApplicationUpdater.Downl
                assembly="Microsoft.ApplicationBlocks.ApplicationUpdater.

            <!-- *************** THE RSA HASHING VALIDATOR     ************
            <validator type="Microsoft.ApplicationBlocks.ApplicationUpdater.Valida
                <key>
                    <RSAKeyValue>
                        <Module>s4+zdlfur9s7olTNopaLNo20+3t3Z7RXe57SO
                        <Exponent>AQAB</Exponent>
                    </RSAKeyValue>
                </key>
            </validator>
            <application name="ServiceTest1" useValidation="true">
                <client>
                    <baseDir>C:\Program Files\Microsoft Application Blocks
                    <xmlFile>C:\Program Files\Microsoft Application Blocks
                    <tempDir>C:\Program Files\Microsoft Application Blocks
```

Figure 7-24. *Sample configuration file for a computer-wide controller*

The configuration file is actually consumed by a section handler in the UAB. This particular configuration file tells the UAB to poll for updates every two minutes (120 seconds) and has two applications configured for updates. Each application has a client-side entry and a server-side entry, wrapped up within the application tag. The baseDir tag tells the UAB the root directory to the application on the client, and the xmlFile tag points to the AppStart.exe.config file we talked about earlier. This is the configuration file that has the latest version number on the client side. tempDir is the location where updates are downloaded prior to installation.

On the server side, xmlFile points to the server-side manifest file. This manifest file tells the UAB the latest version on the server side. The UAB can then compare the client-side version number, by looking the AppState.exe.config file locally, and the server-side manifest information to determine if an update is available. When the UAB finds a difference in version numbers, it will look at the server-side manifest to find the location of the latest version on the server side.

Finally, the maxWaitXmlFile tag tells the UAB how long to wait for the server to return the manifest file; that is, if it doesn't get the file within 1,200,000 milliseconds, it will give up and try again the next time.

That covers how updates are detected and downloaded. We still need to look at how to deploy the application. Recall that the bootstrapper application is the entity that users launch to run the application, rather than executing the real application. Therefore, to keep things simple, the UAB requires you to deploy the bootstrapper within the root of the application's deployment folder. The folder structure is shown in Figure 7-25.

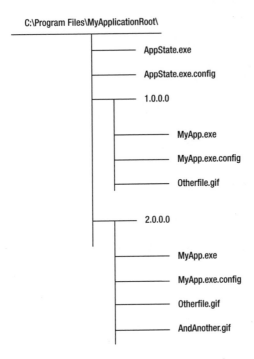

Figure 7-25. *Client-side folder structure when using the UAB*

Figure 7-25 shows that each application can have many versions on the client side. Users launch the application by running the bootstrapper, and the bootstrapper determines which version to run. The bootstrapper's configuration file contains the version number that tells the bootstrapper which version to launch.

UAB QuickStart—SelfUpdating Demo Application

It's also useful to take a peek at how a self-updating application might use the UAB. As noted earlier, self-updating applications don't rely on a controller to manage the update process. Instead, the application itself creates an instance of the `ApplicationUpdateManager` and registers for events to download updates.

The UAB download also comes with a solution that demonstrates how a self-updating application might be implemented. This solution is named QuickStart—SelfUpdating and is located at `C:\Program Files\Microsoft Application Blocks for .NET\Updater\Code\CS`. If you open the solution in Visual Studio 2003, you'll see that the solution has the usual UAB-related projects and one named `SelfUpdatingTest`. This project has a form that is used to demonstrate self-updating.

Note that the application must consume the ApplicationUpdateManager; this is similar to the service we talked about earlier. Also, the application must register for update-related events. Finally, the implementation of the event handlers is important. Listing 7-4 shows code snippets from the self-updating form.

Listing 7-4. *The Initialize() Method*

```
private void Initialize()
{

    //  make an Updater for use in-process with us
    _updater = new ApplicationUpdateManager();

    //  hook Updater events
    _updater.DownloadStarted +=
        new UpdaterActionEventHandler( OnUpdaterDownloadStarted );
    _updater.FilesValidated +=
        new UpdaterActionEventHandler( OnUpdaterFilesValidated );
    _updater.UpdateAvailable +=
        new UpdaterActionEventHandler( OnUpdaterUpdateAvailable );
    _updater.DownloadCompleted +=
        new UpdaterActionEventHandler(OnUpdaterDownloadCompleted);

    //  start the updater on a separate
    //  thread so that our UI remains responsive
    _updaterThread =
            new Thread( new ThreadStart( _updater.StartUpdater ) );
    _updaterThread.Start();

    //  get version from config, set caption correctly
    string version = ConfigurationSettings.AppSettings["version"];
    this.Text = this.Text +
      String.Format("  ****  VERSION {0}  ****  ", version);
}
private void OnUpdaterUpdateAvailableHandler
( object sender, UpdaterActionEventArgs e )
{
    string message = String.Format(
"Update available:  The new version on the server is {0}
and current version is {1} would you like to upgrade?",
        e.ServerInformation.AvailableVersion,
        ConfigurationSettings.AppSettings["version"] ) ;

    DialogResult dialog =
MessageBox.Show( message, "Update Available", MessageBoxButtons.YesNo );
```

```
if( DialogResult.No == dialog )
{
    // if no, stop the updater for this app
    _updater.StopUpdater( e.ApplicationName );
      lblStatus.Text += "Update Cancelled." + Environment.NewLine;
}
else
{
    lblStatus.Text += "Update in progress." + Environment.NewLine;
}
}
private void OnUpdaterDownloadCompletedHandler
( object sender, UpdaterActionEventArgs e )
{
        lblStatus.Text += "Download Completed." + Environment.NewLine;
}
```

The Initialize() method is called from the form's constructor to create the ApplicationUpdateManager and to register for update events. After it creates the manager and registers for events, it starts the update manager on a background thread. When an update becomes available, the UAB notifies the application of the update by firing the UpdateAvailable event. In the UpdateAvailable event handler, the application displays a friendly message to the user indicating that an update to the application is available. The user can then choose to have the update installed.

If the user chooses to install the update, the application tells the UAB to download the update. When the download operation has completed successfully, the UAB notifies the application via the DownloadCompleted event. In this case, the application simply shows a message in the status bar indicating that the new version was downloaded. This indicates that the user should shut down the application and relaunch it to see the updates.

UAB Downloaders, Validators, and Postprocessors

The UAB also defines downloaders, validators, and postprocessors. As you can guess, a *downloader* is something that is used to handle downloading files. The UAB, by default, uses a downloader implementation that is based on Binary Internet Transfer Services (BITS). This implementation, however, is configurable, and the UAB really operates on the IDownloader interface. Therefore, smart clients can implement and configure other downloaders based on their requirements.

Validators play the same role as with the public/private keys you saw used with ClickOnce. They ensure that the application is updated with the same parties who did the installation and that some unknown file has not been introduced to the upload of the application. This essentially guards against tampering with the application and using the UAB as a means of disseminating viruses.

Postprocessors are classes that implement the IPostProcessor interface. These processors are called after downloading updates and can be used to do custom work after downloading new versions.

UAB Wrap-Up

The UAB is very extensible and configurable to meet the needs of most applications. The challenge with using the UAB is the initial installation and configuration required to enable seamless integration with the UAB. To use the UAB, you need to deploy the application with the bootstrapper application next to it, and have the controller running and configured (unless you are using a self-updating approach). With that said, the effort involved for the return is minuscule and when ClickOnce is released with Visual Studio 2005, you should be able to easily migrate the UABs in your applications.

Summary

In this chapter, we discussed various approaches to deploying WinForms smart clients. We covered NTD, OTD, and MSI installer deployment. Then we focused on the next-generation deployment solution called ClickOnce.

You learned that the ClickOnce technology builds on the previous attempts to solve the problems associated with deploying rich clients. We showed examples of deploying and updating smart clients with ClickOnce, and then demonstrated how you can use the ClickOnce API to handle deployment tasks programmatically.

Finally, we discussed the Application Updater component and the UAB. These technologies are useful for cases where you can't use ClickOnce deployment.

In the next chapter, we will introduce XML Web Services and how smart clients can use them.

CHAPTER 8

■ ■ ■

XML Web Services and Smart Clients

As with all new IT approaches and concepts, XML Web Services seem to take on a life of their own. As more and more gets written about XML Web Services, the developers and executive managers need to sift through the fiction, hype, and reality. Fiction is a fabrication, hype is a mixture of truth and falsehoods, and reality is what is left over after the fiction has been uncovered and the truth has been gleaned from the falsehoods. This chapter will get to the reality of XML Web Services and dispel what is hype.

We begin by making the business case for XML Web Services. Next, we will consider both the benefits and drawbacks of using XML Web Services. Then we'll proceed to study the various components that make up XML Web Services. Finally, we'll work through an example of developing an XML Web Service.

Business Case for XML Web Services

This book is about smart clients, so why bring up XML Web Services? The reason is that smart clients give the user a new experience on the client, and XML Web Services extend that user experience when connected remotely.

Prior to XML Web Services, most of the interaction using the Internet involved a thin client tightly coupled to inaccessible back-end services via a web server. As discussed in Chapter 1, the Internet was initially (and still is) used for advertising, publishing, and broadcasting. Other than small requests by thin clients, information flow using the Internet was monodirectional from the advertising firm to the user, as illustrated in Figure 8-1.

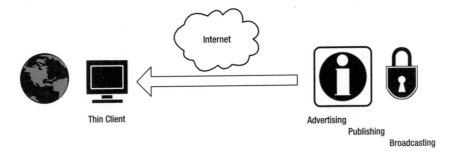

Figure 8-1. *Basic Internet capability*

XML Web Services are a new architectural component that brings together a set of business functions or logic that can be accessed through a standard interface by any consumer. A consumer could be a smart client, another XML Web Service, or any software process that follows the interface standards. XML Web Services allow businesses to aggregate the logic, discover it, and then expose it through a controlled interface via the Internet. This is a large opportunity and can be exploited further with smart clients.

Business is based on financial transactions—the exchange of money for products or services. For this purpose, information flow needs to be bidirectional, as illustrated in Figure 8-2. Also, typically, a larger quantity of information is needed to complete the transaction. No one wants to give up money or hand over a product or service without having a high level of confidence in the other party involved.

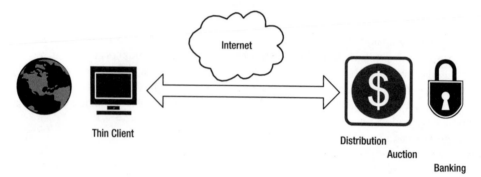

Figure 8-2. *Bidirectional information flow is necessary for Internet transaction processing.*

Many Internet-based companies, such as Amazon and eBay, have developed transaction-based systems on the Internet. However, without XML Web Services, the business functionality contained in back-end services is still inaccessible, unless a system or user goes through the user interface to get it, as shown in Figure 8-3.

A forward-thinking corporation that wishes to prepare its applications for use with smart clients and XML Web Services can maneuver its IT systems to be in a position to take advantage of new markets and opportunities. Let's look at a couple business cases to see how this could work.

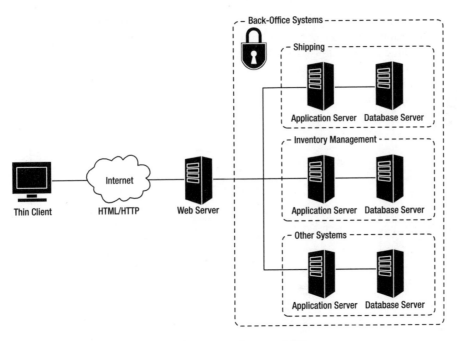

Figure 8-3. *Basic Internet transaction processing capability*

Opening Up the Back Office

Suppose a book distribution corporation's national market is saturated. The corporation can no longer continue to grow without head-to-head competition with its closest competitor. The managers are not prepared to fight a price war just yet, and are strongly interested in developing an international market segment to continue the company's growth. This corporation currently uses thin clients and the Internet to process all of its national market transactions.

Given the typical thin client Internet application architecture, the corporation must either use its current national user interface or create a new international one, typically line by line. Thin clients use HTML over HTTP to access the information in corporate back-office systems. Adjusting the back-office business logic is another problem. To support the international market, the developers will need to isolate the current national business logic, and then construct the new international logic. This is a costly approach and shows the inflexibility of thin clients and the rigidity of the back office.

The corporation could go around these problems by letting the international users access back-office systems through a business-to-business (B2B) connection, but this will need a proprietary adapter, security, and interfaces and a new thin client.

If the corporation invests in smart clients and XML Web Services, a much cheaper solution is available. Using smart clients and XML Web Services unlocks the back office. An XML Web Service aggregates a set of business logic as a service, and then supplies a standard interface to discover and use it. As illustrated in Figure 8-4, if the book distribution company needed an XML Web Service for each of its real-world services, it would need to develop only one smart client, supply it with the necessary business logic for use with the international market, and then directly access the current XML Web Services.

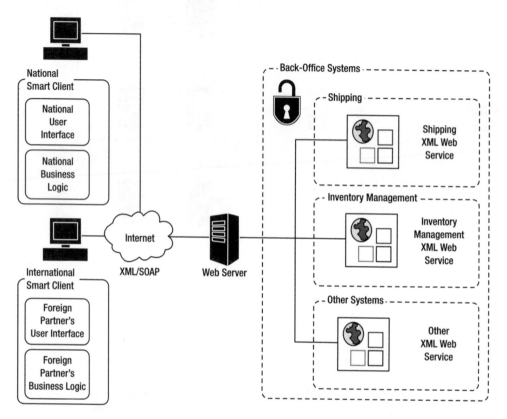

Figure 8-4. *Opening up back-end services*

Opening Up the Enterprise

A second business case example will demonstrate how to get better intranet interoperability by using smart clients and XML Web Services. A corporation has two thick client systems and a single thin client system. All three systems have "silo" architectures, and information is not passed between them, as shown in Figure 8-5. Executive management has passed down a new initiative that will force information sharing between these systems. The external architecture is different, and the internal software architecture can vary between the two thick clients applications. The corporation will need to make modifications in all three systems, along with all three clients.

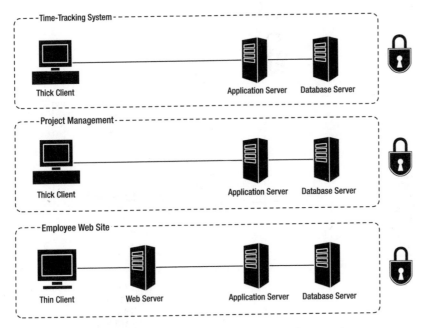

Figure 8-5. *Thin and thick clients configured in a locked enterprise*

Each system has probably placed business logic in different locations within the back office and client. This alone will require additional analysis time and effort to determine the business logic that will be needed for the integrated system. Communications for each of these systems will typically be different—one may work on synchronous transmission, and others may be based on asynchronous communication. Interfaces are probably not standardized between systems, which will make the construction of unique adapters difficult. Each of the clients will also need to change to present the integrated viewpoint. Finally, message formats will also need to be standardized between systems. All these modifications to the current architecture will be costly.

What if smart clients and XML Services are employed by the corporation? Then how hard would this directive be to implement? An XML Web Service can be a consumer to another XML Web Service as well as a client, which can be extremely valuable in developing interoperability across systems. XML Web Services use standardized message formats and interfaces. Using a standardized message format in itself is a large benefit, since no work needs to be done to translate information from one format to another.

Common or defined interfaces make interoperability much easier. Smart clients perform well in an intranet setting and provide more functional capability than either thin or thick clients. XML Web Services aggregate business logic. This grouping of business logic gives the overall architecture the modularity it needs.

If the company used XML Web Services, the software changes could be isolated to the presentation layer of each client. By implementing a smart client coupled with XML Web Services, as shown in Figure 8-6, the modification becomes as simple as integrating some of the logic in the smart client to use the XML Web Service in a different interoperability configuration. Smart clients and XML Web Services offer a low-cost solution and give the overall organization flexibility.

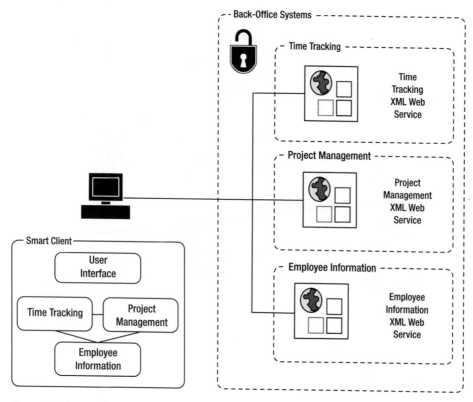

Figure 8-6. *Smart client opening up the enterprise*

XML Web Services Benefits and Drawbacks

XML Web Services are founded on a number of technologies that have matured and have been accepted by the industry as a whole. This maturation and acceptance are what make XML Web Services a real and viable technology.

Benefits of XML Web Services

The primary benefit of XML Web Services is standardization. These standards have been adopted by all major vendors (Microsoft, IBM, and so on) and are governed by the World Wide Web Consortium (W3C). The W3C refines and publishes the specifications for XML Web Services.[1]

XML Web Services are simple to implement. Many of the construction complexities and rudimentary tasks have been handled by Visual Studio .NET, as you will see in the "XML Web Service Development" section later in this chapter. This makes XML Web Services easier and less costly to construct than many other technologies trying to implement the same functionality.

---

1. The W3C defines an XML Web Service as "a software system identified by a URI whose public interfaces and bindings are defined and described using XML. Its definition can be discovered by other software systems. These systems may then interact with the Web service in a manner prescribed by its definition, using XML-based messages conveyed by Internet protocols."

To communicate, XML Web Services use TCP/IP, which gives them wide acceptance over a vast range of technologies. XML Web Services introduce an abstraction layer between the presentation and the business logic layers. This layer gives XML Web Services the ability to connect adapters or translators created for use with technologies not directly aligned with it. XML Web Services can also be discovered, which gives them a dynamic attribute for use in both Internet and intranet applications.

Here is a summary of the benefits of XML Web Services:

- Microsoft and all major vendors have accepted and standardized interfaces and operation of XML Web Services.

- Microsoft's Visual Studio .NET makes it easy to construct XML Web Services.

- XML Web Services are based on solid network technologies, such as TCP/IP.

- XML Web Services place an abstraction layer between the presentation and the business logic layers, which increases interoperability opportunities.

- XML Web Services are dynamic and can be discovered by consumers who need them.

Drawbacks of XML Web Services

XML Web Services are not a panacea; no technological solution ever is. What are some of XML Web Services' drawbacks?

XML Web Services can be slow if large amounts of data must be exchanged between the systems. For better performance, you might choose to use .NET Remoting rather than XML Web Services, if the application architecture warrants it.

Additionally, XML Web Services have more limited capabilities than distributive computing models.

Architecture of XML Web Services

XML Web Services use three principal technologies: XML, SOAP, and UDDI or DISCO files. These technologies initially interact by having the description of the XML Web Service, which is created its using the XML-based Web Services Definition Language (WSDL), published to the UDDI registry. A smart client can then use the WSDL to discover what capabilities the web service provides and how to interface with it. After the discovery process, the smart client is bound to the web service. The smart client and XML Web Service communicate through XML messages using SOAP. Figure 8-7 illustrates this architecture.

The designers of Visual Studio .NET have gone to great lengths to automate many of the underpinning complexities of this architecture. Therefore, you can use XML Web Services without knowing the details of its underlying technologies. However, we discuss XML, SOAP, WSDL, UDDI, and DISCO files here to give you a better understanding of how XML Web Services work, so you can use them effectively in your applications.

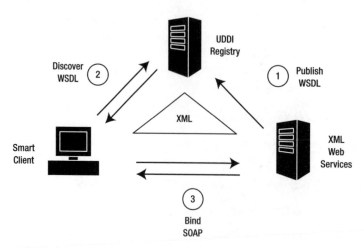

Figure 8-7. *XML Web Services architecture*

XML

XML Web Services are first and foremost based on XML. XML is a nonproprietary language, which contributes to its interoperability. XML is classified as a markup language and is based on encoding tags or elements like HTML, but unlike HTML, whose elements are all static or fixed, the elements in XML can be defined. This makes XML a meta-markup language. The term *meta* means data about data, and in XML, you can use information to define new information, which is why XML has this label.

Microsoft loads the Microsoft XML parser (MSXML) with its Internet Explorer browser. This parser allows the browser to read documents created with XML elements in the appropriate format.

XML Syntax

All XML elements have a similar syntax in that the element name is identified first, followed by its attributes. All elements are enclosed with left and right angle brackets (< >), and each unique attribute name has its value placed in quotation marks (quotes), which follow the equal sign, like this:

```
<ELEMENT-NAME … ATTRIBUTE1="value" ATTRIBUTE2="value">
```

Element names are case sensitive, so ELEMENT-NAME is different from Element-Name.

Elements are grouped in pairs. For every beginning element, there must be an ending element. The ending element has a backslash (/) before the right angle bracket. A typical XML element has this structure:

```
<ELEMENT attribute1="value"> Text <ELEMENT/>
```

An element may take up several lines, like this:

```
<ELEMENT attribute1="value">
      Text
<ELEMENT/>
```

This just makes it easier to read and does not change the functionality of the element.
Elements can be nested inside one another in this fashion:

```
<OUTSIDE-ELEMENT attribute1="value">
        <NESTED-ELEMENT attribute1="value">
        Text
         <NESTED-ELEMENT/>
<OUTSIDE-ELEMENT/>
```

It is best to align element pairs to make sure that you don't make a mistake when creating the file.

The Root Element

All XML files start with a root element. This root element has a slightly different syntax. It uses ?
followed by the key word xml to distinguish it from other elements. This element is also closed
with a ? and uses *single* quotes. It resembles the following line:

```
<?xml version='1.0' encoding='UTF-8' standalone='yes'?>
```

This root element tag has three attributes:

- version: This is the current version the parser is reading. It's best to stick with 1.0, as in
  the preceding example.

- encoding: This identifies the type of character code being used. It is recommended that
  you use the Unicode type of UTF-8 (as in the preceding example) or UTF-16. Other character code types include USC-2, USC-4, ASCII, and a number of ISO-88XX-X standards.

- standalone: This can be set to either yes or no. A value of yes, as in the preceding example, means that this document will not use external document type definitions (DTDs).
  The equal sign and quotes are not considered a part of the value.

The attributes must be placed in order for the parser to read in the line of code. If they are
not in the correct sequence, the parser will not be able to read the file.

Custom XML Tags and Elements

You can create an XML file in Notepad. If you typed the following code into a Notepad file and
saved it as Book.xml, it would be an XML program.

```
<?xml version='1.0' encoding='UTF-8' standalone='yes'?>
<USER-DEFINED-XML-TAG>
Professional Service-Oriented Smart Clients
</USER-DEFINED-XML-TAG>
```

In Internet Explorer, Book.xml looks like Figure 8-8.

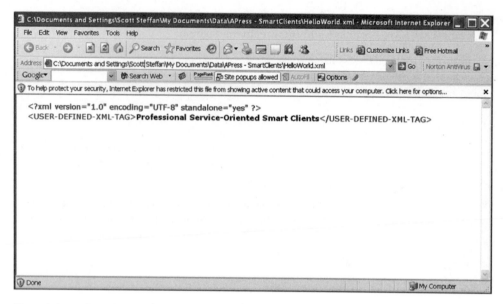

Figure 8-8. *Book.xml, with a user-defined XML element (tag)*

Since this chapter uses a hierarchical data schema, it can also be represented in XML. The contents of the file saved as Chapter7.xml (representing an early draft version of this chapter), generates a partial chapter outline, as shown in Listing 8-1.

Listing 8-1. *Chapter7.xml*

```xml
<?xml version='1.0' encoding='UTF-8' standalone='yes'?>
<!--Chapter Construction-->
<chapter name="Chapter 7">
        <title>XML Web Services and Smart Clients</title>
        <date>March 7, 2005</date>
        <description>Present XML Web Services and Smart Clients</description>
        <section>
                        <name>Business Case for XML Web Services</name>
                          <description>Present business case</description>
        </section>
        <section>
                        <name>What are XML Web Services?</name>
                        <description>Present benefits and drawbacks</description>
                        <subsection>
                                        <name>Benefits</name>
                        </subsection>
                        <subsection>
                                        <name>Drawbacks</name>
                        </subsection>
        </section>
```

```
    <section>
            <name>Architecture of XML Web Services</name>
            <description>Present architecture</description>
    </section>
</chapter>
```

The code in Listing 8-1 results in the output shown in Figure 8-9 when displayed using Internet Explorer.

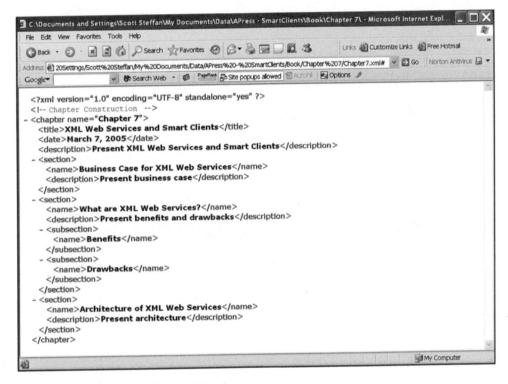

Figure 8-9. *Chapter 7.xml displayed in a browser*

Just displaying the code from Listing 8-1 in a browser is not enough, since it contains a custom element (tag) called `user-defined-xml-tag`. This custom element needs to be defined before it can be used. The element name in this file must match the tag name in `Book.xml`. This is accomplished by defining the custom element using { } and saving it in a file with a `.css` file extension. For this example, save the one line in Listing 8-2 as `format-tag.css` (`format-tag` is just the name we're using in the example; the only requirement is that the file name must have a `.css` extension).

Listing 8-2. *Element Declaration in format-tag.css*

```
USER-DEFINED-XML-TAG {display: block; font-size: 18pt; font-weight: bold;}
```

The last step is to modify Book.xml to inform it where the definition of the custom tag is. You do this with the following tag:

```
<?xml-stylesheet type="text/css" href="format-tag.css"?>
```

The type attribute is set to text or css (for a Cascading Style Sheet), and the href attribute indicates what the file is named.

Listing 8-3 shows the Book2.xml file with the additional line. The format-tag.css file needs to be located in the same directory as the Book2.xml file, or a path to its location needs to be specified.

Listing 8-3. *Book2.xml*

```
<?xml version='1.0' standalone='yes'?>
<?xml-stylesheet type="text/css" href="format-tag.css"?>
<USER-DEFINED-XML-TAG>
        Professional Service-Oriented Smart Clients
</USER-DEFINED-XML-TAG>
```

Assuming you typed everything correctly in Listings 8-2 and 8-3, your Book2.xml file should look like Figure 8-10 when you view it in your browser window. The text has been reformatted using the Cascading Style Sheet.

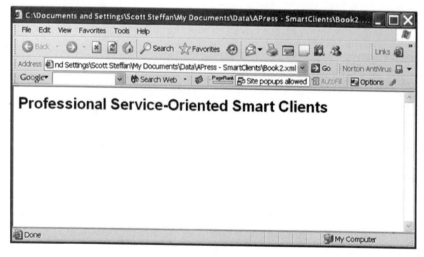

Figure 8-10. *Book2.xml after user tag is declared*

If you get an error, the screen shown in Figure 8-11 appears, indicating where the problem is. In the example, the *e* was left off the encoding attribute name.

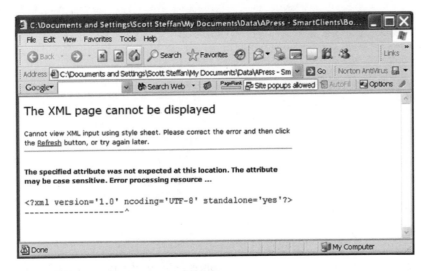

Figure 8-11. *An XML syntax error message*

Namespaces

The elements or tags used in the Book2.xml example might fail, since other XML authors might use tags with the same names, such as <title>, <description>, and <section>. *Namespaces* correct this situation by introducing a unique identifier for each element, removing the duplication of names among documents.[2]

First, you must declare the namespace. For our example, the declaration looks like this:

```
<chp:chapter xmlns:chp="http://professionalSOSC.com/chp"/>
```

After the keyword xmlns, the namespace prefix is chp, and it is defined as the name space identifier (URI): http://professionalSOSC.com/chp. Listing 8-4 shows the Chapter7.xml file with the added line.

Listing 8-4. *Updated Chapter7.xml*

```
<?xml version='1.0' encoding='UTF-8' standalone='yes'?>
<chp:chapter xmlns:chp='http://professionalSOSC.com/chp' name="Chapter 7">
<!--Chapter Construction-->
    <chp:title>XML Web Services and Smart Clients</chp:title>
    <chp:date>March 7, 2005</chp:date>
    <chp:description>Present XML Web Services and Smart Clients</chp:description>
    <chp:section>
        <chp:name>Business Case for XML Web Services</chp:name>
        <chp:description>Present business case</chp:description>
    </chp:section>
```

---

2. The W3C maintains the specification for XML namespaces, which you can find at http://www.w3.org/.

```
    <chp:section>
        <chp:name>What are XML Web Services?</chp:name>
        <chp:description>Present benefits and drawbacks</chp:description>
    <chp:subsection>
        <chp:name>Benefits</chp:name>
    </chp:subsection>
    <chp:subsection>
        <chp:name>Drawbacks</chp:name>
    </chp:subsection>
    </chp:section>
    <chp:section>
        <chp:name>Architecture of XML Web Services</chp:name>
        <chp:description>Present architecture</chp:description>
    </chp:section>
</chp:chapter>
```

The qualified name (also referred to as the *QName*) consists of a *local* part and a *namespace prefix* part. When you run Listing 8-4, the browser displays the screen shown in Figure 8-12.

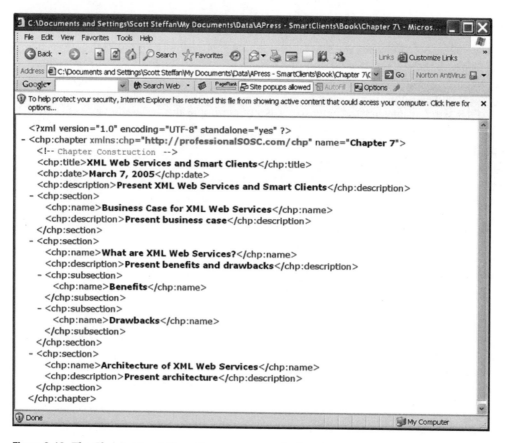

Figure 8-12. *The Chapter7.xml file with a namespace declaration*

If a prefix is not declared, the default namespace will be used. You can have only one default namespace. To declare the default namespace, use this form:

```
<chapter xmlns="http://professionalSOSC.com/chp"/>
. . .
</chapter>
```

Default namespaces are exactly like those with prefixes, but they make the document easier to read. You can declare more than one namespace per element, as in this example:

```
<chapter xmlns="http://professionalSOSC.com/chp"
xmlns:sec="http://documentSOSC.com/sec" />
<sec:section>This section</sec:section>
...
</chapter>
```

The option of declaring namespaces below the root is also allowed. For example, the preceding code could look like this:

```
<chapter xmlns="http://professionalSOSC.com/chp"/>
...
<sec:section xmlns:sec="http://documentSOSC.com/sec" >
This section</sec:section>
...
</chapter>
```

XML Schema Definitions (XSD)

One of the most important aspects of XML is its ability to define schemas. *Schemas* are data structures that increase the quality of service (QoS) of XML. Schemas allow for structure and type validation, which can be very helpful when data is being passed back and forth between the smart client and a web server that uses queries and data binding.

A schema is like a class in object-oriented programming, and a document instance is like an object. The schema defines a document instance, just as the class defines an object. They both serve to document vocabularies.

XML Schema Validation Tools

You need to validate the XML schema with the XML document. One way to validate the schema is to use Visual Studio .NET. Another way is to use a free XML schema validation tool, called Schematron Validator, which is the approach we will demonstrate here.

Before you can get the Schematron Validator tool to work, you need to download and install the MSXML 4.0 (Service Pack 2) Microsoft XML Core Services parser.[3] The file that will be downloaded from the Microsoft site (`http://www.microsoft.com/downloads/details.aspx?familyid=3144B72B-B4F2-46DA-B4B6-C5D7485F2B42&displaylang=en`), shown in Figure 8-13, is `msxml.msi`. Next, double-click the MSI to install it.

---

3. Earlier versions of MSXML (versions 2.0, 2.6, and 3.0) support only the reduced schema definition set.

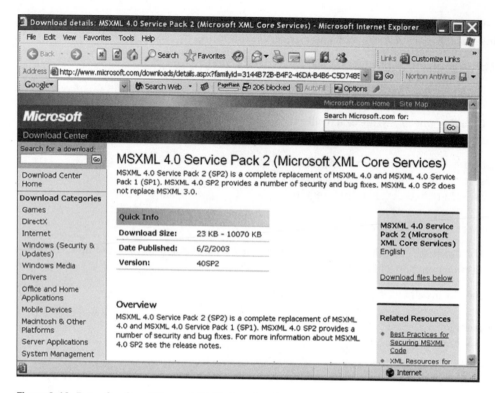

Figure 8-13. *Downloading Microsoft XML Core Services (MSXML 4.0)*

Now you can download the Schematron Validator tool from `http://www.topologi.com/`, as shown in Figure 8-14. After you've downloaded the package, install it.

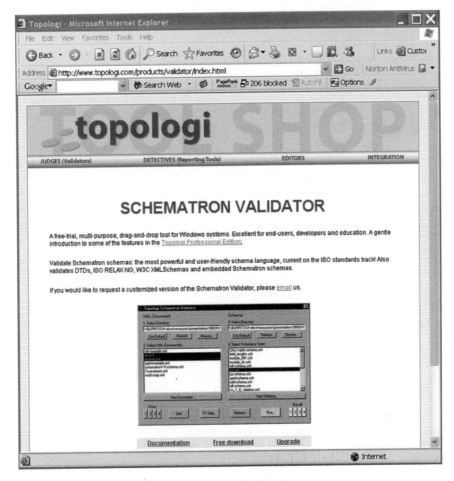

Figure 8-14. *Downloading Topologi Schematron Validator*

XML Schema Construction

To build an XML schema, insert the schema tag below the declaration line. This tag identifies the default namespace xmlns='http://www.w3.org/2001/XMLSchema' for the schema, a prefix namespace xmlns:target='http://www.ProfSOSC.com/name' to override the default if you need it, and a target namespace targetNamespace='http://www.ProfSOSC.com/name' to populate it. The prefix namespace is targetNamespace in this example.

This takes care of the top-level elements, but the local elements are not fully qualified. The final line in the schema tag allows elementFormDefault="qualified" local elements to be populated. A local element can be overridden by using form="unqualified" in the local element declaration. An element by itself is a *simple type*; an element containing other elements is a *complex type*. The element chapter contains the subelements title, section, and subsection, making it a complex type. Listing 8-5 shows the XML schema for Chapter7.xsd. (Schema files have an .xsd extension.)

Listing 8-5. *XML Schema for Chapter7.xsd*

```xml
<?xml version='1.0' encoding='UTF-8' standalone='yes'?>
<schema xmlns="http://www.w3.org/2001/XMLSchema"
      xmlns:target="http://www.ProfSOSC.com/name"
          targetNamespace="http://www.ProfSOSC.com/name"
          elementFormDefault="qualified" >
          <element name="chapter">
                <complexType>
                          <sequence>
                                  <element name="title" type="string" />
                                  <element name="section" type="string" />
                                  <element name="subsection" type="string" />
                          </sequence>
                </complexType>
          </element>
</schema>
```

We also need an XML schema instance document, as shown in Listing 8-6. The chapter element specifies a default namespace and that we are using the schema Chapter7.xsd and associating it with the prefix schema namespace xsi.

Listing 8-6. *XML Schema Instance Document for Chapter7.xml*

```xml
<?xml version='1.0' encoding='UTF-8' standalone='yes'?>
<chapter
    xmlns="http://ProfSOSC.com/chp"
    xmlns:xsi="http://www.w3.org/2001/XMLSchema-instance"
    xsi:schemaLocation="http://www.ProfSOSC.com/chp Chapter7.xsd"
    name="Chapter 7" >
                <title>XML Web Services and Smart Clients</title>
                <section> Architecture of XML Web Services</section>
                <subsection>Drawbacks</subsection>
</chapter>
```

Now that we have our XML schema and instance document, we can validate it using the schema validation tool. Open the Schematron Validator program, browse to the location of the files, and select the Chapter7.xml file in the left pane of the Schematron Validator window, as shown in Figure 8-15.

Click Run. If you typed everything correctly, you'll see the display shown in Figure 8-16.

This has been a brief introduction to XML. Now, we'll turn to another component of XML Web Services: the SOAP protocol.

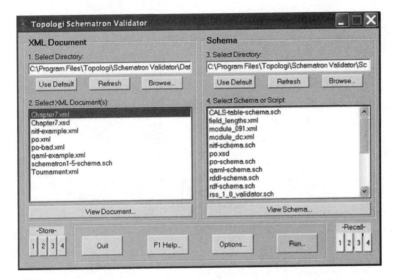

Figure 8-15. *Checking XML schema instance document for Chapter7.xml*

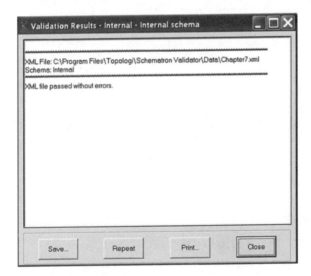

Figure 8-16. *Successful XML schema check*

SOAP

SOAP is message protocol that is used to send messages between the consumer and the XML Web Service. SOAP rides on top of a transfer protocol, such as HTTP, SMTP, or MQ Series. The transfer protocol resides on top of TCP/IP. Figure 8-17 shows this structure, along with the Open System Interconnection (OSI) Reference Model (on the right side of the figure), indicating where the network layer is functionally.

■Note Seven layers make up the OSI Reference Model, the top three layers—Session, Presentation, and Application—are sometimes referred to as the Application layer. The lower four layers are typically where the network administration personnel concentrate and what application developers call *connectivity*. For more information about the OSI Reference Model, visit the Institute of Electrical and Electronic Engineers (IEEE) web site at http://www.ieee.org, and search using the keywords *OSI* and *802* committee (the committee that created the standard).

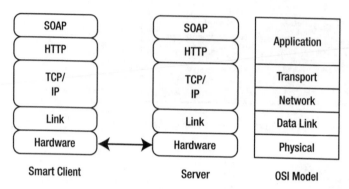

Figure 8-17. *Where the SOAP protocol resides*

SOAP Messages

SOAP is based on XML standards that allow Remote Procedure Calls (RPCs) to be exchanged. An RPC is a request/response message-transmission style, as illustrated in Figure 8-18. The smart client can initiate a request and the XML Web Services can respond, or vice versa.

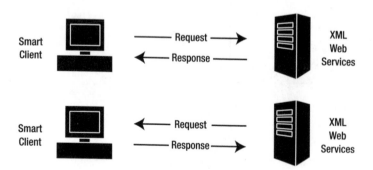

Figure 8-18. *Request/response messaging*

The SOAP request or response message has a general format, as shown in Figure 8-19. The top-level element of a SOAP message is called the *envelope*. The information contained within the envelope is called the *payload*. The payload consists of a header and a body. The *header* is optional and contains information about how the message is to be processed, including routing, security, and transaction information. The *body* is required and contains the information that the smart client and XML Web Services require to perform the discovery, description, binding, and communication.

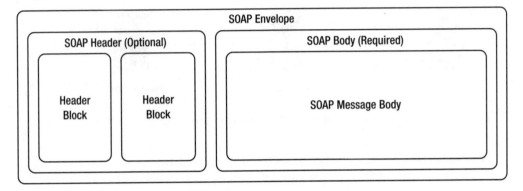

Figure 8-19. *SOAP message header and body*

A typical SOAP message resembles Listing 8-7.

Listing 8-7. *A Typical SOAP Message*

```
<env:Envelope xmlns:env="http://www.w3.org/2003/05/soap-envelope">
  <env:Header>
    <hdr:aHeaderElement xmlns:hdr="http://www.ProfSOSC.com/msg"
            env:mustUnderstand="true"
            env:relay="true"
            env:role="http://www.w3.org/2003/05/soap-envelope/role/next">
    </hdr:aHeaderElement>
  </env:Header>
  <env:Body encodingStyle="http://www.w3.org/2003/05/soap-encoding">
    <ws:name xmlns:ws="http://www.ProfSOSC.com/msg">
            <ws:title>ProfessionalSOSC</ws:title>
    </ws:name>
  </env:Body>
</env:Envelope>
```

You can see the basic components of a SOAP message in Listing 8-7. The Envelope element typically consists of the namespace for the envelope. The Header element in this example contains the namespace for the header and three attributes:

- The mustUnderstand attribute, when set to true, requires the recipient of the message, specifically the header, to be able to process the message. Failure of the recipient to process the message results in a failure message being sent back to the sender to indicate what could not be processed, as described in the next section.

- The `relay` attribute, when set to `true`, indicates to an intermediary that it can process the message or leave it alone. An intermediary is a computer between the sender and its final destination, as shown in Figure 8-20. Typically, the default value for the `relay` attribute is `false`.

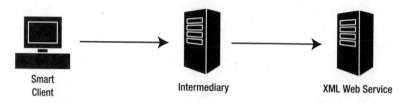

Figure 8-20. *SOAP message header working with intermediary*

- The `role` attribute supports having the header processed with the next computer (intermediary) or final destination, or turns off the header for processing, as follows:

```
role="http://www.w3.org/2003/05/soap-envelope/role/next"
role="http://www.w3.org/2003/05/soap-envelope/role/ultimateReceiver"
role="http://www.w3.org/2003/05/soap-envelope/role/none"
```

The `Body` element uses the `encoding` attribute, which establishes the type of encoding style that the body is going to use. To ensure interoperability, use the standard style:

```
<env:Body encodingStyle="http://www.w3.org/2003/05/soap-encoding">
```

SOAP Faults

This basic message assumes everything will work okay, but what happens if there is an error? Let's assume the message shown in Listing 8-8 was sent to an XML Web Service.

Listing 8-8. *A SOAP Message with a Problem*

```
<?xml version="1.0" encoding="UTF-8" standalone="yes"?>
<env:Envelope xmlns:env="http://www.w3.org/2003/05/soap-envelope">
  <env:Header>
    <hdr:aHeaderElement xmlns:hdr="http://www.ProfSOSC.com/msg"
        env:mustUnderstand="true"
        env:role="http://www.w3.org/2003/05/soap-envelope/role/ultimateReceiver"
      env:encodingStyle="http://www.w3.org/2003/05/soap-encoding">
    </hdr:aHeaderElement>
  </env:Header>
  <env:Body xmlns:book="http//www.ProfSOSC.com">
    <book:title>Smart Client and XML Web Services</book:title>
  </env:Body>
</env:Envelope>
```

The failure message returned to the smart client could resemble Listing 8-9.

Listing 8-9. *A SOAP Failure Message*

```
<?xml version="1.0" encoding="UTF-8" standalone="yes"?>
<env:Envelope xmlns:env="http://www.w3.org/2003/05/soap-envelope">
  <env:Body>
    <env:Fault>
      <env:Code>
              <env:Value>env:Receiver</env:Value>
      </env:Code>
      <env:Reason>
          <env:Text xml:lang="eng">
                     Title unavailable
          </env:Text>
      </env:Reason>
    </env:Fault>
  </env:Body>
</env:Envelope>
```

Error handling is accomplished with the Fault element. This element can assist the sending application in the determination of the error. The Fault element has two required subelements and three optional subelements:

- Code: A required top-level element. It has two lower-level elements: Value (required) specifies the fault code, and Subcode (optional) specifies the fault response back to the application. Several fault codes are automatically defined for the Value element:

    - VersionMismatch means that the namespace for the envelope element was not recognized.

    - MustUnderstand means that the mustUnderstand attribute was set to true in the original message and the receiver could not process it.

    - Sender means that the problem is with the sender.

    - Receiver means that the problem was with the receiver.

    - DataEncodingUnknown means that there was a message-encoding error.

- Reason: A required element that contains a natural language message about the fault.

- Node: An optional element that contains the URI of where the failure occurred.

- Role: An optional element that contains a URI of what failed.

- Detail: An optional message that presents the details of what failed in the application processing of the message.

Web Services Definition Language (WSDL)

WSDL is used to describe the XML Web Services.[4] The WSDL document is the backbone of XML Web Services. It describes the interface, its bindings, and the location of the XML Web Services. The WSDL document is a contract between the smart client and the XML Web Service.

A WSDL document can bind to SOAP, or it can use the HTTP and SMTP protocols. The most common practice is to use SOAP, because SOAP currently offers more functionality than the other protocols.

The document is developed in XML and has a specified format. All WSDL documents begin with the root element and the `definitions` element. The `definitions` element declares the namespaces that will be used within the document, as follows:

```
<?xml version="1.0" encoding="utf-8"?>
<definitions xmlns:http="http://schemas.xmlsoap.org/wsdl/http/"
xmlns:soap=http://schemas.xmlsoap.org/wsdl/soap/
xmlns:s="http://www.w3.org/2001/XMLSchema"
xmlns:s0="http://tempuri.org/"
xmlns:soapenc="http://schemas.xmlsoap.org/soap/encoding/"
xmlns:tm="http://microsoft.com/wsdl/mime/textMatching/"
xmlns:mime="http://schemas.xmlsoap.org/wsdl/mime/"
                       targetNamespace="http://tempuri.org/"
xmlns="http://schemas.xmlsoap.org/wsdl/">
```

The remainder of the WSDL document is divided into two sections, which contain seven required elements. The top section contains the abstract definition, and the bottom section is called the concrete section. The separation is made because separate concrete sections can be applied to the abstraction section.

The abstraction section documents the data types, the request/response messages formats, and the functionality the XML Web Service. It contains the following four elements:

- `<types>`: Declares the data types that will be used by the request and response messages. The `type` element is used with both simple and complex types.

- `<message>`: Declares the request, response, or fault messages. The `message` element is usually used with SOAP.

- `<operation>`: Declares the message associated with the operation.

- `<portType>`: Declares the number of operations that the XML Web Service supports.

The concrete section describes how to physically connect to the XML Web Service. It contains the following three elements:

- `<binding>`: Supports a particular `portType` and identifies the address and the protocol that will be used to communicate with the XML Web Service.

- `<port>`: Identifies the URI where the XML Web Service is located.

- `<service>`: Declares the `port` elements.

---

4. The current version of the WSDL specification is version 1.1.

The WSDL document generated by Visual Studio .NET is shown in Listing 8-10.

Listing 8-10. *WSDL Document Generated by Visual Studio .NET*

```
<?xml version="1.0" encoding="utf-8"?>
<definitions xmlns:http="http://schemas.xmlsoap.org/wsdl/http/"
xmlns:soap=http://schemas.xmlsoap.org/wsdl/soap/
xmlns:s="http://www.w3.org/2001/XMLSchema"
xmlns:s0="http://tempuri.org/"
xmlns:soapenc="http://schemas.xmlsoap.org/soap/encoding/"
xmlns:tm=http://microsoft.com/wsdl/mime/textMatching/
xmlns:mime="http://schemas.xmlsoap.org/wsdl/mime/"
targetNamespace="http://tempuri.org/" xmlns="http://schemas.xmlsoap.org/wsdl/">
  <types>
    <s:schema elementFormDefault="qualified" targetNamespace="http://tempuri.org/">
      <s:element name="HelloWorld">
        <s:complexType />
      </s:element>
      <s:element name="HelloWorldResponse">
        <s:complexType>
          <s:sequence>
            <s:element minOccurs="0" maxOccurs="1"
                                    name="HelloWorldResult" type="s:string" />
          </s:sequence>
        </s:complexType>
      </s:element>
    </s:schema>
  </types>
  <message name="HelloWorldSoapIn">
    <part name="parameters" element="s0:HelloWorld" />
  </message>
  <message name="HelloWorldSoapOut">
    <part name="parameters" element="s0:HelloWorldResponse" />
  </message>
  <portType name="Service1Soap">
    <operation name="HelloWorld">
      <input message="s0:HelloWorldSoapIn" />
      <output message="s0:HelloWorldSoapOut" />
    </operation>
  </portType>
  <binding name="Service1Soap" type="s0:Service1Soap">
    <soap:binding
                transport="http://schemas.xmlsoap.org/soap/http" style="document" />
    <operation name="HelloWorld">
      <soap:operation
                   soapAction="http://tempuri.org/HelloWorld" style="document" />
```

```
  <input>
    <soap:body use="literal" />
  </input>
  <output>
    <soap:body use="literal" />
  </output>
  </operation>
 </binding>
 <service name="Service1">
   <port name="Service1Soap" binding="s0:Service1Soap">
     <soap:address location="http://localhost/WebService2/Service1.asmx" />
   </port>
 </service>
</definitions>
```

Universal Discovery, Description and Integration (UDDI)

As explained earlier in this chapter, you can discover XML Web Services by communicating with a UDDI registry. UDDI registries can be public or private, depending on the business purpose. A public registry allows everyone to discover and access the web services. A private registry may be set up for a particular corporation's intranet or extranet solutions. Although most XML Web Services use UDDI for discovery, a DISCO file is another mechanism available to Visual Studio .NET developers. DISCO files are easier to use than UDDI, but they have more limitations. Here, we'll look at discovery with UDDI. The next section covers using DISCO files.

■**Note** Although many companies may not have jumped on the bandwagon to use public UDDI registries just yet, this situation may still change. As the acceptance of XML Web Services continues to increase and considering the backing from prominent industry IT leaders, its mainstream adoption still may be realized. However, private UDDI corporate registries that deal with business alliances are more likely to succeed at first, since they could alleviate some of the fears involving security issues.

UDDI Business Registry (UBR)

A group of corporations has amalgamated public registries into a single UDDI Business Registry (UBR). Four UBR nodes exist, operated by Microsoft, IBM, SAP, and NTT Communications.

All nodes are identical copies of each other. Additional UBR nodes are added only to assist with performance and access, since a change in one UBR is propagated to all others.

To allow others to discover the XML Web Services, you must comply with the public or corporate requirements of the registry. The Microsoft public registry (UBR) is located at http://uddi.microsoft.com,[5] as shown in Figure 8-21. This facility allows businesses to discover other businesses, as well as have their business be discovered. The UBR makes available a set of sophisticated APIs that define how information will be exchanged, updated, and used in a standardized format with XML Web Services.

---

5. Microsoft has a corresponding test site located at http://test.uddi.microsoft.com/.

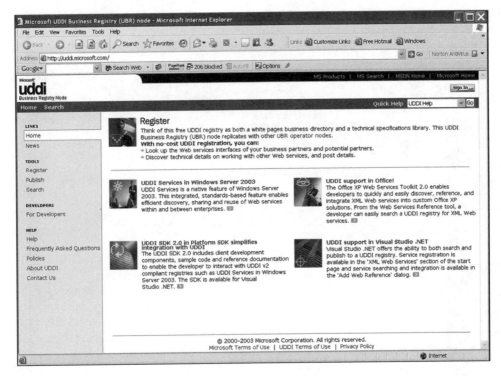

Figure 8-21. *Microsoft public UDDI registry*

UDDI Specification Version 3

The UDDI specifications are managed and developed in a collective open forum known as OASIS, which stands for Organization for the Advancement of Structured Information Standards. OASIS is a consortium of businesses, which includes Microsoft, IBM, Sun Microsystems, and more than 70 other corporations. UDDI specifications have undergone three versions. Its final version 3.0.2 was ratified in February 2005 by OASIS. You can find information about the UDDI specifications at http://www.uddi.org/, as shown in Figure 8-22.

The UDDI specification version 3.0.2 is presented in the following documents:

- The UDDI Version 3.0 Features List document lists the new features not previously available in versions 1 and 2. The standards community recommends reading this document first, before delving into the standard itself.

- The UDDI Version 3.0.2 document contains the OASIS standard that was ratified.

- The UDDI Version 3.0.2 XML Schema document presents the formal XML data structures used with UDDI version 3. Those familiar with the standards for the XML schemas and WSDL service interface descriptions will be interested in this and the next document.

- The UDDI Version 3.0.2 WSDL Service Interface Descriptions document contains WSDL definitions used with UDDI version 3.

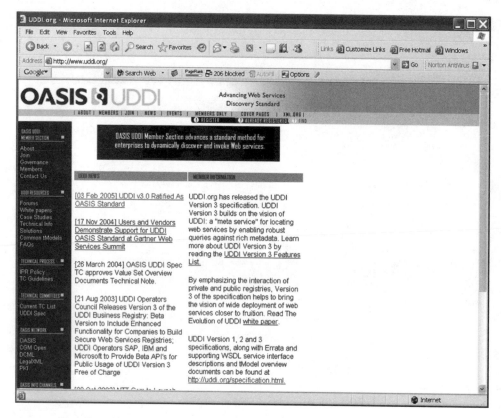

Figure 8-22. *OASIS web site*

UDDI Data Types

The UDDI information model consists of instances of entities. UDDI uses six XML data schemas to define persistent entities for use within this model. Each entity has a purpose and relationship to support the registry and its operations, as follows:

businessEntity: This data type provides information in multiple real-life languages about the corporation or business that is going to provide the XML Web Service. For example, it may include the name, contacts, and descriptions. The businessEntity is a top-level data structure in the UDDI information model.

businessService: This data type provides information such as the name, description, and classification of the collection of XML Web Services that the business entity is offering. The businessService entity is contained within the businessEntity.

bindingTemplate: This data type provides technical information such as the XML Web Service access point or the indirection of how to get to it, as well as information about how to use a particular XML Web Service. The bindingTemplate entity is contained within a businessService entity.

tModel: Short for "technical model," this data type represents the unique "contract" of the XML Web Service's requirements, transport, protocol, and namespace of the particular functionality being offered. The tModel entity is used by the bindingTemplate. A single tModel can be used by multiple bindingTemplate entities, so it is a reusable entity. The technical model can be based on WSDL, XSD, and other documents that specify and make the contract distinct. The tModel entity, however, does not actually contain the documents, since they are not stored within the UDDI registry. Instead, it contains references or addresses to those documents. How tModel entities represent the data and metadata in the information model is important to UDDI.

publisherAssertion: This data type describes a relationship between one businessEntity and another businessEntity. The publisherAssertion entity is associated with the businessEntity data type.

subscription: This data type keeps track of changes to the other entities.

UDDI API

The UDDI API contains two major parts: the inquiry API and the publish API. These two APIs are used within a WSDL document to discover the XML Web Services.

The inquiry API has three patterns associated with it:

- The browse pattern allows the examination of data, which is typically in a hierarchical format.

- The drill-down pattern gives the system the capability to transverse a hierarchical tree to get to the particular piece of information.

- The invocation pattern prepares the XML Web Service for use with the consumer requesting it by invoking the appropriate prerequisite components.

The publisher API is used to publish and update information contained in the UDDI registry. Table 8-1 lists the functions in the UDDI API.

Table 8-1. *UDDI API Functions*

Inquiry API Functions	Publisher API Functions
find_binding	add_publisherAssertions
find_business	delete_binding
find_relatedBusinesses	delete_business
find_service	delete_publisherAssertions
find_tModel	delete_service
get_bindingDetail	delete_tModel
get_businessDetail	discard_authToken
get_businessDetailExt	get_assertionStatusReport
get_serviceDetail	get_authToken
	get_publisherAssertions
	get_registerInfo

Continued

Table 8-1. *Continued*

Inquiry API Functions	Publisher API Functions
	save_binding
	save_business
	save_service
	save_tModel
	set_publisherAssertions

DISCO Files

Visual Studio .NET developers have an alternative XML Web Service discovery technology available. This technology uses a DISCO (short for discovery) file, which has a .disco extension.

Using UDDI, you can discover XML Web Services without prior knowledge of them. DISCO differs from UDDI in that you must know that the XML Web Service exists. Initially, this may seem like a major drawback, but many business alliances are based on known exchanges of data. The fact that you may need to have prior knowledge of XML Web Services may not be a critical issue, even though it does limit the intelligence and agility of the XML Web Service. One distinct advantage of using DISCO files is that the corporation does not need to maintain a central registry.

DISCO files are XML documents that use a proprietary Microsoft format and contain URL references to WSDL documents or URL references to other DISCO files. As an XML document, a DISCO file can be created using a standard text editor, but the easiest way to create one is to let ASP.NET do it for you. ASP.NET will automatically create the DISCO file for an XML Web Service when the developer appends ?DISCO to the URL of the xmlwebservice.asmx file. Listing 8-11 shows an example of a DISCO file.

Listing 8-11. *A DISCO File*

```
<?xml version="1.0" encoding="utf-8"?>
<discovery xmlns:xsd=http://www.w3.org/2001/XMLSchema
                  xmlns:xsi="http://www.w3.org/2001/XMLSchema-instance"
                  xmlns="http://schemas.xmlsoap.org/disco/">
<contractRef ref=http://localhost/WebService2/Service1.asmx?wsdl
                  docRef="http://localhost/WebService2/Service1.asmx"
                  xmlns="http://schemas.xmlsoap.org/disco/scl/" />
<soap address=http://localhost/WebService2/Service1.asmx
          xmlns:q1="http://tempuri.org/" binding="q1:Service1Soap"
          xmlns="http://schemas.xmlsoap.org/disco/soap/" />
</discovery>
```

Visual Studio .NET processes DISCO files through the Add Web Reference command, as shown in Figure 8-23. This command will automatically look at the .disco file and search through its references for other .disco files.

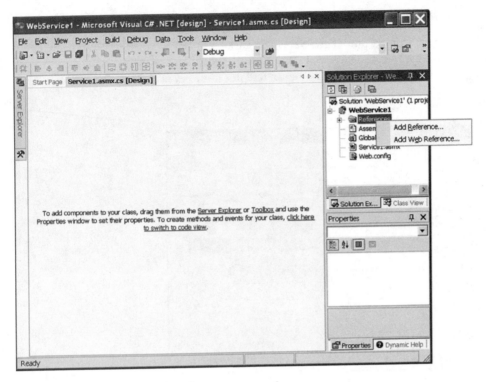

Figure 8-23. *Using the Add Web Reference command*

Note ASP.NET has an automatic discovery feature that will discover XML Web Services. Microsoft does not recommend using this feature for production systems, because it can compromise what you want to publish publicly. However, this feature can assist developers in discovering all available XML Web Services within a corporation. This is accomplished by creating .vsdisco files on the IIS server. The .vsdisco file searches all folders and subfolders for XML Web Service documents and generates a DISCO file that contains all the references to those documents.

XML Web Service Development

Now that we have discussed the fundamentals of what make up a XML Web Service, let's develop a simple one with Visual Studio .NET. You'll see how many of the complexities have been automated in this IDE. For this example, we assume that you have installed IIS and Microsoft FrontPage Extension and Visual Studio .NET 2003 or 2005.

Launch Visual Studio .NET and follow these steps:

1. Start a new project, and then select to create an ASP.NET Web Service,[6] as shown in Figure 8-24. Note the location `http://localhost/WebService2/`. This is the directory where the files will be loaded. You can find this directory at `C:\Inetpub\wwwroot\WebService2\`.

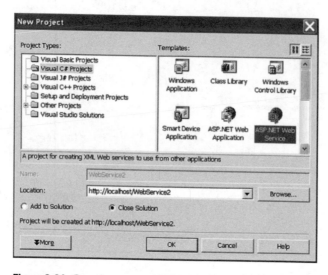

Figure 8-24. *Creating a new ASP.NET Web Service project in Visual Studio .NET*

2. Visual Studio .NET automatically generates the `AssemblyInfo.cs`, `Global.asax`, `Web.Config`, and `Service1.asmx` files. We're interested in the `Service1.asmx` file, with which the web service is associated. Right-click `Service1.asmx` and select View Source. Even though the file has a quantity of information, only the end of it is of interest to us at this time.

```
// WEB SERVICE EXAMPLE
// The HelloWorld() example service returns the string Hello World
// To build, uncomment the following lines then save and build the project
// To test this web service, press F5

//[WebMethod]
//public string HelloWorld()
//{
//        return "Hello World";
//}
}
}
```

---

6. Even though you're developing an XML Web Service, you select ASP.NET Web Service in Visual Studio .NET, because ASP.NET actually creates it.

3. Uncomment out the following lines:

```
// WEB SERVICE EXAMPLE
// The HelloWorld() example service returns the string Hello World
// To build, uncomment the following lines then save and build the project
// To test this web service, press F5

[WebMethod]
public string HelloWorld()
{
        return "Hello World";
}
}
}
```

4. Build the solution by selecting Build ➤ Build Solution.

5. After the build, press F5. You'll see the screen shown in Figure 8-25.

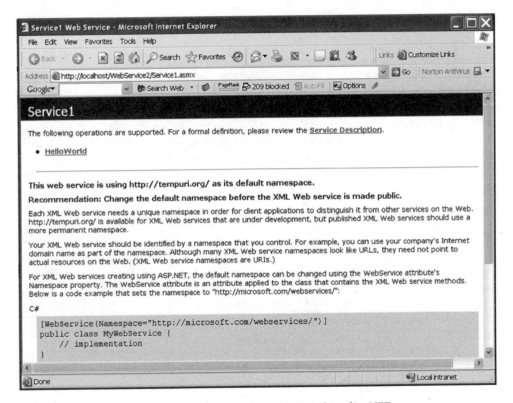

Figure 8-25. *Service1.asmx and its namespace built by Visual Studio .NET*

6. Select the HelloWorld link, and you'll see the screen shown in Figure 8-26.

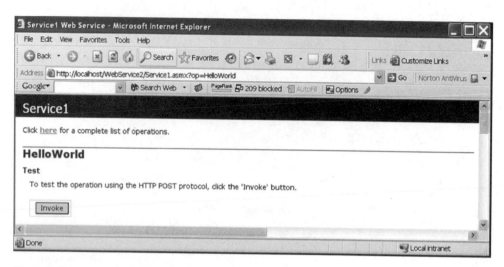

Figure 8-26. *Testing the helloworld web service*

Your XML Web Service is complete. Visual Studio .NET makes it that easy.

A closer look at the web service reveals some of the complexities generated automatically. Click the back button in your browser to return to the screen shown in Figure 8-25. Now let's look below the HelloWorld link. The default namespace is defined as `http://tempuri.org`.

You'll need to change this namespace to work in a public setting. Click the back button in your browser and select the Service Description link on the page. The WSDL file for this XML Web Service is automatically generated, as shown in Figure 8-27. Note the `http://localhost/WebService2/Service1.asmx?WSDL` in the URL. The `?WSDL` generates the WSDL file.

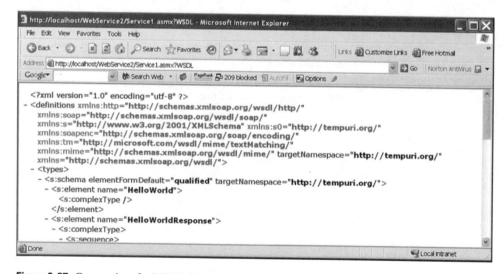

Figure 8-27. *Generating the WSDL document*

The complete WSDL file is shown in Listing 8-12.

Listing 8-12. *The WSDL File for the Sample Web Service*

```
<?xml version="1.0" encoding="utf-8"?>
<definitions xmlns:http=http://schemas.xmlsoap.org/wsdl/http/
xmlns:soap="http://schemas.xmlsoap.org/wsdl/soap/"
xmlns:s="http://www.w3.org/2001/XMLSchema" xmlns:s0="http://tempuri.org/"
xmlns:soapenc=http://schemas.xmlsoap.org/soap/encoding/
xmlns:tm="http://microsoft.com/wsdl/mime/textMatching/"
xmlns:mime="http://schemas.xmlsoap.org/wsdl/mime/"
targetNamespace="http://tempuri.org/" xmlns="http://schemas.xmlsoap.org/wsdl/">
  <types>
    <s:schema elementFormDefault="qualified" targetNamespace="http://tempuri.org/">
      <s:element name="HelloWorld">
        <s:complexType />
      </s:element>
      <s:element name="HelloWorldResponse">
        <s:complexType>
          <s:sequence>
            <s:element minOccurs="0" maxOccurs="1"
                            name="HelloWorldResult" type="s:string" />
          </s:sequence>
        </s:complexType>
      </s:element>
    </s:schema>
  </types>
  <message name="HelloWorldSoapIn">
    <part name="parameters" element="s0:HelloWorld" />
  </message>
  <message name="HelloWorldSoapOut">
    <part name="parameters" element="s0:HelloWorldResponse" />
  </message>
  <portType name="Service1Soap">
    <operation name="HelloWorld">
      <input message="s0:HelloWorldSoapIn" />
      <output message="s0:HelloWorldSoapOut" />
    </operation>
  </portType>
  <binding name="Service1Soap" type="s0:Service1Soap">
    <soap:binding transport="http://schemas.xmlsoap.org/soap/http"
                          style="document" />
    <operation name="HelloWorld">
      <soap:operation soapAction="http://tempuri.org/HelloWorld"
                                          style="document" />
      <input>
        <soap:body use="literal" />
      </input>
```

```
    <output>
      <soap:body use="literal" />
    </output>
  </operation>
</binding>
<service name="Service1">
  <port name="Service1Soap" binding="s0:Service1Soap">
    <soap:address location="http://localhost/WebService2/Service1.asmx" />
  </port>
</service>
</definitions>
```

Now, click the back button in your browser again, and append ?DISCO at the end of the URL in the browser. The DISCO file has been automatically generated, as shown in Figure 8-28.

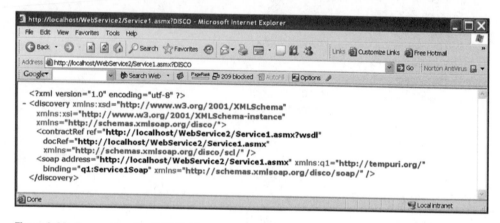

Figure 8-28. *Generating the DISCO file*

The contents of the DISCO file are shown in Listing 8-13.

Listing 8-13. *The DISCO File for the Sample Web Service*

```
<?xml version="1.0" encoding="utf-8"?>
<discovery xmlns:xsd=http://www.w3.org/2001/XMLSchema
 xmlns:xsi=http://www.w3.org/2001/XMLSchema-instance
xmlns="http://schemas.xmlsoap.org/disco/">
<contractRef ref="http://localhost/WebService2/Service1.asmx?wsdl"
        docRef="http://localhost/WebService2/Service1.asmx"
        xmlns="http://schemas.xmlsoap.org/disco/scl/" />
<soap address=http://localhost/WebService2/Service1.asmx
        xmlns:q1="http://tempuri.org/" binding="q1:Service1Soap"
        xmlns="http://schemas.xmlsoap.org/disco/soap/" />
</discovery>
```

Summary

This chapter provided an overview of XML Web Services. We began with a review of two business cases that demonstrated how using XML Web Services and smart clients can lower future development costs and give applications a broader reach. Next, we summarized the benefits and drawbacks to using an associated technology with XML Web Services. Then we reviewed each of the technologies used by XML Web Services: XML, SOAP, WSDL, UDDI, and DISCO. Finally, we went through the steps to develop an XML Web Service with Visual Studio .NET 2003 or 2005.

In the next chapter, we will explain how integrating these elements into a service-oriented architecture will enhance your smart client application.

CHAPTER 9

■ ■ ■

Service-Oriented Architecture

Component architectures, based on aggregating functions into small entities called components, have been around for quite some time. The bulk of thick and thin clients were developed using component architectures. Unfortunately, components are very fine-grained. Although they present an opportunity for reuse, this is a small advantage typically seen by the developer or designer on a single solution. Focusing on services, rather than components, offers a greater opportunity for the enterprise.

Corporations have always made an effort to align their computer systems with their real-world business processes or services, but technological systems of the past tightly coupled the user interface and business logic of a single system. For example, business functionality cannot be shared between user interfaces or systems except for simple cut-and-paste operations.

A service-oriented architecture (SOA) supports the enterprise with greater interoperability and integration, but more important, it extends the enterprise beyond the corporate walls. Using industry-wide standards, mechanisms, and techniques, the corporation is no longer forced to build translators and adapters to communicate with outside partners, allies, and customers. A customer using a smart client can explore, communicate, and exchange information with corporations who have developed an SOA.

This chapter focuses on the SOA. We will start with the crucial step of service identification, and then talk about SOA communications. Finally, we will explore the steps in developing an SOA.

Service Identification

Being service-oriented requires a business to understand its real-world services. Each business will have different services, and developing an architecture to support them can be a complex task.

Business Modeling and Requirements Analysis

Identifying unique and separate real-world services is essential to SOA development. You can accomplish this through a business modeling and requirements analysis. The tool for this analysis is the Rational Unified Process (RUP), a formal methodology that identifies the activities, documents, deliverables, and roles. After identifying the services, the next step is to detail each interface and the processing that must be accomplished to perform its business objective.

■**Note** Many books and other sources cover RUP in detail. If you're not familiar with RUP techniques, a starting place is http://www-306.ibm.com/software/awdtools/rup/. Also, a good book to start with is *The Rational Unified Process, An Introduction, Third Edition*, by Philippe Kruchten (Addison-Wesley, 2004).

As an example, suppose that a small company that ships out-of-print movies to resellers decides it wants to develop an SOA. Internally, the company has multiple real-world departments. The business has some easily recognizable services, as illustrated in Figure 9-1.

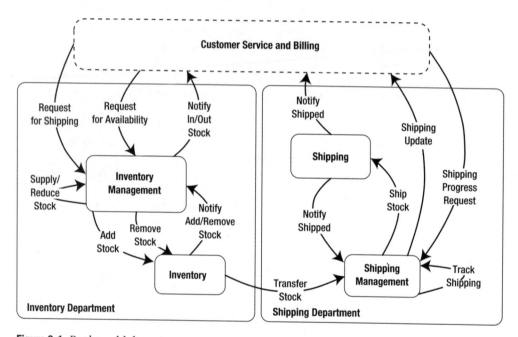

Figure 9-1. *Real-world departments*

The front office manages customer service and billing, and the back office manages the inventory and shipping. The inventory department allows two requests from customer service: one for availability and the other for shipping. If the inventory department receives an availability request, it reviews the inventory and tells the customer service department whether this item is in or out of stock. As availability requests are processed by the inventory department, decisions are made to balance stock to keep marketable material in-house. If the customer requests shipping, a stock-removal request is made, and the stock will be removed from inventory and transferred to the shipping department. Periodically, add-stock requests are processed to resupply or supply selected titles. The inventory department notifies inventory management to confirm any additions or deletions to inventory.

The shipping department is notified about the transfer of stock, and shipping management arranges for the shipment. When the item is ready to be shipped, shipping management requests that the stock be shipped. After that, the shipping department notifies the customer service department and shipping management that the stock item has been shipped. Shipping management then tracks the shipment. The customer service department may require a shipping-progress request, and shipping management will supply an update on the shipping progress.

Each department in this example has three isolated older systems performing the required functionality, as shown in Figure 9-2. The goal is to interoperate the systems and develop an SOA.

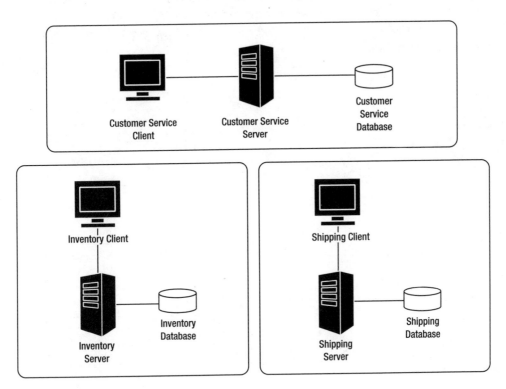

Figure 9-2. *Isolated system architecture*

Setting up an SOA would be easy if the company had no IT systems, but this is rarely the case in the real world. With three isolated systems, we can only hope that duplication of data and business logic is minimized. The company could have combined one or more of these into a single system, which would have minimized the duplication and potentially tightly coupled the business logic and data. However, a tighter coupling of business logic and data can also hinder service orientation, because internal software structures may need to be torn apart to determine which services are being supported. Service orientation offers a loosely coupled set of services while minimizing duplicity. These issues are common in the corporate landscape today. When you're rearchitecting a group of systems, each system should be handled one at a time, instead of trying to do all of them at once.

In analyzing the functionality of the shipping department, we see that its primary objective is to manage shipping and ship the stock. Shipment management includes arranging shipping, shipping the items, and tracking the progress of shipping. The inventory department balances the inventory and manages the request for shipping and availability. Preparing a UML sequence diagram presents the interfaces for each department clearly, as shown in Figure 9-3.

Note The Unified Modeling Language (UML) is used for modeling applications. If you're new to UML, you can start at the Object Management Group's (OMG's) UML Resource page, at http://www.uml.org/. Some good books on UML include *Enterprise Development with Visual Studio .NET, UML, and MSF*, by John Erik Hansen and Carsten Thomsen (Apress, 2004); *UML Applied: A .NET Perspective*, by Martin L.Shoemaker (Apress, 2004); and *Fast Track UML 2.0*, by Kendall Scott (Apress, 2004).

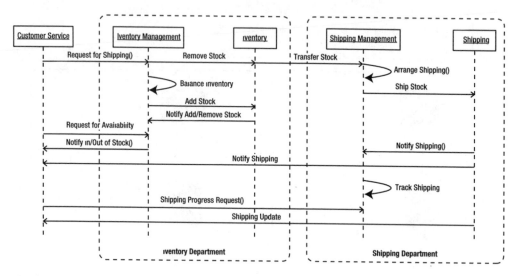

Figure 9-3. *UML sequence diagram*

The shipping department has two primary functions: one to arrange shipping and the other to track it. It uses two inbound messages (transfer stock and shipping progress request) and two outbound messages (notify shipping and shipping update). The inventory management department has one primary function: balancing inventory. It has two inbound messages (request for shipping and request for availability) and two outbound messages (notify in/out of stock and transfer stock). In the real world, these messages are paper documents that are generated by the individual departments using their respective systems.

Data Analysis

As noted in the previous section, a data analysis of heterogeneous systems that have been isolated typically reveals duplication of data and business logic, since core or critical data is required by each system to run independently. Duplication is not regulated in isolated systems, because each application responds to different business requests and matures along different timelines.

Data duplication decreases efficiency and productivity within the corporation. For example, a single change that impacts a critical set of data used by all three systems in our example (inventory, shipping, and customer service) will require the corporation to pay additional costs to modify each system. The need to consolidate information forces businesses to integrate systems. Once the systems are integrated with each other, this abuse is more evident from the lack of synchronization between the data. Initial corrections introduce master/slave relationships called "systems of record" to try to curtail misuse. However, denormalization is still rampant, due to the performance issues of joining multiple tables or databases across systems, which can slow down a particular system. Convenience of development and testing is another contributing factor in the denormalization of data, because it's easier to test and develop a local system when it has the data.

If the duplication of data is minimal, as illustrated in Figure 9-4, the overlap of common data is manageable. But it may turn out that data duplication more closely resembles Figure 9-5. The level of overlap depends on the systems and how they are supporting their current business solutions; either of these two situations could exist.

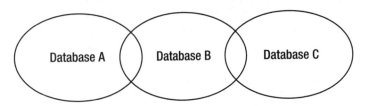

Figure 9-4. *Manageable data duplication*

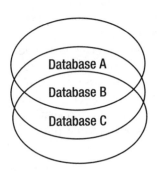

Figure 9-5. *Unmanageable data duplication*

Duplication of the magnitude shown in Figure 9-5 can force all three systems to move at the pace of the slowest system's release schedule, which results in the delay of critical enhancements and upgrades for the other two systems. An old naval statement reminds us that "the convoy moves at the speed of the slowest ship." Most enterprises support many more than three systems, and data duplicity across systems can cripple the overall enterprise.

The timeliness of the data is also a concern for the enterprise, since one system usually precedes the others in updating information that has been duplicated across systems. Once the systems are coupled, the lack of timely data updates can lead to incorrect business decisions, since information could be stale in one or more systems. Ideal systems hold state in the database, but a single enterprise system must often place state closer to the user to enhance performance and responsiveness. Caching state to increase performance can force a system to exceed business or technical latency thresholds in other partnered or integrated systems.

An SOA developed with XML Web Services adds a critical abstraction layer that allows duplicity to be removed from databases, but supports the aggregation of business logic if required by the XML Web Services. This means that a single XML Web Service can be supported by multiple normalized databases and be developed in denormalized fashion, if necessary, to support the service. Additionally, an XML Web Service can support data caching to give it the necessary performance boost and provide a timely data solution. As an enabler of an SOA, XML Web Services can also exchange information to minimize duplicity.

SOA Communications

Service orientation is not just simply aligning systems directly with real-world business services. Business applications that are distributed on multiple platforms by their nature are heterogeneous; they supply different functionality to different customers who have different needs. Point-to-point communications will not work for enterprise interoperability. Message-oriented middleware (MOM) provides the solution.

The Problem with Point-to-Point Interoperability

To see why point-to-point communications don't work, let's continue with our example of the out-of-print movie supplier with three departments. Assume that three users in the company are using three heterogeneous systems that were built at various times, and they would now like to share data and business logic between these systems. User A is in the customer service department, User B is in the inventory department, and User C is in the shipping department.

The problem is that each system will require an individual connectivity solution to allow interoperability between multiple dissimilar environments. This could potentially require a total of three new protocols and six separate adapters. If the communication format is not standardized, this could require message translators to support processing the transmissions and receptions. Adding to this complexity are the significant changes in the programming logic of the clients and business logic servers to absorb the new information, since the client architecture of many legacy distributive systems are typically tightly bound to the server.

If systems using point-to-point interoperability also use synchronous protocols, this could lead to slow response time for all users. A synchronous protocol requires the application to suspend its work until the transmission request has been processed and a response is received. If User A requested information from Database C, he might need to wait for a communication over both protocols 1 and 6. Figure 9-6 illustrates the point-to-point interoperability components.

As more and more systems are added to this architecture, the number of connections increases in accordance with the following formula:

$$Connections = \frac{[Node \times (Node - 1)]}{2}$$

You can see that the number of nodes must remain small if this architecture is to succeed. Even a slight increase in the number of nodes will yield an unwieldy and unmanageable situation, as illustrated in Figure 9-7.

System reliability is also an issue with point-to-point interoperability. Up to four translators would be involved, which could potentially reduce the reliability of the overall system. The more translations and the greater the variation of each translation for a connection, the more chances there are for problems to occur during the communication transmission.

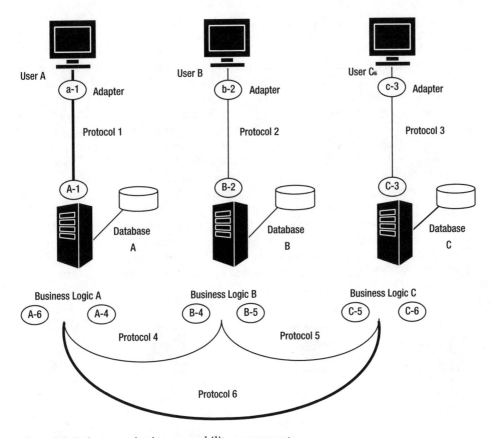

Figure 9-6. *Point-to-point interoperability components*

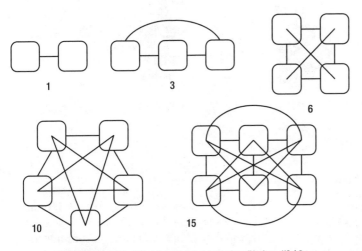

Number of Point-to-Point Connections = [Node x (Node − 1)] / 2

Figure 9-7. *Point-to-point connections*

The MOM Interoperability Solution

As you've seen, developing communications with multiple systems is the biggest drawback of point-to-point communications. Maintaining unique adapters, protocols, and translators for each system only serves to add to cost and effort while reaping no benefit. Point-to-point interoperability tightly couples the enterprise together. In contrast, a MOM solution supports multiple connections across the enterprise while loosely coupling the architecture. This simple approach to interoperability reduces integration costs and the time to interconnect new systems.

With MOM, the abstraction of a message layer makes connectivity available while allowing each system to perform individual functions. As in a football team, an individual with the ball can perform his function and allow other team members to carry out assigned duties, without hindering the overall team objective or performance.

Converting the point-to-point solution using MOM interoperability would resemble Figure 9-8. The most obvious change is that only one protocol is needed to connect all the systems. This by itself generates a significant reduction in maintenance costs. With only one protocol, adapters need only to convert to the common "x" format when coupling to the middleware layer. The result is that any user connected to the MOM can communicate with any server or client that is already connected.

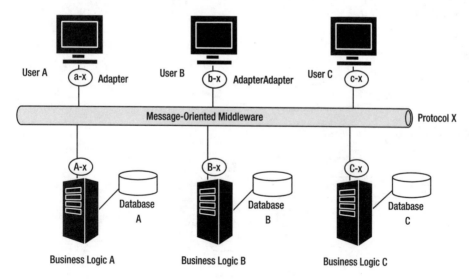

Figure 9-8. *Message-oriented middleware interoperability*

MOM Publish/Subscribe Model

Simple point-to-point communications that use a request/response synchronous communication transmission style may affect the overall performance of the enterprise. Broadcast and asynchronous communication offer an advantage in that a client or server can continue to process information after the message has been sent, giving the user or system the freedom to perform other critical business objectives. If a response is to be delivered, the user or system can return to the previous business objective seamlessly once that response arrives. Since clients and servers both benefit from these communication styles, designing broadcast or asynchronous communication into an application is a critical factor in developing smart clients that use both remote and local resources.

Because MOM is constructed using queues, using MOM gives a single system the capability to easily send a message to multiple destinations. Broadcasting from a single publisher to multiple subscribers is known as *publish/subscribe*. In this model, subscribers register with the publisher to receive messages. Once subscribers are registered, publishers send all published messages to the appropriate inbound queues of subscribers. This mechanism allows each of the receiving applications to process its messages in turn. Additionally, after sending the messages, the publisher can continue to support other business functionality. Using this mechanism, the queues act as an abstraction layer between the applications employing it, as illustrated in Figure 9-9.

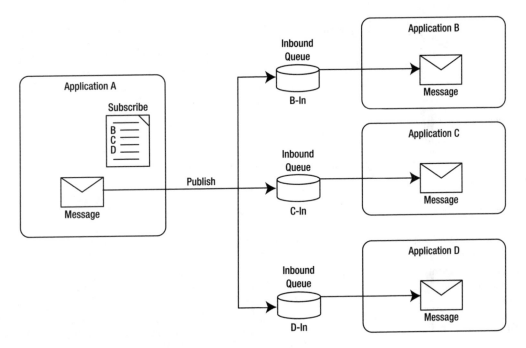

Figure 9-9. *Publish/subscribe model*

MOM Queues and Delivery Levels

A queue is a permanent storage device, which is typically a file on a disk. Queues are managed by a separate system and not coupled to the application. Messages sent from an application are written from memory to the queue, and then sent to the recipient. After the message is written to a queue, if the application exits or crashes, when the application restarts, it can pull the message off the queue and proceed as if the event did not happen.

This isolation from the application has many benefits. A MOM system can support various levels of service delivery by using different queue configurations.

The highest level of delivery is guaranteed message delivery. This delivery mechanism is also called *store and forward* and uses four queues, as shown in Figure 9-10. A set of queues is set up for each application. One set is configured for inbound traffic, and another is set up for outbound traffic. The key to guarantee the delivery is to always have the message in two isolated spots during its transmission in case of a system failure. If either application fails, messages will be safe in one or more of the queues.

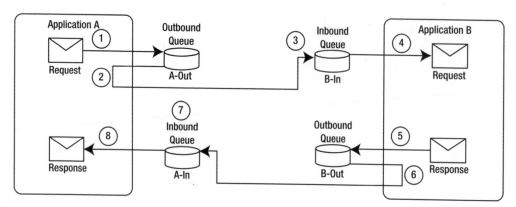

Figure 9-10. *Guaranteed delivery service level*

The steps to process a guaranteed delivery are described in Table 9-1.

Table 9-1. *Guaranteed Delivery Steps*

Step	Message Location
1. Request message is written to application A's outbound queue.	Message is in application A's memory space and its outbound queue.
2. Request message is sent and written to application B's inbound queue.	Message is in application A's outbound and application B's inbound queues. Message is deleted from application A's memory space.
3. Request message is requested by application B from its inbound queue.	Message is in application B's inbound queue and application B's memory space. Message is deleted from application A's outbound queue.
4. Request message is processed by application B, and response message is generated.	Message is in application B's inbound queue and application B's memory space.
5. Response message is written to application B's outbound queue.	Message is in application B's memory space and its outbound queue.
6. Response message is sent and written to application A's inbound queue	Message is in application B's outbound queue and Application A's inbound queue. Message is deleted from application B's memory space.
7. Response message is requested by application A from its inbound queue.	Message is in application A's inbound queue and application A's memory space. Message is deleted from application B's outbound queue.
8. Response message is processed by application A.	Message is in application A's inbound queue and application A's memory space. After processing, message is deleted from application A's inbound queue.

Guaranteed delivery can impact performance for a large quantity of messages due to the number of file reads and writes. If necessary, you can reduce the level of service level by using virtual queues and synchronous communication. For example, Figure 9-11 illustrates how the setup shown in Figure 9-10 could be modified by removing both of the outbound queues and converting both inbound queues to virtual ones. For a lower level of service (and increase in performance), you could use synchronous communication, eliminating the writing to the queue or performing it after the message has been sent, read, or processed. MOM software products such as IBM's WebSphere MQ, TIBCO Rendezvous, and SONIC's SonicMQ offer robust capabilities and let you decide on the trade-off necessary for the appropriate level of performance for service.

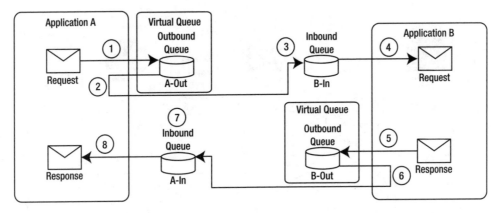

Figure 9-11. *Increasing performance with virtual queues*

MOM Messages

Along with queues, MOM is also based on messages. Messages are succinct data packets that are easy to manage and offer more flexibility when working with multiple applications. MOM messages have the following attributes:

- A message can be time-independent or time-dependent. Messages that are time-dependent are known as *events*. An event can be processed to give the application an understanding of sequencing and state.

- Messages can be organized and processed by classifications, priorities, and functionality.

- Messages can be transmitted using synchronous, asynchronous, or broadcast communication styles.

Messages offer a flexible way to transfer data, and adding the abstraction layer supported with queues delivers a better solution for enterprise interoperability. Messages, queues, and transmission styles benefit the enterprise holistically with greater interoperability.

MOM Wrap-Up

Using MOM for connectivity eases communication with multiple systems, as shown in Figure 9-12. Once connected, each system communicates seamlessly with any other system that is already connected. This interoperability offers a huge enterprise integration advantage.

However, one critical drawback is that a MOM product typically uses proprietary interfaces and message formatting. Each system must develop and use separate adapters, as indicated in Figure 9-12. While using a MOM is acceptable for a localized solution and establishes a foundation for the enterprise, it alone cannot provide the interoperability level required for an SOA. Proprietary communication structures and messages inhibit the extension of the architecture beyond the corporate enterprise.

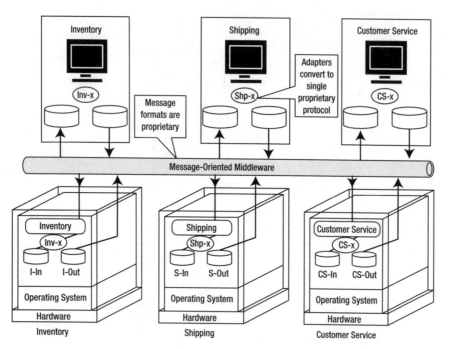

Figure 9-12. *Interoperability using MOM*

The other part of the solution is XML Web Services. Coupling a MOM product with the open standards developed for XML Web Services gives you an SOA that extends the architecture beyond the corporate walls. The remainder of this chapter is devoted to presenting how these two technologies are pivotal in developing an enterprise SOA.

Service-Oriented Architecture Development

Now that you understand the fundamentals of an SOA (MOM and XML Web Services), let's walk through the steps to build the architecture. We'll continue with the small out-of-print movie supplier company example that we've used in previous sections.

As described earlier in the chapter, before beginning SOA development, you need to perform a business modeling and requirements analysis to identify the services and their functionality and interfaces. Figure 9-13 highlights significant requirements, indicating the information exchanges (paper or electronic) and the principle functionality in our example.

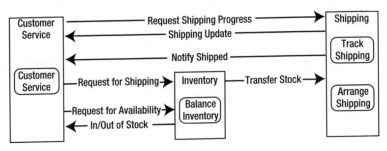

Figure 9-13. *Information exchanges and principal functionality*

After you've identified the services and their functionality and interfaces, SOA development involves the following tasks:

- Create XML Web Services.

- Build a message-oriented architecture (MOA), using a horizontal service bus, which employs standardized XML Web Services, XML interfaces, and SOAP messages.

- Configure XML Web Service discovery and publication, through DISCO files or UDDI, to extend information within the corporation and to external partners.

Creating Web Services

XML Web Services, detailed in Chapter 8, are the enabler of an SOA. Selecting a department or a subset of functionality that represents a single service is a good starting point. If we use the boundary of the shipping department as the XML Web Service public interface, we have the initial steps toward defining a web service, as shown in Figure 9-14. In the initial steps, we do this using point-to-point communication.

From our simple requirements analysis, we know that the shipping XML Web Service itself must perform the functionality of arranging shipping and tracking shipping. This functional alignment helps the architecture ensure that the business objectives of the XML Web Service will be achieved. The inventory and customer service XML Web Services are similarly developed based on the requirements analysis.

No interdepartment communication is initially needed, but messages should be constructed in XML using SOAP formats to standardize communication between the client and the XML Web Service within the department. The XML Web Service needs to be constructed using the standards as defined by the industry. Standardizing the XML Web Service construction will help when using many of the advanced XML Web Service functionalities. See Chapter 8 for details on creating and using XML Web Services.

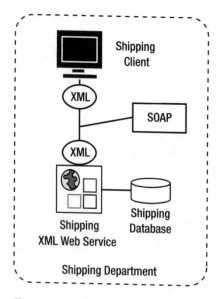

Figure 9-14. *Point-to-point XML Web Service using SOAP*

Building a Message-Oriented Architecture

The next step involves developing a *horizontal service bus*, which is the SOAP or HTTP protocol running on top of a MOM product. The bus is referred to as *horizontal* because it connects across systems, which are usually thought of as vertical entities, also known as vertical *silos*.

Although this step does not give an immediate benefit, its justification is that it is the catalyst for the SOA. Overcoming the issues of simple point-to-point communication early in the adoption cycle is essential to the success of developing an SOA. A horizontal service bus is the mechanism that provides the interoperability desired for an SOA.

The communication system of a horizontal service bus is also based on messages. The horizontal service bus sends and receives messages to be transmitted from one to many recipients simultaneously. This simplifies the process and reduces the cost as other systems are introduced to the SOA. Figure 9-15 shows how a point-to-point mechanism that was based on XML and SOAP can be converted to use a horizontal service bus.

The next step in the metamorphosis is to convert another department to an XML Web Service in isolation or directly add it to the horizontal service bus. Adding an XML Web Service to the horizontal service bus, as shown in Figure 9-16, does not require the new web service to interact with the others that are already on it. By configuring the communication style as publish/subscribe, as described earlier in the chapter, the shipping XML Web Service (subscriber) does not need to register with the inventory XML Web Service (publisher). Thus, this will prevent any interaction until integration is desired.

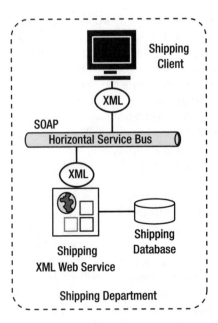

Figure 9-15. *XML Web Service using a horizontal service bus and SOAP*

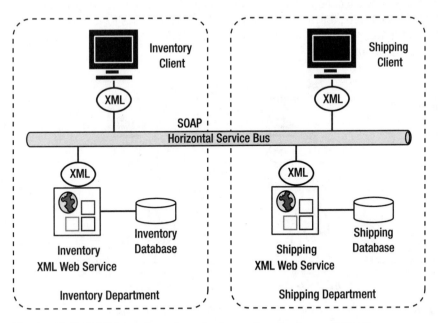

Figure 9-16. *XML Web Service using a horizontal service bus and SOAP*

Prior to integration, you should perform a data analysis on the two XML Web Services to determine compatibility and how to deal with duplicate data. Any duplicate data should be assigned to one or the other XML Web Services. If you were to discover large amounts of duplicate data, you would need to construct more messages to be exchanged between the two services. In this example, we will assume very little or no duplicate data exists.

In our example, the requirements indicate that the transfer stock documentation currently used will be converted to a new single electronic XML message. This message will be sent from the inventory system to the shipping system using the SOAP protocol. The transfer-stock message will include information about the customer name, customer shipping address, and the stock item. The shipping XML Web Service will process this message and allow the shipping client to arrange shipping.

Next, convert the customer service department to an XML Web Service using the requirements analysis, and then connect the XML Web Service to the horizontal service bus. Again, before integrating this web service, perform another data analysis to check for compatibility and duplication.

The requirements indicate that a request for shipping, shipping progress request, and availability documents currently being sent from the customer service department to the inventory and shipping departments will be changed to XML messages. Likewise, notify shipping, shipping update, and notify in/out of stock documents sent from the shipping and inventory departments will also be switched to XML messages.

The enterprise is now configured with a horizontal service bus. These systems can now interact and exchange data effectively. This type of architecture is known as a *message-oriented architecture* (MOA). The MOA has been coupled with XML Web Services, as shown in Figure 9-17. The standardized XML Web Services, XML interfaces, and SOAP messages ensure an industry-wide acceptance of the architecture.

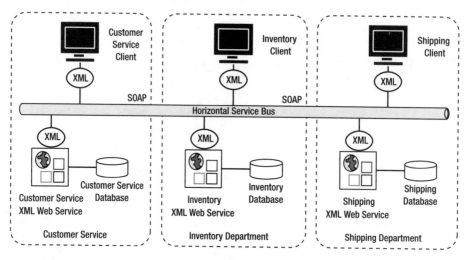

Figure 9-17. *Message-oriented architecture using XML Web Services*

SOAP allows a message to be relayed and processed by an intermediary. In our example, the notify shipping message is used in the shipping XML Web Service and is currently being sent to the customer service XML Web Service, as shown in Figure 9-18.

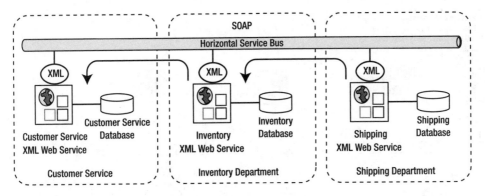

Figure 9-18. *Intermediate delivery using SOAP*

We use SOAP to alert the inventory department by sending this message to the inventory XML Web Service and then relaying it to the customer service XML Web Service. Instead of creating a separate message, the SOAP message allows a single attribute change in its header, which will force all intermediaries to process the message and relay it onward. For messages such as the notify shipping one, this can be done for multiple XML Web Services along the way. This kind of flexibility gives SOAP a distinct advantage over many communication protocols.

Discovering and Publishing XML Web Services

Two critical features of an SOA are discovery and publication of the XML Web Services. These capabilities allow a corporation to expose XML Web Services to its enterprise. This exposure establishes the interface, the interface binding, and the location of the XML Web Service. As you learned in Chapter 8, UDDI and DISCO files are two mechanisms for web service discovery.

Microsoft DISCO Files

A small corporation, such as the movie supplier in our example, may want to use the simple DISCO file approach to publishing and discovering XML Web Services. Once constructed, the DISCO files are loaded in the Inetpub/wwwroot directory of the IIS web server. The DISCO files reference the WSDL files for each of the XML Web Services, which can also be located on the web server.

For our example, we would generate DISCO and WSDL files for each of the customer service, inventory, and shipping XML Web Services, as shown in Figure 9-19. As new systems are placed on the horizontal service bus, the developer can quickly accommodate interfacing to each of the existing XML Web Services.

Microsoft's DISCO files suffice for small endeavors, but as noted in Chapter 8, using them requires that the developer already be aware that the XML Web Service exists. This approach is also limited because it is a Microsoft proprietary solution.

However, using a DISCO file does ensure that a set of standards is being maintained. When you're ready to move to a private UDDI registry, as described in the next section, the migration will be easier.

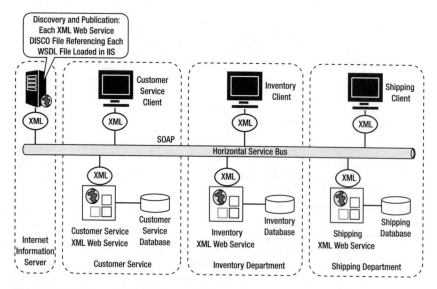

Figure 9-19. *Using DISCO files for publish and discovery services*

DISCO files also allow developers to use an auto-discovery feature, which is useful for development or test pipelines (server's environment), but should not be used for production systems. This feature can notify the developer about the creation of XML Web Services and identify the phase of development.

Private UDDI Registry and Server

The core component that glues an SOA together is a UDDI registry. As you learned in Chapter 8, these registries come in two flavors: public and private. The private registry is developed for a corporation's intranet solutions or XML Web Services. The public registry is to expose services to the Internet.

The private UDDI registry is housed within a UDDI server. The UDDI server offers more sophisticated features than the DISCO files approach. UDDI servers support a hierarchical data model that identifies the business, the classification of the type of service, the access point, and the technical model (which identifies the WSDL and specifics about the XML Web Service). The UDDI data model is presented in Figure 9-20.

The UDDI data model represents all the information necessary to discover, understand, and connect to an XML Web Service. The UDDI registry acts as a central repository for all this information—a kind of a one-stop shopping approach, like an information booth in a mall that contains a reference to all the stores, a classification of their services, and a map showing where to find them. The UDDI server uses a public SOAP XML API, which exposes to clients or XML Web Services a set of commands to inquire, update, and delete information about the XML Web Services in its repository. This API traverses this data model to accomplish this mission.

For example, if our sample company's inventory XML Web Service were published to the UDDI server, when a customer service client wanted to connect with the inventory XML Web Service, it would inquire the UDDI server for the inventory service. Finding it, it would retrieve the necessary information to interface, locate, and bind with it. This process could be repeated over and over again with any newly developed services.

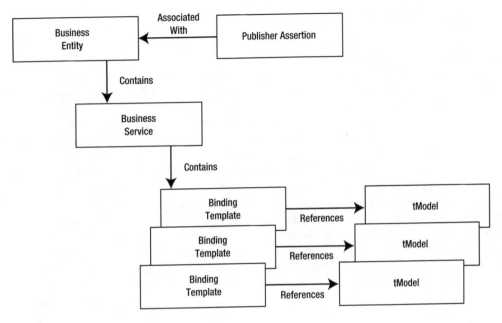

Figure 9-20. *UDDI data model*

Our sample company has now achieved an SOA, as illustrated in Figure 9-21. Such an architectural evolution takes time, beginning with developing standardized XML Web Services, then deploying an MOA that uses a horizontal service bus, and finally employing a UDDI server for discovery and publication.

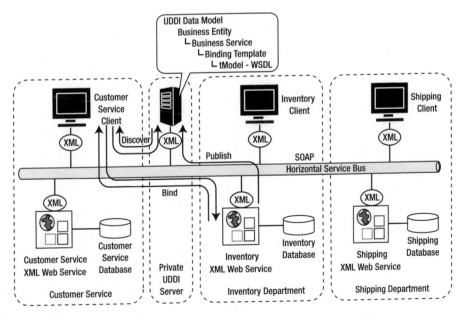

Figure 9-21. *Private UDDI server*

Exploiting the SOA

Once an SOA has been constructed within a corporation, a number of business opportunities become available. Major computer vendors such as Microsoft, IBM, SAP, and NTT Communications have set up global UDDI Business Registries (UBRs), as described in Chapter 8. These public UDDI registries are all based on a single set of standards, and they exist to support global publishing and discovery of services.

Our sample company has a limited market reach and is known by only a few distributors. Publishing its inventory XML Web Services to the UBR (http://uddi.microsoft.com) may yield many new customers seeking products that the company sells.

Also, consider that our small supplier needs to arrange shipping. This service currently requires the shipping clerk to get on the phone with a few shippers the company knows to establish the cost and pickup time. A more competitive rate and quicker delivery may be vailable. This limitation may be costing the corporation unnecessarily. The corporation could look for more competitive shipping services by exploring the UBR to determine if cheaper or faster services exist (for example, potentially located at www.fedex.com).

Using the UBR is not the only avenue available. Setting up an alliance with another partner can also be a cost-effective approach. For example, the corporation could set up an alliance or partnership with a global inventory distributor such as www.amazon.com, which could use another corporation's private registry to find the XML Web Service.

Using a UBR or partnership with another corporation's private registry allows automatic discovery and binding to be executed in real time. Once bound, the inventory system could manage inventory directly with the Amazon XML Web Service to expand its distribution market.

As illustrated in Figure 9-22, an SOA gives a corporation a global reach and a strategic enterprise viewpoint.

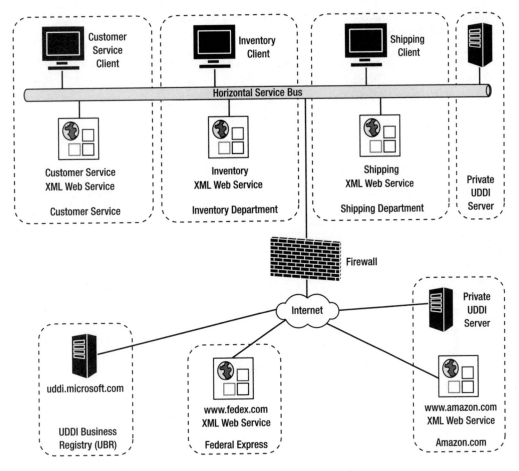

Figure 9-22. *Private UDDI server*

Summary

This chapter described how to develop an SOA. As you learned, an SOA is an architecture that
extends beyond the corporate walls by using industry-level standards. By coupling MOM and
XML Web Services, you develop an MOA. Then you add discovery and publication services,
either through DISCO files or UDDI.

As we noted, although using DISCO files is a simpler solution, this approach is limited.
A large corporation, or one wishing to be efficient, should invest in building or purchasing a
private UDDI registry. Large corporations invest millions of dollars in developing IT solutions.
In many situations, a corporation has a hard time inventorying solutions or services that it
has developed and provided. Greater still is the challenge of informing the various parts of
the development community about these services, their capabilities, and how to interface
with them. Most companies today cannot afford the inefficiency attributed to duplication

or the failure to exploit current resources to the fullest. UDDI gives the corporation an appropriate tool to publish and discover services, which can also remove duplicity of effort and save money.

The next chapter puts together the topics covered in this and previous chapters. It presents how you can use smart clients with an SOA to develop a powerful new client: a service-oriented smart client that gives the user more capabilities and extends the reach to the global market seamlessly.

CHAPTER 10

■ ■ ■

Service-Oriented Smart Clients

The client evolution has matured through four forms: stand-alone, thick client, thin client, and now smart clients. A service-oriented smart client (SOSC) is based on two principle technological advances: smart clients and the service-oriented architecture (SOA). Smart clients offer benefits of both thick and thin clients, and the SOA allows effective interaction when using remote resources. Companies can gain a great business advantage by leveraging the capabilities supported by these two technologies and integrating them into a single solution.

As you learned in the previous chapter, the SOA supports interoperability across systems and clients using standards. With the interoperability that can be achieved with the SOA, smart clients can become pervasive and ubiquitous, giving the user a better experience. Because smart clients can use local resources, they can exploit both persistence and concurrency. Additionally, smart clients can be multithreading, allowing them to support foreground activities while processing background requests at the same time. Smart clients are easy to deploy on both portable and stationary devices.

In this chapter, we'll cover SOSC development and characteristics, beginning with a basic framework for SOSC application design.

Service-Oriented Smart Client Model

In Chapter 9, we detailed the SOA and how it provides interoperability between clients and remote resources. An SOA aligns real-world services with technology systems that work with functionality that has been aggregated at an enterprise granularity. At the foundation of this enterprise is a horizontal service bus, which places an abstraction between services and clients to loosely couple these two entities. This abstraction allows developers to use advanced communication techniques that enhance the interactivity, intelligence, and agility between the clients and services.

An SOSC model organizes the primary components of the smart client in an SOA framework of abstractions and aggregations that centralize functionality and business logic. By following the modeling guidelines presented here, you'll be able to develop SOSCs that are easy and cost-effective to maintain and enhance.

Now, we'll look at the SOSC components, and then present some examples of practical SOSC applications.

SOSC Components

The SOSC framework consists of a local data store, service repository, service registry, and smart agent. Figure 10-1 illustrates the basic architectural model for an SOSC, with its relationship to the components on the server and third-party web services.

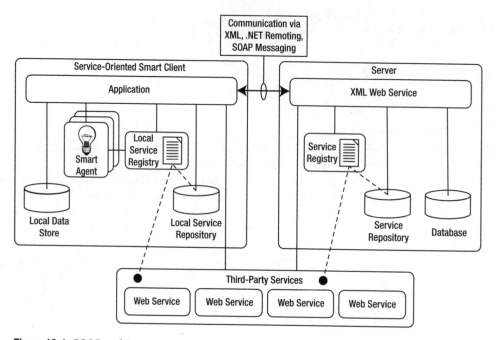

Figure 10-1. *SOSC architecture*

Local Data Store

The local data store gives the SOSC the ability to store state and maintain persistence. If the SOSC is operating as a data gatherer, it can use this data store to safely store its information, in case the portable device is powered off. On the other hand, when the SOSC is acting as a "terminal" for remote-user access and is updating a remote resource, the data store can be used as a backup in case communications fail. The data store acts as the principal baseline when an SOSC is in disconnected mode, as explained in the "Smart Client State and Persistence" section later in this chapter.

Local Service Registry and Repository

The local service registry and repository need to resemble their server counterparts to preserve the interoperability of the client with the server. The service registry and repository allow the application to discover, describe, and integrate web services that can be downloaded or to keep references to remote services. By designing an SOSC that employs standards and contexts that adhere to WSDL, UDDI, and DISCO, you can redeploy localized XML Web Services intended for the SOSC to centralized services, at little or no cost.

Smart Agent

A critical aspect of the SOSC is the smart agent, which gives the SOSC the ability to adapt automatically. For example, by adding adaptive intelligence to a particular function, you can make the SOSC more aware of its environment or able to support a better decision for the application. The smart agent is the component that ensures that the adaptive intelligence will be amalgamated and not distributed within the client.

You should develop a smart agent for each service that needs to bolster its intelligence. The level of intelligence required depends on your particular application and varies from setting up a simple classic feedback loop to providing artificial intelligence or fuzzy logic. The sky truly is the limit, but as the client becomes more complex, you must ensure that the time, effort, and expense of developing its level of intelligence deliver the return on investment for the application users and the business case.

In the next sections, we'll look at some business case examples and illustrate the SOSC model to accommodate them.

Gaming SOSC Example

Most role-playing games (RPGs) or real-time strategy (RTS) games save game preferences, character state, or selected inventory in a nonstandardized or proprietary form of smart clients. Even though a game developer, such as Microsoft, produces hundreds of games each year, each game yields a unique and isolated gamer experience.

Smart clients offer a rich user interface experience, as well as easy deployment via the Internet; however, they do not address many of the other issues associated with configuring and maintaining games. Different games require the gamer to set up different financial accounts. The gamer must also adjust environment configurations and preferences for the keyboard, joystick, mouse, monitor, graphics resolution, and sound for each game each time. A gamer may also spend a significant amount of time developing friendships, character skills, and experience in one game, only to find that this information cannot be used in another game.

A more versatile game experience is available using the basic SOSC framework and smart agents. The SOSC could address the environment issues, as well as some of the in-game experiences. Using a single SOSC to manipulate all games developed by the company would minimize the effort required by the user to set up multiple games from the same company. Aligning remote resources as services and using smart agents to provide the adaptability to particular gaming functions are the keys to giving the user the next level of interoperability.

As illustrated in Figure 10-2, a gaming SOSC could be modeled with three sets of smart agents, a local data store, and a local service registry, as follows:

- A local data store and local service registry maintain the playtime communication and gamer's account information, with the appropriate remote financial and availability services, to present a seamless integration with the corporation's financial systems.

- The game environment set of smart agents supports the graphic rendering, keyboard configuration, mouse configuration, joystick alignment, and sound support for all games.

- The in-game information set of smart agents supports game information such as the characters, playing time, friends, and gamer preferences (for movement, combat, and so on). These in-game information smart agents could be used by all games to increase their appeal to the gamers of a particular corporation's gaming market. For example, a group of friends who own more than one game could collaborate in multiple games and become part of a larger corporate gaming community.

- The game-specific set of smart agents holds information specific to a particular game. Game-specific information is isolated to a particular agent to make it easier to maintain and upgrade the game.

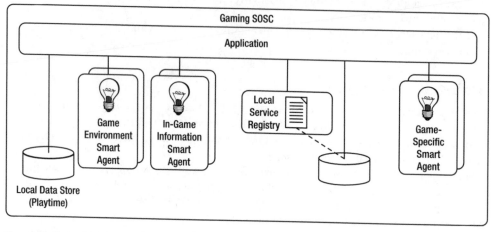

Figure 10-2. *An SOSC gaming example*

Each of the three types of smart agents would know if information is local or if they needed to connect to a server to get to remote services. As new features or games are released, only the affected agents need to be upgraded.

Logistics SOSC Example

A logistics company provides rapid transit of a high volume of raw materials or goods. To stay in business, a logistics company relies on getting the cheapest transit rates coupled with the shortest timetables to support just-in-time (JIT) delivery. A smart client could assist a logistics company in achieving its goals, but an SOSC can give the company an edge over the competition.

Inbound logistics track parts to the factory, and outbound logistics track products from the factory to a dealer. An SOSC could align the inbound and outbound services and smart agents to the departments. As shown in Figure 10-3, a logistics SOSC could be modeled as follows:

- The local data store holds persistent information such as vehicle types.

- The local service registry maintains the currently selected set of transit rates and timetables.

- An inbound smart agent tracks part movement and optimizes delivery to plants.

- An outbound smart agent calculates the optimum routes for products based on available rates, vehicle types, and timetables. Daily, both the inbound and outbound smart agents use intelligence and agility to check remote services for cheaper rates and shorter timetables, and download them.

- An inventory smart agent updates the client local services with approved transactions and sends the remote services the requested information.

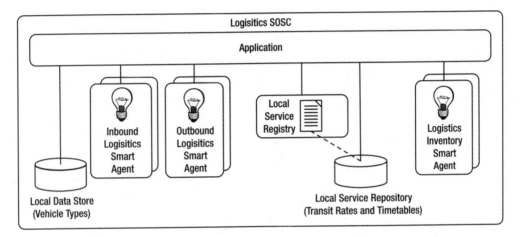

Figure 10-3. *An SOSC logistics example*

Pervasive and Ubiquitous Smart Clients

Today, corporations expect computer systems to be pervasive and ubiquitous. Consider how the current technology of cell phones has freed people from anchoring or limiting their phone conversations to wire-connected phones. Similarly, people and corporations are on the move, and they want their data to be available anywhere and all the time. Without pervasive systems, companies will be out of touch with their customers, and today, that means they may soon be out of business.

The SOA enhances system integration, but it does not directly address the client-connectivity challenges. Pervasive and ubiquitous smart clients require more intelligence to handle the use of multiple technologies and integration with different capabilities.

The SOSC, with its smart adaptation capabilities, is the best candidate for pervasive and ubiquitous computing. The complexity of smart agents operating in multiple environments is too challenging for a simple thin client to do the job. An SOSC supports the mobility using smart agents and intelligence to provide media and communication agility, giving all applications a boost from a user's perspective.

Media Agility

Clients based on a single medium develop a conflict between bandwidth and mobility. Wired clients have great bandwidth, but lack mobility. Isolated clients have great mobility but lack bandwidth. As illustrated in Figure 10-4, stuck in the middle are clients using wireless media.

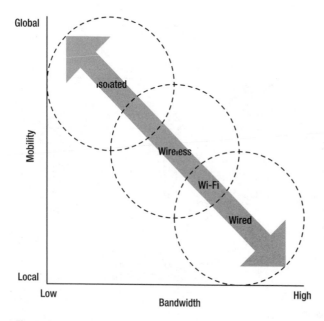

Figure 10-4. *Comparison of bandwidth and mobility for various media*

Many static solutions exist to solve this problem, but today's business environment is very dynamic, and static solutions do not give the flexibility required to meet the expectations of users or customers. Smart clients solve this problem by giving the business the "intelligent" choice. Since smart clients can call on local resources, they can offer the needed flexibility to maneuver between types of network connections or the total lack of a network connection. This flexibility is called *media agility*.

As an example, let's return to the hypothetical small movie supplier's SOA that we developed in Chapter 9. There, most of the modifications were made to the back-office area; the enhancements to the client were limited. Now, let's suppose that this company has a sales force, which uses the inventory and shipping systems, as shown in Figure 10-5. The company equips the salespeople with laptops (or other portable devices), and wants to configure the system so that the salespeople can get information when they travel to client sites.

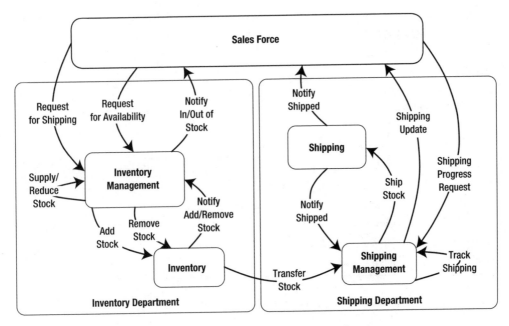

Figure 10-5. *Sales force interaction with inventory and shipping departments*

By developing a media-agile SOSC, the company can provide its agents with the maximum flexibility. For example, a sales agent working from an office in the company can use the smart client to connect using wired connectivity. If the sales agent then goes to the cafeteria and wants to continue working, he can connect using the wireless LAN supplied by the corporation. When the sales agent leaves the office to call on customers, the smart client could operate in either an isolated mode or connect via a wireless network. If the customer's site has wireless coverage, the smart client can gain network access using the wireless connection. If the sales agent is in a location without wireless coverage, the smart client will configure itself to work in an isolated mode. Table 10-1 shows the range of options for the smart client in this example.

Table 10-1. *Smart Client Media Agility*

Smart Client Location	Resource Usage	Media
Office	Use local/office resources	Wired
Office area	Use local/office resources	Wi-Fi wireless
Travel (coverage)	Use local/office resources	Wireless cellular/satellite
Client site (coverage)	Use local/office resources	Wireless cellular/satellite
Home (no coverage)	Use local resources	Isolated

With media agility, a smart client uses its intelligence to manipulate the available media as appropriate. Staying connected as much as possible gives users access to the resources they need to make timely business decisions. However, when a connection is unavailable, users should not be left stranded without information; instead, they should have the opportunity to use the latest possible information stored on a portable device to make the most informed decisions. Employing a smart client using a media-agile approach keeps users productive.

Types of Media

The main types of media are wired, wireless, and isolated. Wireless media can be further divided into Wi-Fi, cellular, and satellite. Table 10-2 summarizes the characteristics of each type.

Table 10-2. *Wireless Media Types*

Media	Mobility	Client Functionality	Operational Cost	Bandwidth
Wired	None	Varies (thick vs. thin)	$	High
Wireless (Wi-Fi)	Low	Varies (thick vs. thin)	$	Medium
Wireless (cell)	Medium	Lean	$$	Medium
Wireless (satellite)	High	Lean	$$$	Low
Isolated	High	Rich	$$$	None

Now let's take a closer look at each connectivity option.

Wired Connectivity

Wired connectivity describes a client that is using a network interface card (NIC) to connect to an Ethernet or a Token Ring network. The bandwidth of these wired networks is 10 or 100 megabits per second (Mbps). Connecting to a 100 Mbps network offers minimal latency and maximum throughput. Most clients that are stationary (either constantly or temporarily) use wired media to connect to the Internet or an intranet, as illustrated in Figure 10-6, since this is the most cost-effective solution.

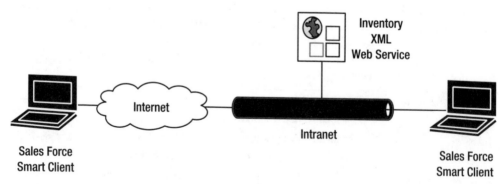

Figure 10-6. *Smart client using wired media*

Wireless Connectivity

Clients have several choices for wireless connectivity, as shown in Figure 10-7. Wi-Fi products occupy the low end of the mobility spectrum; cellular and satellite infrastructures support the high end. Wi-Fi[1] products give the user mobility at a specific location and basically extend a wired local area network (LAN). Coverage for Wi-Fi products is measured in terms of feet or meters, not miles or kilometers, and gives the user mobility while at the office or home where the wireless access point has been set up. The bandwidth for Wi-Fi network products ranges from 0.38 to 54 Mbps.

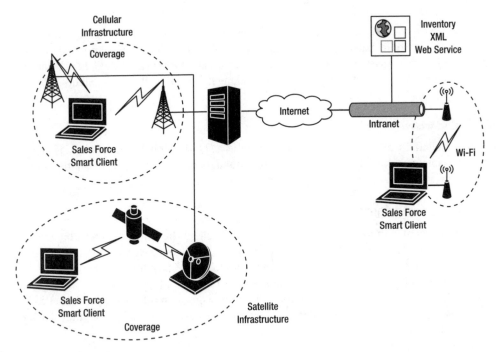

Figure 10-7. *Smart clients using wireless media*

Wireless cellular technology is supported by a host of cellular companies such as Verizon, Cingular, Sprint, and so on. These companies have developed an infrastructure that allows users to move around and stay connected. Coverage for wireless cellular is measured in miles or kilometers, and most significant metropolitan areas have one or more competing infrastructures. Outside these metropolitan areas, coverage becomes intermittent. Wireless cellular supports a bandwidth range from 19.2 to 56 Kbps. Each cellular service provider charges a fee based on actual usage to send/receive data or voice over its infrastructure. This infrastructure is connected to the Internet to complete the pathway to desired services. You need to take into account the coverage area and the operational cost when considering this solution.

---

1. Wi-Fi represents a consortium of companies that sets standards for wireless LAN products based on the IEEE 802.11 specification. Three specifications are standard in the industry: 802.11a (24 Mbps), 802.11b (11 Mbps), and 802.11g (54 Mbps).

■Note Wireless cellular connectivity is subject to coverage, which is based on the location of the towers, the signal strength they output, and the sensitivity of the device to pick up the signal. The proximity of the device to the towers is crucial for the technology to work properly. Although this technology is constantly improving, the reliability of wireless cellular communication can be suspect.

Wireless over satellite connectivity offers the best mobility, since the coverage area is literally global. As you would expect, this is the most costly solution, so it should be reserved for only the most critical transmissions and/or applications. (The sales force example would not warrant satellite connectivity, unless the sales agents were selling movie originals in the million-dollar price range.)

Isolated Connectivity

Isolated connectivity refers to a client that operates as a stand-alone device. The cost is highest with an isolated solution, since all logic or functionality must be kept locally all the time. However, an isolated solution gives the user the most mobility.

A Media-Agile Smart Agent

Using a smart agent with intelligence can give the smart client the ability to determine media agility, as illustrated in Figure 10-8. You could preset this intelligence with default metrics, or allow the user to dynamically adjust a set of heuristics to get the best business benefit. For example, you could set up these heuristics or metrics to support range values or fuzzy logic to deal with cost, criticality, or fault conditions. In this way, you can reduce the operational costs for pervasive and ubiquitous computing by using expensive resources only when they deliver a strategic business value.

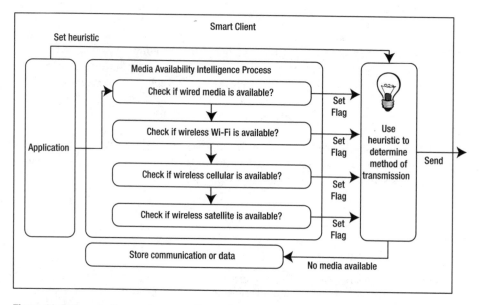

Figure 10-8. *Smart client using a media-agile smart agent*

Communication Agility

A smart client will need information from a variety of remote sources, so it should use a variety of communication styles, just as people do in the real world. Communication styles depend on how quickly the information is needed, how important the information is, and whether the information is static or dynamic, as illustrated in Figure 10-9.

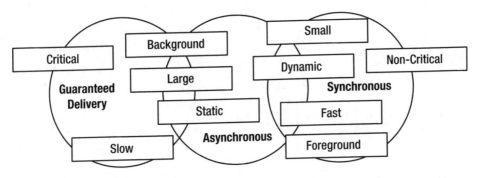

Figure 10-9. *Communication styles and types of messages*

If you need a quick response, you pick up a phone and start a conversation to get the information immediately. This corresponds to synchronous computer communications. If the information requires analysis or effort before you receive it, you might leave a message and do other things while you wait for the response. For example, you might leave a note for someone to complete a list of work around the house, and then focus on other activities while the chores are being completed. This is analogous to asynchronous communications.

The importance of the information also affects your choice of communication channels. If the information is critical, you want to relay it over the most reliable channel available to ensure it gets to its destination; in other words, you want guaranteed delivery. If the information were of low importance, you would choose to send it over the least reliable channel. For example, you might send information regarding a summer holiday resort in the middle of winter over a channel with low reliability, since it isn't critical and you could resend it if necessary.

When choosing a communication style, you also need to consider the propensity of the information to change state. For example, if an application is requesting geographic information about a continent, the data can be considered static. This kind of information rarely changes, and additional requests for this data can use a slower communication channel. Financial data, such as that in the stock market, changes by the second, and this type of information is dynamic. Dynamic information should use a communication channel more aligned to the timeliness of the information.

Table 10-3 shows the characteristics of the three main communication styles: synchronous, asynchronous, and asynchronous with guaranteed delivery.

Table 10-3. *Communication Styles*

Communication Style	Remote Information Processing	Reliability	Multitasking
Synchronous	Limited, dynamic, noncritical	Low	No
Asynchronous	Large, static, noncritical	Low	Yes
Asynchronous (guaranteed)	Large, static, critical	High	Yes

Now, let's see when to implement these types of communication in a smart client.

Synchronous Communication

The smart client using synchronous communication expects the connectivity to the remote resource to be consistently available. This type of communication requires the smart client to wait for the remote resource's response (or vice versa). As indicated in Figure 10-10, Task A on the smart client needs Task A' on the remote resource to finish before it can continue. Task A is stopped until the response is delivered.

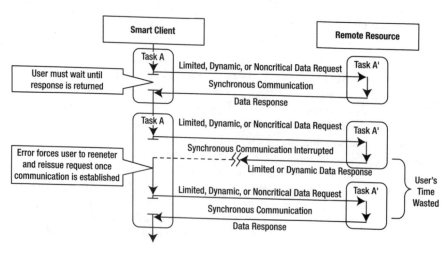

Figure 10-10. *Synchronous communication*

Because of the waiting involved, only limited data exchanges should be implemented with synchronous communication. Large data should always be broken into manageable chunks if sent synchronously, or the user will experience delays and notice a lack of responsiveness in the application.

Failure or interruption of communication can be another problem when using synchronous transmission. An interruption of synchronous communication results in the complete loss of the transaction, which forces the user to restart the request from the beginning once the communication channel has been reestablished. Task A is dependent on Task A' processing and returning information. If the communication is interrupted during the response, the user must send the request to Task A' to process the information again. If manual input were required, this information would need to be resubmitted. Figure 10-10 indicates the amount of time wasted in this case.

Synchronous communication requires fast and reliable media, and you should use it to deliver only limited, dynamic, or noncritical information.

Asynchronous Communication

Asynchronous communication allows the user to continue to perform local functions while making background requests.[2] A request for data that requires analysis or processing should use this style of communication. For example, if a user wishes to execute a task that requires a large amount of data processing, asynchronous communication allows that user to start the desired processing and go on to another task using local or other remote resources. Once the data processing is complete, the user can use the results.

As illustrated in the example in Figure 10-11, Task A requires Task A' to perform a significant amount of processing on the remote resource. The user starts Task A, and then starts Task B, which could employ another remote resource or use local resources. Once Task A' is finished, the user has the option to work with those results immediately or finish Task B.

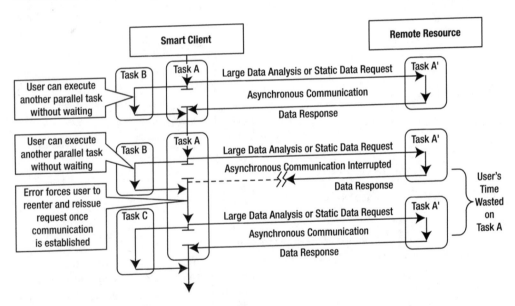

Figure 10-11. *Asynchronous communication*

Asynchronous communication by itself does not necessarily imply reliability. An interruption in connectivity can result in the loss of the transaction and force the user to restart the process. The good news is that the user could start Task B and then Task C in the interim while waiting for Task A to finish, so only the time related to Task A is wasted.

---

2. Asynchronous communication is not viable with a traditional thin client, since it is typically stateless unless it uses COM objects.

Asynchronous communication keeps the user productive. Asynchronous communication should be used with sizable remote processing, noncritical communications, or static data. It assumes the user has other more critical tasks to accomplish.

Guaranteed Asynchronous Communication

Using asynchronous communication coupled with a guaranteed delivery mechanism increases reliability. The guaranteed message delivery mechanism, also called *store and forward*, uses queues to store messages. (See Chapter 9's discussion of message-oriented middleware inter-operability for details on how guaranteed message delivery works.)

As illustrated in the example in Figure 10-12, Task A starts Task A'. Once the remote Task A' is complete, it stores the response in its outbound queue first, and then transmits the data. If the communication is interrupted and restored later, the information stored in the outbound queue of the remote resource is automatically retransmitted to the smart client. This minimizes the time lost due to the interruption.

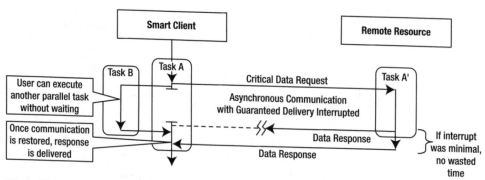

Figure 10-12. *Asynchronous communication with guaranteed delivery*

This form of communication is appropriate when the information is critical and must reach its destination. Also, the smart client should employ this type of communication when in an isolated or disconnected mode. In this situation, the smart client, once disconnected, sends all information directed to the remote resource to its own outbound queue. After recon-necting, the smart client will automatically transmit the information to the remote resource.

A Communication-Agile Smart Agent

A smart client can use these different communication styles appropriately to fit the situation. With intelligence located in local resources, it can balance the nature of data being channeled with the corresponding communication style to elevate the user's quality of service. The smart client can also allow users to contribute their understanding of the situation to determine how the adjustments are to be made, to ensure remote information is requested with the right crit-icality, speed, and timing.

You will need to reconcile your smart client's communication style with media choices, because different media have different characteristics, as summarized in Table 10-4. The smart client can use synchronous and asynchronous communication with wired connectivity, which also offers good reliability. Smart clients using wireless media can employ synchronous communications in areas where the signal strength is strong. If the media reliability is questionable, the smart client should use asynchronous communication. In isolated mode, the smart client cannot use synchronous communication. It can use only asynchronous communication with a store-and-forward configuration (as described in Chapter 9).

Table 10-4. *Media and Communication Reconciliation*

Media	Synchronous	Asynchronous	Asynchronous (Guaranteed Delivery)
Wired	Yes	Yes	Yes
Wireless (Wi-Fi)	Yes	Yes	Yes
Wireless (cellular, strong signal)	Yes	Yes	Yes
Wireless (satellite)	Yes	Yes	Yes
Wireless (cellular, weak signal)	No	No	Yes
Isolated	No	No	Yes

Figure 10-13 shows a general flow diagram for a smart agent that supports communication and media agility.

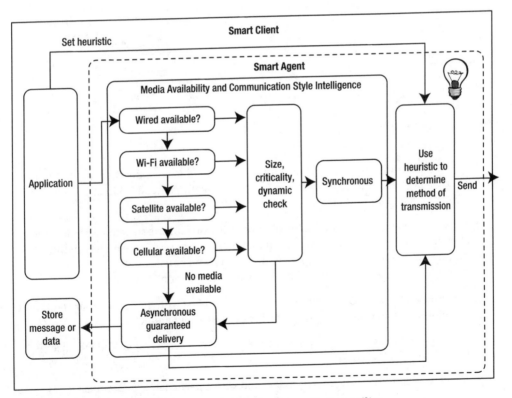

Figure 10-13. *Smart agent supporting media and communication agility*

Smart Client State and Persistence

In a classic sense, *state* is information that needs to exist beyond a particular event or time frame. *Persistence* gives information life beyond a particular event. Persistence is accomplished by writing the information to a file or database. This ensures that the information is retrievable if the device loses power. The smart client will be required to maintain state when interacting with remote data stores used by XML Web Services in both connected and isolated modes.

An ideal configuration places state in a single central location. This ensures no duplicate information exists to produce a conflict for a piece of information that is critical to an application. For most wire-connected clients, this is typically implemented by locating persistent information in a database. As the user updates or modifies the value, the information is stored at a particular time. Everyone on the system evaluating that same piece of information in the future views the time (t_1) and value (S_1) as it was written identically, as illustrated in Figure 10-14.

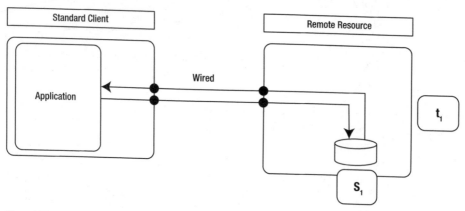

Figure 10-14. *Simple state with time (t_1) and value (S_1)*

To avoid maintaining useless or stale data, you also need to consider the length of time that state must be maintained. The duration of state is usually generalized in four classifications, as illustrated in Figure 10-15:

- *Server:* The first classification has the longest duration and is associated with data that should be kept while the hardware is operational. This state is associated with the server and exists to support multiple applications running on or using the particular device, or to extend the information beyond the life of a particular application.

- *Application:* The next classification of state is associated with the application and is used for information that survives within the life of a particular application.

- *Session:* The third classification is associated with the user's session (time the user is logged in).

- *Request:* The final classification is associated with a particular user's request.

These state classifications are just guidelines, but they do indicate how different information has a particular life expectancy and value.

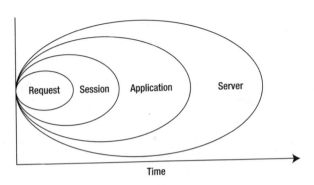

Figure 10-15. *Duration of state*

Smart clients present an interesting challenge when persisting state because they can operate in multiple modes using both local and remote resources. Maintaining state in two or more locations results in conflict and ambiguity, unless you manage the configuration carefully. When dealing with a smart client at a single instance in time, the states of each device typically will not coincide. Storing state in a single location is the ideal situation, but this requires a continuously connected solution, which limits the business opportunity.

State Maintenance with a Wired Connection

A pervasive smart client needs a local data store to maintain state and to interoperate with state that is located on the remote resource. Assuming the remote resource is the repository where the information will be deposited, the smart client will need to treat the remote resource as the primary holder of state. In the earlier example of a smart client for a sales force, this is the case, since the sales agent's purpose is to collect information and deliver it back to the corporation.

However, sometimes the smart client is the primary holder of state. For example, if the user is an independent researcher who deposits data on the mobile device, then the smart client is the primary holder of state. Whoever is the primary holder of state will need to contain the business logic to ensure that the data collected will not be replaced or updated erroneously. For the rest of the discussion, we will assume the remote resource is the primary holder of state.

In Figure 10-16, the darkly shaded data store on the remote resource is the primary holder of state. When connected in a wired configuration, the smart client will use the remote data store to maintain state S_1, which will be backed up on the smart client. This means that at any particular time t_1, as the user makes a change in state, the value S_1 is simultaneously updated to both the remote data store and the smart client data store. The backup of state data on the smart client is used when it disconnects from the remote resource. The remote resource data store maintains state for all smart clients connected to it.

■**Note** The local data store could also serve as a cache for static data. This is data that is not likely to change on the remote resource. Using a cache on the smart client could present problems if the data that was considered to be static does change. You should make sure that only static data will be cached on the smart client. See Chapter 6 for guidelines on the type of data suitable for a local data store.

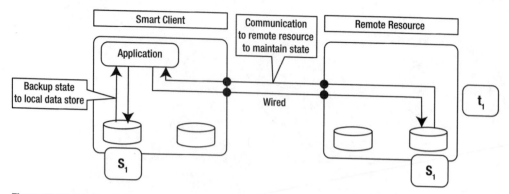

Figure 10-16. *Maintaining state in a smart client with wired connectivity*

State Maintenance with a Wireless Connection

When the smart client reconfigures itself to use wireless media, assuming the signal strength is strong, this situation is identical to the wired connection, as illustrated In Figure 10-17. When connected in a wireless configuration with a strong signal, the smart client will use the remote data store to maintain state S_2 and will be backed up on the smart client. In Figure 10-17, the darkly shaded data store on the remote resource is considered the primary holder of state. Once again, at any particular time t_2, as the user makes a change in state, the value S_2 is simultaneously updated to both the remote data store and the smart client data store.

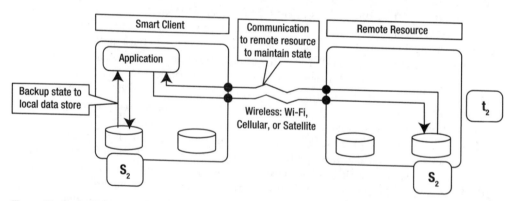

Figure 10-17. *Maintaining state in a smart client with wireless connectivity*

The backup of state data in this situation serves to support the smart client when disconnected. It can also be used to cache static information to the smart client. All state in this configuration is maintained on the remote resource for all smart clients connected via wireless and wired connectivity.

State Maintenance Without a Connection

When the smart client does not have a wired or wireless connection, it operates in an isolated mode. If, once disconnected from the network, the smart client never reconnected, state would not be a problem, but this is rarely the case. Moving from a disconnected mode back to a connected one is much more complex than just maintaining state in a single location in a connected mode. The data stores on the smart client and remote resource will need to record the time in which the data is written. These timestamps are critical to allow the application to determine how fresh or stale the data is. The user should be made aware of the timeliness of the data so that correct business decisions can be made.

Figure 10-18 illustrates how state is maintained when the smart client is disconnected. When the smart client is isolated at a particular moment t_3, the state in the smart client is identical to the state S_3 in the remote resource. The state S_3 that had been backed up to the local data store until the connection was terminated is now used to support the smart client. This information can be read as appropriate to assist the user while being disconnected. As the user makes changes (creating, deleting, and modifying data) at a future time $t_{3.1}$, the smart client must save changes to state $S'_{3.1}$ to the alternate data store located on the smart client. This additional data store is used *only* to temporarily hold modifications and acts as a change-audit trail for information on the smart client. All changes must be made to this new data store, and the user can retrieve and modify the data again, if desired. The bulk of information that has not changed is stored in S_3.

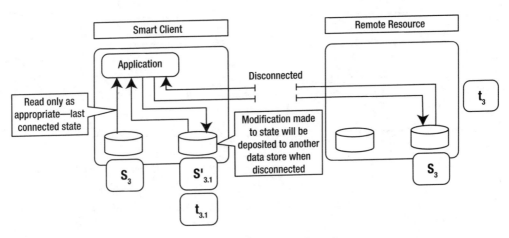

Figure 10-18. *Maintaining state in disconnected or isolated mode*

At a future time t_4, other smart clients will make changes to the state S_4 being held on the remote resource, and the smart client that is disconnected will continue to deposit changes to the alternative data store S'_4. These two data stores, S_4 and S'_4, will continue to diverge as they stay disconnected; similarly, the data store holding state S_3 at the time of the disconnection will grow stale. The disconnected smart client uses both local data stores S_3 and S'_4 to make as complete a picture as possible for the user, as shown in Figure 10-19.

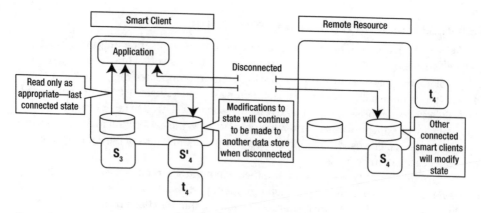

Figure 10-19. *Continuing to maintain state in a disconnected (isolated) mode*

At some point, the smart client user will reconnect to the network. When this happens, the smart client will need to reestablish state with the remote resource. The first step of this process is to transfer the state changes to another alternative data store located on the remote resource, as shown in Figure 10-20. This step ensures all changes have been written to the remote resource and that the network is not tied up moving data back and forth.

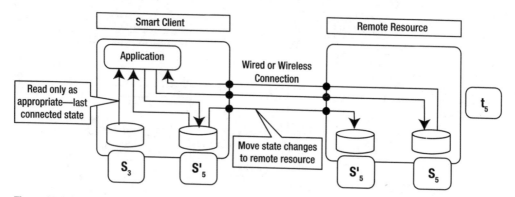

Figure 10-20. *After reconnecting, the smart client moves state changes to an alternative data store on the remote resource.*

Once the data has been moved to the remote resource, it will then need to go through a process of *reconciliation*,[3] as illustrated in Figure 10-21. The inputs to this process are the two different views of state, which are the changes made by the smart client S'_5 and the changes made by the remote resource S_5.

---

3. This process is sometimes called *synchronization,* but it is actually a comparison that resolves conflicts to bring state into equilibrium between the two devices.

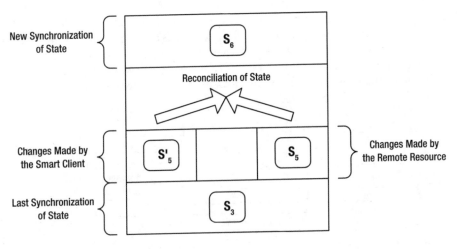

Figure 10-21. *Reconciliation process*

The actual reconciliation is a step-by-step process that evaluates each change that the smart client executed when in a disconnected mode, as summarized in Figure 10-22. This reconciliation can be accomplished through an automated process using business rules, or it can be done manually. For example, you could resolve conflicts automatically using business rules based on time dependence (the smart client data is or is not more current than the remote resource) or based on criticality, priority, or other metrics (for example, the smart client data does or does not have higher priority than the remote resource). Manual reconciliation requires a human to intervene in the process to choose to overwrite data or reject changes.

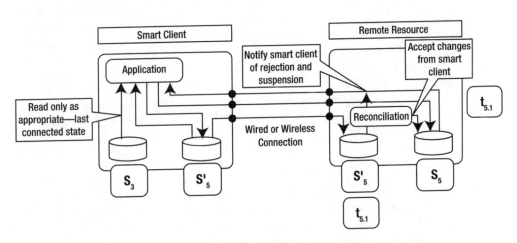

Figure 10-22. *Reconciliation of state between smart client and remote resource*

If any changes cannot be reconciled, they are typically placed into a suspense state, where they await manual approval or rejection by someone in a supervisory role. In all cases, the rejection or acceptance of a change is relayed to both the remote resource and smart client (and to the user).

The reconciliation is executed at time $t_{5.1}$ by a process that has the step-by-step logic (based on self-contained or accessible business logic) and resides on the remote resource. At the completion of the process, a single state S_6 will again exist. This single state will be used to synchronize between the smart client and the remote resource. This new state S_6 will then be loaded on to the smart client, as shown in Figure 10-23, which allows the process to repeat if the smart client is once again disconnected.

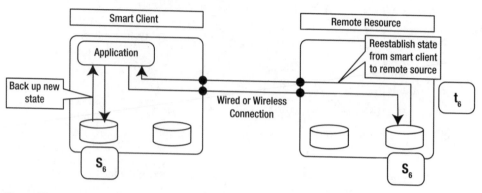

Figure 10-23. *New state is updated to the smart client*

Concurrency with Smart Clients

Smart clients can also use concurrency effectively to give the user a better experience in both connected and disconnected modes. *Concurrency* is the concept of executing things simultaneously. Doing more than one thing at time is a natural for people. In a single instant, the heart beats, eyes take in light energy, and the individual uses her mind and muscles to accomplish voluntary tasks simultaneously.

Connecting and communicating with remote resources such as web services can take time and impact the QoS that the user experiences if only one operation can be processed at a time. Fortunately, the computer can do things simultaneously, and many operations can be executed in parallel while the user works on another task. Concurrency uses the mechanisms of multitasking and multithreading.

Multitasking and Multithreading

Multitasking is executing more than one process at a time. A *process* is a binary set of instructions that follows a flow of logic sequentially, and then terminates when the last instruction is reached.[4] A process is an executable and is associated with the memory space that has been allocated for it and is sometimes referred to by the resources that use it. Scheduling for a process is done by the operating system, such as Windows 2000 and Windows XP. Processes use shared memory, shared files, and interprocess communication (IPC) to interact.

---

4. This happens unless an earlier instruction forces the logic to return to the starting point or an intermediate point to prevent the process from executing.

A *thread* allows a small amount of logic to execute separately. Every process has a single primary thread that is started during its creation and initialization.

Whereas processes are controlled by the operating system, threads are controlled by an application or *AppDomain*. AppDomains are the logical partitions within the memory space allocated for a process. Multiple AppDomains can be contained within a single operating system process. Each process has a default AppDomain defined for it. AppDomains offer performance enhancements over traditional operating system processes, because it takes less time for the Common Language Runtime (CLR) to load and unload them.

To further the segmentation, AppDomains are subdivided into *contexts*. Contexts allow similar logic to be handled by the CLR appropriately. Not all logic requires a specific context to be developed, but each AppDomain has a default context defined for it. Figure 10-24 illustrates the relationship between processes, AppDomains, and contexts.

Using a threading execution model allows AppDomains to work on separate sets of logic in parallel. Thus, an AppDomain can execute multiple threads simultaneously. Another interesting point is that a thread is not associated with a single AppDomain. This means that a thread can cross AppDomain boundaries and be associated with more than one AppDomain.[5] This migration is the responsibility of the thread scheduler and the CLR.

Figure 10-25 shows multiple AppDomains executing within a single process, and three threads interacting between the two AppDomains. Both AppDomains are running multiple threads, and Thread B executes in the top AppDomain before moving to the bottom AppDomain.

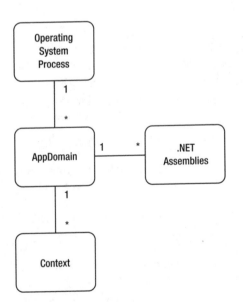

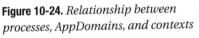

Figure 10-24. *Relationship between processes, AppDomains, and contexts*

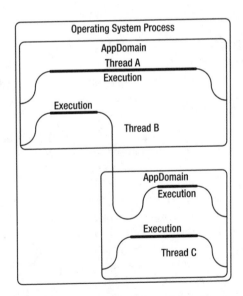

Figure 10-25. *Threads and AppDomains*

---

5. This capability should not be confused with the fact that the execution of the thread will occur in only one AppDomain at a time. This capability is different from operating system process threads, which are associated with and execute in only one process.

Background and Foreground Execution

Although all threads share the same characteristics, threads are categorized in two classifications.

- *Foreground threads*, also called *UI threads*, have a user interface component.

- *Background threads* are not associated with the user interface.

All threads are initiated as foreground threads unless delegated as background threads by the developer.

Foreground threads are allocated for use with the user interface. Most work for the user interface is done on the primary foreground thread. Some operations, such as printing or writing information to files based on user input, are good candidates for worker, or secondary, threads in the foreground. Foreground threads should be used with operations that require interaction with the user. You should avoid using foreground threads to perform extensive data retrieval or remote processing, because as UI threads, these types of operations would consume user interface processing resources and cause the application to "freeze" (and frustrate the user).

Background threads support operations that are not related to the user interface and use secondary (worker) threads. Inquiries for remote data retrieval, resource processing, XML Web Services, or process-intensive calculations should be executed with background threads. This will give the users the flexibility they need to perform other critical tasks while the background thread is executing.

Note A failure of a background thread may involve a number of courses of action. If the failure is associated with the retrieval of data or remote processing, the background thread may elect to attempt to retry the inquiry or relay the request again. Ultimate failure should result in the notification of the failure to the user.

As you've learned, smart clients can make both synchronous and asynchronous calls. Synchronous calls initiated from a foreground thread will cause the user interface to halt and be unresponsive, since the request must wait for the response. If a synchronous call must be made, it needs to be done very quickly. This restriction is also applicable to secondary threads running in the foreground.

Using an asynchronous style from a foreground thread is more acceptable, because this forces the processing onto the remote resource and allows the user to continue to use the application's foreground thread for other purposes.

Background threads can use asynchronous or synchronous communication, but since they are operating on the smart client, you need to be careful that you don't spawn too many threads. A smart client making multiple synchronous requests could spawn a number of background threads, which would end up lowering the overall performance of the client. Again, asynchronous requests place the burden of processing on the remote resource and free the smart client for the user's operations.

Foreground threads are associated with the application. This means that while a foreground thread is running, the application cannot terminate. In the example in Figure 10-26, two foreground threads have been initiated, and when the primary foreground thread finishes, the application will terminate. If the secondary foreground thread were to live longer than the primary thread, the application would not terminate until the secondary thread finished. Once all foreground threads terminate, the application will be shut down, which will automatically end all background threads, even if the background threads have not finished processing. This means that you must be careful in determining what information will be processed by a background thread.

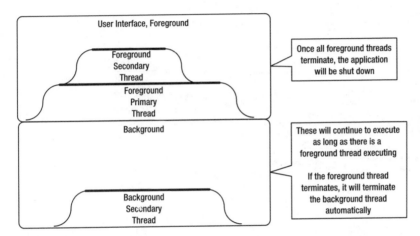

Figure 10-26. *Foreground and background threads*

Background threads are not considered when terminating the application. As long as there is a foreground thread running, the background thread will continue. Once all foreground threads have finished, the background thread will automatically be terminated. Table 10-5 summarizes foreground and background thread capabilities.

Table 10-5. *Foreground and Background Thread Capabilities*

Thread	UI	Synchronous	Asynchronous	Application Control
Foreground	Yes	No (yes, if quick)	Yes	Yes
Foreground (secondary)	Yes	No (yes, if quick)	Yes	Yes
Background (secondary)	No	Yes	Yes	No

Thread Management

Getting logic to run in parallel in a multithreading system takes more analysis and understanding than setting up single threading. Certain situations may require a resource to be accessed one thread at a time or serially. In those cases, having two threads enter the logic will be detrimental to the application. To prevent this, a *lock*, or token, is made available to a thread; other threads will not be able to enter the resource or logic until the lock is released. In this manner, only a single thread at a time can use the resource, and then that thread will release the resource for another thread to use. Locking a resource has an impact on performance, since it inhibits the other threads from performing their objective. Therefore, you need to be careful when locking a resource for serial usage.

Another problem that can arise from indiscriminant locking is a situation called a *deadlock*. As illustrated in Figure 10-27, deadlock exists when Thread A locks Resource 1 and is waiting to use Resource 2. Thread B locks Resource 2 and is waiting to get to Resource 1. Neither thread can accomplish its mission, and the application locks up.

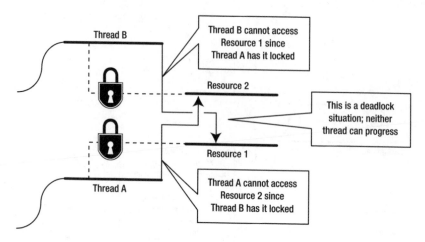

Figure 10-27. *Deadlock situation*

Thread management is critical to maintaining the health of an application. For example, locking inappropriately or for too long a period can have dire consequences. Resources should be locked only if a serial operation is needed, and once the operation is over, the resource should be released.

A Review of Smart Client Configurations

Most corporations have made a significant investment in desktops and/or laptops for internal and external staff. When this equipment is assigned to support a single application, most of the capability of these devices is being restricted. Many corporations accentuate this by building thin clients to support internal applications. A personal computer configured with the Windows operating system, Microsoft Office, and a browser primarily being used for thin-client activities to support an intranet application is a bad investment of equipment, time, and resources.

As we've demonstrated throughout this book, the next generation of clients—smart clients—provide the optimal solution, offering many advantages for both small and large organizations. Here, we'll review each of the smart client configurations.

Single-Application Smart Clients

The smart client can be used with single solutions to give corporations a competitive advantage. As shown in the sales force example in this chapter, the smart client offers media and communication agility, which gives the sales agents a pervasive and ubiquitous solution. The sales agents are no longer required to stay glued to their chairs when reaching out to the customer.

Smart clients offer intelligent solutions that maximize the use of all applications or local resources present on the platform. The mobile world is moving to more intelligent devices, and smart clients are just the start.

Multiple-Application Smart Clients

Developing a smart client that supports more than one solution and giving it access to more than one back-end service increases the smart client's scope. For example, developing a smart client that supports the customer service, inventory, and shipping departments reduces the cost of supporting three distinct and unique applications.

The company can minimize integration issues and development resource requirements by employing Visual Studio .NET universally throughout the organization. The company can also develop a technical center to give any user access to all corporate services available.

Using a multiple-application smart client greatly reduces integration and interoperability costs in resources, time, and money. Additionally, supporting multiple applications with a single smart client allows the user to reach multiple systems and formulate better decisions.

SOSCs

Developing smart clients that support more than one solution and giving them access to SOAs expands their capability in multiple dimensions. The SOA allows a single set of tools to loosely couple the back-end and make it interoperable. It also extends the reach of the corporation to global markets. Smart clients accomplish a similar type of interoperability across applications within the client.

Using an SOA develops standards that give a smart client the ability to interchange between local services, as well as extends the smart client's access to external services. A smart client with access to the Internet as well as corporate services can give users a global viewpoint in all aspects of their business decisions. Interoperating with local resources on the smart client and remotely accessing corporate and global services ensures that users are well informed about the business decisions at both the operational and strategic levels.

Figure 10-28 shows how the example we used in the previous chapter can be extended with a single smart client that can support multiple applications. To ease development costs, our small company decided to use a smart client to support customer service, inventory, shipping, and sales force automation. The smart client can interoperate with local resources on the client with regard to each of these services. Since the corporation developed an SOA, the smart client can automatically check for internal services by intelligently inquiring directly with the private UDDI server in the corporation or the partnered corporation (Amazon.com). If a new service is needed, the smart client could inquire the UBR to see if a service of that type is available. This could be something as simple as assisting a customer with directions to get to the corporate facility.

The mobile salespeople have all the capabilities that their stationary counterparts have. If they need directions or need to inquire to either public or private UDDI registries, they can. At the same time, the smart client can be working on proposals to determine if the inventory is in and alert the customer service, inventory, and shipping departments when they need to perform their necessary actions to meet the customer's commitment.

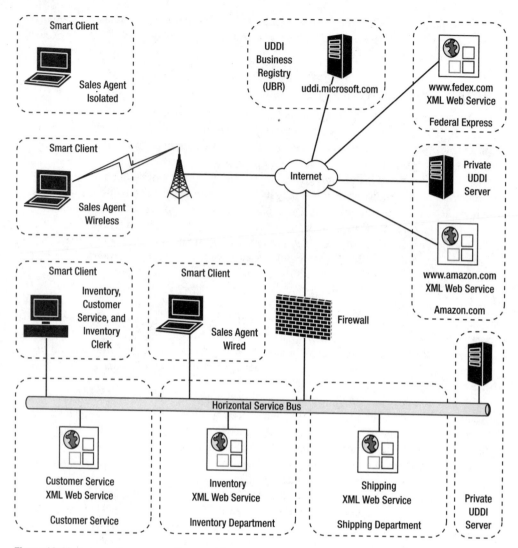

Figure 10-28. *Integrating smart clients with an SOA*

User mobility is the direction for technology, and interoperability is required to ensure the data users are reaching for is not isolated. SOAs and smart clients are two technologies that are on convergent paths. Coupling a smart client with pervasive and ubiquitous technology and service orientation gives the user global reach anytime and anywhere.

Summary

In this chapter, we described how to develop an SOSC by combining the SOA and service client technologies. You learned how adding a smart agent, a special component of an SOSC, can enhance media and communication agility for a smart client. We then discussed how to maintain state and use concurrency within this environment. We concluded by returning to the example developed in the previous two chapters to show how XML Web Services and an SOA can be leveraged by a smart client. The example demonstrated how SOSCs can reduce the duplication of clients and provide a seamless solution that allows users to reach both local and global resources. In the next chapter, we will discuss some of the difficulties in testing an SOSC in this environment.

CHAPTER 11

■■■

SOSC Testing

The architecture of an application plays a significant role in how the testing is organized and executed. For most *n*-tier systems, the user interface is the facade of the system, the business logic is located in a middle layer, and the data is stored in a back-office database. Dividing the application across three platforms should support compartmentalizing the logic by functional area. This localization makes the overall testing process easier. The database can be constructed and tested, even when the rest of the application is incomplete. Starting with the data constraints identifies the metadata and range of data values that the system will use. Using this approach, you can test the functionality of a significant amount of business logic before the user interface is finished. Finally, you can introduce parts of the user interface, until you have tested the entire end product.

Unlike an *n*-tier system, which typically has centralized business logic, the architecture of an SOSC distributes business logic and persistence in both local and remote components, adding to its complexity. This and other characteristics of SOSCs make testing them more challenging than testing traditional applications. In this chapter, we'll first review software testing stages and test data selection, and then focus on more specific requirements for testing SOSCs.

Software Testing Stages

Software functional testing is typically accomplished in three stages: unit testing, integration testing, and system testing. These stages build upon one another, until the complete system is integrated and tested.

Unit Testing

The first stage of testing involves reviewing individual units of code and is generally called *unit testing*. This stage of testing is accomplished using a "white box" test approach, in which the developer uses a debugger to walk through the code, setting breakpoints and watch variables to check all primary paths within the code. Visual Studio .NET offers a complete set of debugging tools to fully test the code using a white box approach, as shown in Figure 11-1.

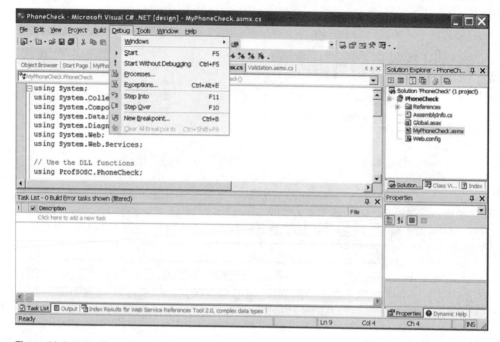

Figure 11-1. *Visual Studio .NET debugging capabilities*

Obviously, with very complex code, unit testing can take a significant amount of time. In many cases, the developer tests only the critical paths with a limited set of data.

Integration Testing

In the next stage of functional testing, a number of units are integrated together and then tested as a whole entity. Referred to as *component* or *integration testing*, this stage uses "black box" testing. Black box testing is based on a stimulus/response approach. A set of data is identified and introduced as input into the component, which performs operations on the input, and then the output data is compared with the expected results, as illustrated in Figure 11-2.

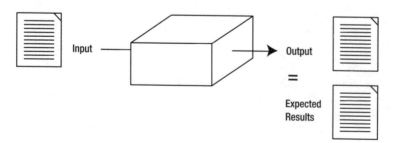

Figure 11-2. *Basic black box testing principles*

When the output data generates the expected results for a particular test, then the test is said to have passed; if it does not, the test is said to have failed. When the complete data domain of output data yields expected results based on input data, the testing is complete.

Setting up component tests that will validate a robust solution can be difficult. A tester not familiar with or unable to approximate the functionality of the module or component is at a serious disadvantage. As an example, let's look at what can go wrong when a tester does not have complete information.

Suppose a tester is told by the development team to test a function that determines whether a user's account is active based on an overdrawn or surplus balance. If the account is zero, the assumption is the account is not being used. The active-account balance function takes a single-input value with a valid range from –10,000 to +10,000, with 0 indicating the account is not active. With valid input, the function should return the value of 1, indicating the account has a balance and is active, or 0 if the account is inactive, as shown in Figure 11-3. The tester sets up a test to check the validity of this function based on this input.

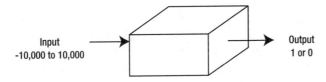

Figure 11-3. *A sample black box test*

Using a common approach, the tester introduces a set of values into the function to check its validity. The tester first picks two values that exceed each boundary value. This is a *negative test*, which checks for values that the application should not accept, with the expectation that a warning will be generated.

The tester next inputs a set of values at each boundary value (–10,000 and +10,000). These data tests are called *boundary value tests* and are considered to be positive tests, because they should yield an acceptable result.

Then the tester inputs two values in the nominal data range, and they also should return an acceptable value. Since only one constraint, which is the value 0, has been presented by the development team, this also is tested. This test should return the value of 0. Diligently, the tester sets up and executes the test, as presented in Table 11-1.

Table 11-1. *Sample Component Test*

Input Value	Reason	Output Value	Expected Result
–50,000	Exceeds low boundary value	Warning	Warning
–10,000	Low boundary value	1	1
–1,000	Valid data range	1	1
0	Known constraint	0	0
1,000	Valid data range	1	1
10,000	High boundary value	1	1
50,000	Exceeds high boundary value	Warning	Warning

Given that the output matches the expected results, the tester will pass this test. But what if the function being tested were actually f(x) = [x / (x – 10)], whose output was then rounded and wrapped in a conditional from –10,000 to +10,000? It might look like this:

```
[WebMethod (Description="Active account balance.")]
public float ActiveAccountBalance(float fBalance)
{
        if (fBalance >= -10000.00 || fBalance <= 10000.00)
        {
                fBalance = round(fBalance / (fBalance - 10));
        }
        else
        {
                Show warning that values are not supported.
        }
        return fBalance;
}
```

For the values input, this function would return the expected results of the test, and the tester would be unaware of the error. The round() function masks the problem by removing the granularity of the division, and the narrow asymptote at positive 10 is all but invisible given the input values. The range of the value also plays a part. Since the numbers are in thousands, there is a tendency to check for values in that range. Using more input values with a wider range of numbers, including smaller ones, would probably catch the problem. For this approach to be successful, the tester would need to employ automated testing tools with finer granularity; manual testing with course granularity is unlikely to catch the error.

System Testing

System testing, the final stage, is executed when all the components have been integrated together. System testing, like component testing, uses a black box testing approach.

One primary difference between system testing and component testing is that the number of exposed interfaces is reduced. Many times during system testing, the only interface available for use is the user interface. Extensive component testing can simplify system testing in this regard.

In many cases, automated tools allow testers to set up the input data stream and validate the output data stream against the expected results. These tools typically are used with the user interface and automatically run via generated scripts that attempt to simulate a user working with the system.

Test Data Selection

The data domain for any application always consists of all data that is valid and invalid. This assumes a set of metadata has been defined and established with an acceptable range of values. In most n-tier systems that serve a single or set of databases at a particular point in time, the amount of valid data can be considered to be finite, even if there is a considerable amount of it, as illustrated in Figure 11-4.

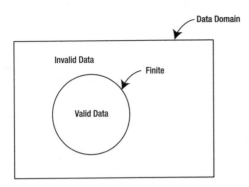

Figure 11-4. *Subset of valid data in the data domain*

Selecting which data in the data domain will be used for testing is critical to achieving the desired result, which is to build and deploy a robust system. Given that the subset of valid data within the domain is finite, the tester must determine which valid data and invalid data to use for input, as shown in Figure 11-5. The coverage of this data is important; if only valid data is chosen as input, the application will not be exposed to user-input errors. If noncritical valid data is used, critical functions may break when the user employs them. Testers should use a combination of critical, noncritical, boundary value, valid, and invalid data.

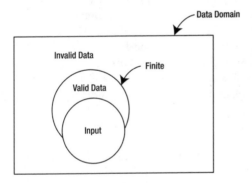

Figure 11-5. *Input parameters of a system having finite valid data*

The process of selecting data for testing is based on the metric of common usage and/or mission-critical information. Once this data is selected, it will be used to support positive and negative testing. For specific tests, the tester chooses values that will check boundaries and the validity of a particular piece of metadata. If the tester used a subset of input data to test *all* valid data, its boundary values, and the immediate invalid data surrounding the valid data, this would result in a very robust product. When a static subset of valid data exists, it is possible to fully test all of the data within the system. If the subset of valid data is small enough, this becomes a feasible exercise for the tester.

In reality, even within static subsets of valid data, only a selective group of data points is typically tested in each individual test. Actual coverage resembles the area shown in Figure 11-6. Each test uses mostly valid input values and a few boundary and invalid values.

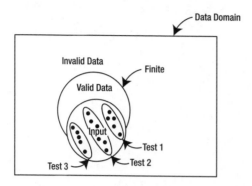

Figure 11-6. *Each test checks a subset oft valid, boundary, and invalid values.*

SOSC Testing Requirements

An SOSC presents a number of challenges from a testing perspective because it is more complex and deals with more variables than a traditional application. One aspect of an SOSC that will improve testing is the alignment of departmental business processes with IT services. This will make it easier to ensure requirements are being satisfied and that the user will be pleased with the application.

As thick client developers know, supporting an application that uses a local environment can prove difficult. Local resources may not be configured identically on the different machines and platforms in the environment. This can make test results erratic, indicating the application has problems, when, in fact, the environment is the culprit. You must perform tests with local resources using a variety of versions to ensure compliance with the user base.

When testing an SOSC, you need to pay particular attention to its communication, state maintenance, and concurrency mechanisms, as well as its smart agent functionality.

Communication Testing

As you learned in Chapter 10, an SOSC can use three communication styles, each of which requires a different approach to testing:

- Synchronous communication requires connectivity and gives immediate results when a failure occurs. This makes this style of communication the easiest to test.

- With asynchronous communication, the communication channel itself must be checked out. In addition, functions that are dependent on communications must be checked out independently from those that are not, since the SOSC must be able to operate in a connected and disconnected mode with both local and remote resources.

- Guaranteed delivery will require the tester to ensure the delivery reaches its destination after a hardware failure or communication interruption. Significant negative testing is required for an SOSC that employs guaranteed delivery.

State Maintenance Testing

The ability of the SOSC to operate in isolation introduces two data stores that can potentially hold state. This requires you to fully test the SOSC with and without connectivity to a back-end. You also need to test the interoperability between the data stores.

As explained in Chapter 10, both persistent data structures need timestamps to use in the reconciliation process (when a disconnected client reconnects). To test the local-to-remote configurations, you will need to create sequenced event-based component tests. This requires a thorough understanding of how to order test operations to validate the functionality of the smart client in both connected and disconnected modes. You must coordinate test management, strategy, and execution to ensure that tests are not performed out of sequence.

Concurrency Testing

An SOSC can employ concurrency by using multiple threads for different functions. Testing multithreaded stand-alone applications can be difficult. When multithreading is coupled with local and remote resource usage in the SOSC, this type of testing can be extremely challenging. You need to configure and generate tests to verify concurrency, and then troubleshoot any errors that arise.

You'll need special tools, such as execution profilers, to ensure that timing is not distorted during the test execution. You'll also need to check threads for deadlock or race conditions. As explained in Chapter 10, a *deadlock* occurs when two threads are waiting for a resource locked by the other thread. A *race* condition is when two running threads want to access the same resource that are dependent on the order of execution and results in blocking the running of critical code.

Smart Agent Testing

The intelligence of the smart agent within the SOSC presents another testing challenge. A smart agent can elect to override local resources or common remote resources and connect to new multiple remote services to obtain optimum data for the SOSC and the user. When the SOSC connects to new multiple remote services or resources, the subset of valid data increases, as illustrated in Figure 11-7. Since the valid data domain is extended each time the SOSC uses a new remote service, testing this intelligence requires planning and standards.

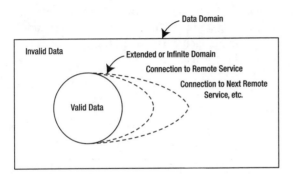

Figure 11-7. *The valid data domain increases with each new remote resource connected to the SOSC.*

One way to reduce the amount of testing required is to classify the remote services by the types of data being exchanged. For example, multiple remote services might be dealing with phone number data, so a single set of tests could be run against each of these remote services. However, even with such classification, the data domain is still hard to pin down. The intelligent SOSC uses its agility to hop from one service to another, making it more difficult to determine results. This directly extends the valid data domain from a fixed domain to an extended or potentially infinite one. You need to account for the heuristics used to provide this agility and set up tests to ensure the smart agent maneuvers within an expected pattern.

Corresponding to the increase in the valid data domain, the input data must also increase to support testing the SOSC, as illustrated in Figure 11-8. Even though input data increases, it is proportionally smaller than the increase in available valid data. Since input data is always a limited subset, you must be very careful to select the most optimal values. Also, as with all dynamic or intelligent software systems, a conflict can arise when what was originally invalid data later becomes a part of the valid domain. For example, the original domain of colors might be red, green, and blue, but after visiting an additional remote resource, the SOSC adds the color yellow to its valid data domain.

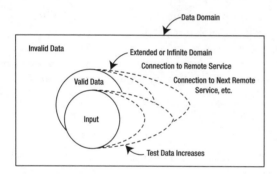

Figure 11-8. *Input data increases with dynamic capability of the SOSC.*

Smart Test Component

To help you meet the SOSC testing challenges, you can construct a smart test component as an integral piece of the smart agent, as illustrated in Figure 11-9. This component will ensure testing is being done after deploying an SOSC with smart agents. The smart test component acts like a self-test component, as well as a health-check test and monitor.

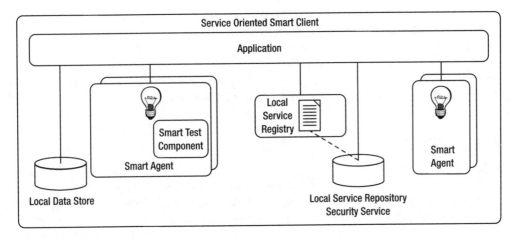

Figure 11-9. *Smart test component*

The smart test component is a set of logic that understands the heuristics used by the smart agent. It uses a set of health-check messages to determine the status of the local and remote resources. For example, the smart test component for the media-agile smart agent described in Chapter 10 would periodically send a self-generated SOAP test message to pre-determined remote resources through each medium and evaluate the responses. If further health checking is required, the smart test component could send other sets of messages to the local and remote resources to verify that the smart client's vital functions are operating. The user does not need to be aware of the checking going on in the background when the SOSC is idle. However, the user could choose to request a series of checks (which would give the user confidence that the SOSC is performing at optimum level).

The smart test component also checks for initialization and environment issues once the smart agent is plugged into the application. This can be accomplished by the smart test component checking for a change of state in the SOSC, similar to the way Microsoft Windows uses Plug-and-Play to check for new hardware.

The smart test component should use a black box test approach to perform its functional check. By supplying the local data store with a set of critical test data and messages, the smart test component could use this information to determine the state of the SOSC's local environment by comparing it with a set of predetermined results. Simple tests could use ordinal or static values, whereas more complex checks could use algorithmic or fuzzy logic to perform their operational checks.

■**Tip** A great place to start developing a smart test component for a smart agent or SOSC is the system test scripts or procedures that were written to check out the system. Many of these scripts or procedures indicate the input data and expected responses needed to validate that the system is operating correctly. Most simple heuristics can be dealt with in this manner.

The type of logic that you will need to construct within the smart test component is directly related to the level of the smart agent's intelligence. For highly intelligent smart agents, you'll need to develop your smart test component to test algorithmic or complex patterns with state-of-the-art techniques to avoid overtaxing the processor or hardware, which would degrade the user experience. For a better understanding of these complex patterns, the reader should reference material on artificial or machine intelligence.

Summary

In this chapter, we reviewed the three phases of software testing: unit, integration, and system tests. Next, we discussed some of the difficulties associated with selecting test data in a "smart" environment. Then we detailed the challenges of testing an SOSC's mechanisms for communication, state maintenance, and concurrency, as well as smart agent functionality. Finally, we presented how to construct a smart test component to check the SOSC and the smart agent during runtime, and alert the user of any critical situations.

In this book, we've covered what smart clients are, how they can be constructed, the ease in which they can be deployed, their ability to interoperate with a XML Web Services, and how they can be tested. You're now ready to develop your own smart clients. We are sure your customers will be extremely pleased with your SOSCs, just as our clients were very satisfied with the ones we developed.

Index